"Lyn Cote's *Echoes of Mercy* tells a tale with all the mystery and intrigue of New Orleans coupled with the redemption and grace of a beautiful love story. Such exquisite research—and such a compelling story. It's absolutely wonderful."

—Lenora Worth
author of *The Wedding Quilt*

"Lyn Cote skillfully weaves the power of love, the trials of faith and prejudice, and the suspense of a legal thriller against a lavish Mardi Gras setting in Prohibition-era New Orleans. *Echoes of Mercy* is a page-turning drama deserving of the silver screen."

—Linda Windsor
author of *Not Exactly Eden*

BLESSED ASSURANCE SERIES • VOLUME 3

LYN COTE

ECHOES OF MERCY

A NOVEL

BROADMAN
&HOLMAN
PUBLISHERS

NASHVILLE, TENNESSEE

0–8054–1969–1

Published by Broadman & Holman Publishers,
Nashville, Tennessee

Scripture quotations marked NASB are from the New American
Standard Bible, © Copyright The Lockman Foundation, 1960, 1962,
1963, 1968, 1971, 1972, 1973, 1975, 1977, 1995. NIV, the Holy
Bible, New International Version, © copyright 1973, 1978, 1984.
NKJV, the New King James Version, copyright © 1979, 1980, 1982,
Thomas Nelson, Inc., Publishers. TEV, The Good News Bible. The
Bible in Today's English Version, © American Bible Society 1966,
1971, 1976, used by permission.

Dewey Decimal Classification: 813
Subject Heading: FICTION

Library of Congress Cataloging-in-Publication Data

Cote, Lyn.
    Echoes of Mercy : a novel / Lyn Cote.
      p.   cm. (Blessed assurance series; v. 3)
    ISBN 0–8054–1969–1 (pb)
    1. New Orleans (La.)—Fiction. I. Title.
PS3553.O76378 E33   2000
                                                              00–023679

            1 2 3 4 5 04 03 02 01 00

Dedicated to Judith Ireland Roemerman,
Thanks for being a great friend and encourager.

With fond memories of Mrs. Ethel Henning and
the stories she told me about her beloved WWI "flying ace"
Quincy, Illinois, 1970

Angels descending bring from above
Echoes of mercy, whispers of Love.
Watching and waiting, looking above,
Filled with His goodness, lost in His love.
—Fanny Crosby, "Blessed Assurance"

"THE LORD DOES NOT SEE AS MORTALS SEE;
THEY LOOK ON THE OUTWARD APPEARANCE,
BUT THE LORD LOOKS ON THE HEART."
—FIRST SAMUEL 16:7

PROLOGUE

Tremble, O earth, at the presence of the Lord.
Psalm 114:7, NIV

San Francisco
April 18, 1906

MEG COULDN'T GET THE screaming out of her head. Shivering, she clung to Aunt Susan's black hand with both of her small white ones. The warmth of the old woman's plump hand felt good. Aunt Susan would take care of her and Del, but . . . "Did the earthquake hurt my papa?"

Aunt Susan answered between deep breaths. "Your Papa . . . is . . . in God's hands."

Meg didn't like those words. When her mama died, people had said the same thing. But surely God wouldn't take both her mama *and* papa, would he? *I'm just a little girl, Jesus. I need my papa.*

"Grandma, I can't believe Kang died," Del said as he glanced around Aunt Susan to catch Meg's eye. His dark face looked downcast, sad.

"We can't think about that now, child," Aunt Susan said.

Meg closed her eyes for a second, trying to block out the memory of seeing the roof fall on their Chinese houseman. It had been awful.

Now the houses that lined both sides of the street looked as if they were leaning over Meg. Would the earth shake again and make the houses fall down on them like they had on Kang? Meg quivered. The screeching in her ears got louder. "I want Papa," she whimpered.

A woman passed right in front of them, pulling a goat behind her. The woman was wearing only a blue nightgown. The sight startled Meg. She looked down and realized she was in her nightgown, too, and her feet were bare. Why hadn't she felt the cold sidewalk before? "I don't have a dress on."

"That don't . . . matter . . . today."

But it always mattered to dress proper, didn't it? Meg shook her head, trying to make herself think better. She hadn't been able to dress this morning. The quake had thrown her right out of bed. Aunt Susan had dragged both her and Del down the front stairs into the street. Then their front porch had torn away from the house as if it were chasing them. The old lady from across the street had stumbled out her front door and had stood in the middle of the street—shrieking.

Only when the quake had finally stopped did Meg realize that Aunt Susan had put her hand over Meg's mouth—Meg had been screaming too. Maybe the noise in her head was really her own voice.

"How will Meg's papa find us?" Del asked from the other side of Susan.

"He'll find us." Suddenly Aunt Susan slowed down. She let go of Meg's hand.

A man carrying a basket of bread rushed by them. Aunt Susan stopped. She staggered to the curb, then slumped down. "Oh, Lord, not now. Please. The children . . ." She doubled over.

"Grandma!" Del bent over her.

"What's wrong?" Meg fell to her knees. "Aunt Susan!"

"Stay . . . together," Aunt Susan gasped.

"Help!" Shouting over and over, Del looked around frantically while Meg clung to Aunt Susan's hand.

Del grabbed the arm of a passing gentleman whose white hair stuck out wildly. "Help us, please!"

The man halted. "What's the matter?"

"Mister," Aunt Susan gasped. "Take . . . children . . ."

"What?"

Aunt Susan slid down off the curb and collapsed onto the street.

"Grandma!" Del knelt and wrapped his arms around her.

"Is she breathing?" the man asked.

Meg looked up at him. Why was he asking her? *I'm only eight years old!* "Do something, Mister. Get a doctor."

The man didn't answer her. Del began to whimper.

"Mister," Meg shouted, "I *said*, get a doctor!"

The man hurried away.

Meg knelt opposite Del and threw her arms around Aunt Susan. "Please, Aunt Susan, don't die."

She and Del waited and waited. No doctor came. No one would stop to help them. Aunt Susan didn't move.

Del stroked Aunt Susan's head, his dark hand looking darker against the silver hair, and whispered over and over, "Grandma, wake up."

Meg remembered when her mother had died, Papa had led her to the bedroom to say good-bye. Mama had been still like this then. Mama's hand had been cold too—just like Aunt Susan's was now. Tears welled up into Meg's eyes. *Aunt Susan. Aunt Susan.*

Meg sat back on her heels. Still remembering the night she lost her mother, she echoed her father's words about Mama, "She's with Jesus now, Del."

With tears running down his dark face, Del nodded.

Meg reached over and touched Del's black, woolly hair gently. "I won't leave you, Del."

The earth shifted beneath her. A terrible groan worked through the nearby houses—creaking and moaning. She and Del lurched together, throwing their arms around each other.

3

The awful twisting and rolling under them went on and on, but Meg's hold on Del and his on her didn't falter. The street swirled and jolted. Still, Meg clung to Del. She shouted, "Stop! Stop!"

The earth stilled.

Meg swallowed a sobbing hiccup. This was worse than losing Mama. She felt flattened, shrunken like a punctured balloon. Had Del and she lost everyone? Trembling, Meg looked at Del. "It's just you and me now."

Del nodded, rubbing his eyes.

"We've got to stick together until we find my papa. Promise?"

Del agreed solemnly, "Promise. I'm bigger. I'll take care of you."

Meg nodded. "That's right. We still have each other." *We won't die,* she told herself. *We won't die. Jesus, take care of Papa. Don't let us die.*

CHAPTER 1

New Orleans
January 2, 1920

THE DOOR SPLINTERED AND broke apart. In the midnight blackness, men shouted, "Police!"

Del reared up in bed. But before he could say a word, a fist caught him sharp in the eye, then hands clutched his throat. Another unseen blow landed hard. His lip split. Shouted curses hurt his ears. *What's happening? Help me! God!*

The single light dangling from the ceiling exploded into blinding radiance.

Through a haze of pain and fear, Del glimpsed three uniformed policemen. One gripped him by the throat. One pointed a gun to his head. One was pawing under his mattress. "Well, look at this." He waved a thick wad of greenbacks.

"Money? What?" Del gasped.

The three policemen laughed. The officer who had Del by the throat dragged him off his bed. Del gagged. The one holding up the money felt under the pillow. "And here's the gun."

Del tried to speak, but the pressure on his throat choked him. He clawed at the fingers on his neck. *Dear God, are they going to kill me?*

Another blow landed like a brick to his temple. Another. Streaks of light flashed in front of his eyes. He scrabbled harder at the fingers around his throat. Pain shot through his head. Finally—blackness.

❀ ❀ ❀ ❀ ❀

Cold water doused Del's face.

"Why'd you kill Mitch Kennedy?" a voice growled in the dim light.

Del tried to focus his eyes. He throbbed, ached . . . everywhere.

"Why'd you shoot your boss?" another harsh voice demanded.

Del shook his head, trying to make sense of what was going on. His arms were bound behind him to the hard chair he sat on.

"We're gonna get a confession outta you or else. Hear me, boy?"

A hard fist crashed into Del's jaw. Pain rattled through his skull.

An image flashed in his memory. The Argonne Forest in red-orange flames. German shells bursting around him. The incredible explosions reverberating through his bones. Earth blasting skyward, pelting down on him like dirty hail. Deafening German shells. A man blew apart. Warm blood splattered Del's face.

Cover! Where could he hide? Another shell detonated only feet away. The shock threw him high in the air. *Stop! Before I fly apart!*

The man cursed him. "Why'd you shoot Mitch?" Someone shook him. Pain zigzagged through his head and face.

The voice, the faces faded. . . .

❀ ❀ ❀ ❀ ❀

"Delman. Delman DuBois?" Gabriel St. Clair—New Orleans Parish Attorney—intoned over the unconscious prisoner.

The man blinked, opened his eyes, but his head lolled to the side on the chair where he slouched.

Gabe hated the dirty, drab anteroom to the city jail. He couldn't wait to get back to the white stone courthouse and his neat office. "Delman DuBois?"

Delman looked up.

The sight of the black prisoner's battered face—one eye swollen shut, lacerated lips, and a swollen jaw—turned Gabe's stomach. "Rooney, you've got to keep your men from roughing up prisoners so badly."

"He resisted arrest," Deputy to the Chief of Police Rooney said. His fat lips twitched in a nasty grin.

"This is America. Innocent until proven guilty."

Rooney snorted. "He's guilty."

"What?" the prisoner muttered.

"Delman, do you know the charges against you?" Gabe asked sharply.

"No."

Gabe grimaced. The boy was obviously in a great deal of pain. He didn't like this. Even a colored deserved to have his charge explained to him. A dog would have been treated better than this. "You have been arrested for the theft of two hundred dollars and the murder of your white boss, Mitch Kennedy."

"Mitch's dead?" The prisoner licked his lips.

"You know he is," Rooney snapped. He reached to strike again.

Gabe caught his arm.

Rooney glared at him, but pulled back.

"Delman, can you afford to hire counsel?"

"The likes of him? Afford a lawyer?" Rooney snorted again. "He's just a cheap black piano player."

"Fam'ly," the man muttered. With effort, he focused on Gabe. "Sir, please . . . word . . . my fam'ly."

Gabe studied the prisoner. Why batter a man's jaw, then try to question him? Beating a helpless man made Gabe sick. But what could he do about it? And legally, there was so little he could do for this colored. The money and the gun had been found in his room. An easy conviction. Just another cheap, nasty crime in Storyville.

The prisoner's head sagged forward. He jerked it up again, pain etched on his bruised face. "Sir, . . . you in France?"

Gabe wondered why this question. He nodded slowly.

The man pointed to himself. "Nine . . . ty-second."

"You served too?" Gabe stirred just saying these words. The man's question about France brought back instant memories—the view of Gabe's squadron's air base from above, the buzz of airplane engines, rapid gunfire, the stench of decaying flesh buried in trench mud. Sweat beaded on Gabe's palms. His stomach roiled. The man had been right to appeal to esprit de corps. Gabe couldn't turn down another soldier, another survivor. The man deserved at least a chance to defend himself. "What's your family's address?"

The prisoner nodded feebly. "Telegraph . . . Linc Wagstaff, 143 Cal . . . fornia Street . . . San Fran . . . cisc . . ." He passed out.

Gabe gazed at him. "See that he gets a clean bed and a doctor. I'll stop and see him tomorrow."

Rooney scowled at him. "That's the problem with lettin' blacks serve as soldiers. He'd never thought of shootin' a white man here if he hadn't shot white men over there."

Gabe was familiar with the sentiment but didn't believe it. He closed his mind as well as he could against the past. "He faced death for his country." *And worse.* "He gets a bed and a doctor."

Rooney nodded sulkily.

Straightening his stiff, white collar, Gabe walked away. He repeated the San Francisco address to himself. He recalled seeing black doughboys with the French Croix de Guerre medal on their drab uniforms. More war images crowded into his mind—flying over trenches teeming with soldiers huddled under enemy fire; bodies slowly rotting in no man's land; the rush of adrenaline, panic when an enemy plane came into sight, then range . . .

His heart pounding, he closed his eyes, willing the images away. He'd send the blasted telegram and get busy with his other parish prosecuting duties. Keeping busy was the only antidote now. That confounded Prohibition was only weeks away! How would he get to sleep nights without two shots of bourbon to numb the pain, to keep him in his right mind?

* * * * *

San Francisco, January 3, 1920

In her red silk robe, Meg Wagstaff sat in the darkened nursery and rocked Kai Lin's infant son. Though Kai Lin and her husband kept house for her parents, they were more like family. Meg had insisted on helping care for their little son during the night to help them out. She did it to help them out, of course, but she also did it to help herself. Home from war-ravaged Europe for little more than three months, Meg still suffered sleepless nights. Rocking the almond-eyed infant was the only sedative that worked. After soothing the child, she was always able to pass out for a few hours of sleep.

The baby had just fallen asleep. She felt herself relaxing, too. She bent her head and breathed in the scent of baby powder and innocence. Rocking rhythmically, she hummed a song Aunt Susan, the dear old family friend who'd helped raise her, had sung to her many bedtimes: "Swing low, sweet chariot...." Aunt Susan's round black face smiled in Meg's memory. Meg could almost feel the old woman's plump arms surrounding her, rocking her.

The front doorbell rang, startling her. The chiming echoed through the silent, sleeping house. Who would ring their bell at nearly four in the morning? Automatically, she edged forward on the chair, but Kai Lin's husband would get it. In the early morning silence, Meg leaned back. She heard the front door downstairs being unlocked. She tried to close her eyes to rest, but worry twisted her stomach.

The front door closed firmly.

Who had come? She rose. Bending, she kissed the baby's soft, small forehead, then carried him into the darkened upstairs hallway where she met the houseman. "What is it?"

"Telegram for Mr. Linc." The man, in a blue cotton Chinese robe, wore a concerned expression.

"I'll take it to him." After exchanging the baby for the telegram, Meg walked to her parents' door. "It's Meg. I've got a telegram."

In his navy pajamas, her father opened the door and took the yellow envelope from her. Suddenly feeling chilled, Meg moved into the large ivory-and-blue bedroom and sat on the huge high bed beside her stepmother, Cecy.

"Meg?" Cecy, blind since an accident years before, felt for Meg, then hugged her closer as she pulled her satiny blanket over Meg's lap. "You're chilled, dear. Linc, I fear it is bad news. Good news could have waited until dawn."

Meg nestled close to Cecy, breathing in her light floral perfume. Under her arm, Meg felt Cecy's pregnant abdomen stir. *Little dear one, did we wake you too?* "Who's it from, Father?"

"A Gabriel St. Clair in New Orleans."

"New Orleans?" Meg echoed. "That's where Del is."

Her father opened the telegram.

She watched his handsome face widen into shock. "What is it?"

"Del's been charged with murder." Disbelief laced her father's voice.

Meg stood up, pulling away from Cecy's affectionate embrace.

"Linc! No!" Cecy reached out for her husband, and Linc hurried forward to catch her hand.

"Read it," Meg demanded.

Her father took a labored breath. "Mr. Wagstaff, Delman DuBois has been arrested for murder. Stop. He's being held at the New Orleans city jail, awaiting arraignment. Stop. Signed, Gabriel St. Clair, New Orleans Parish Attorney." Father looked at Meg over his reading glasses. The worry in his eyes shook her out of denial.

But Cecy voiced it: "It must be a mistake."

"Del wouldn't murder anyone," Meg agreed.

"I warned him against going south." Linc scowled. "I told him he was putting himself at risk. In the South, lynchings have exploded since the war——"

"He was at worse risk in France," Meg snapped, then felt ashamed. Her father had only meant the best for Del. "Sorry."

"That's all right, sweetheart." Handing Meg the telegram, he took both of his wife's hands, then leaned his head against hers.

Meg stared at them, her father's graying blond hair next to her stepmother's auburn beauty. Their love for each other and concern for Del showed plainly.

"We should call Fleur Bower," Cecy said. "Maybe she knows the St. Clair family in New Orleans. It sounds like a Creole name."

"What difference would that make?" Meg bit out, then was ashamed again of her sharp tone. "I'm sorry, Cecy. I don't know why I can't seem to keep my temper lately."

Neither of her parents spoke a word of censure, but their worried faces said much——*We shouldn't have let her go to war. What can we do to help her? Oh, Lord, we love her so much.*

Meg looked away. She hated wounding them, but she would never again be the naive twenty-year-old girl who had put off law school to go to France. And no matter how much they loved her and she loved them, she couldn't fit back here as though nothing inside her had changed. She pushed aside all these worrisome thoughts. "What are we going to do?"

Her father looked sick.

"Linc," Cecy urged, "you'll have to go——"

"No! I can't leave you! You could go into labor any day."

"Yes." Resting a hand on her large abdomen, Cecy replied calmly, "But that can't be helped. Del needs us. We're the only family he has."

"We'll get him legal help. The best. But I can't leave you. Don't ask me to. I won't." Her father's face, though harassed, was determined.

Meg understood why he couldn't leave Cecy. Though Meg had only been seven when her own mother had died in childbirth, she had vivid memories of her father's wrenching grief.

Then after the 1906 earthquake, he'd married Cecy, an heiress half his age. They'd worked together as journalists, championing laws against child labor. Now, after fourteen years of marriage and two miscarriages, Cecy was finally carrying a child to term. But the doctor was worried and visited weekly. Meg crushed the telegram in her hand.

"As soon as it's light outside," Linc said, "we'll call the Bowers. Fleur knows New Orleans, and Clarence will know what to do legally."

Cecy wiped away a tear. "I feel so helpless."

Meg nodded, then left her parents. Feeling oppressed by the appalling news but oddly distanced from it, she walked to her room to sit and watch the sun come up. She knew exactly what she'd do. Only one of them could go, and she wanted to be the one.

✺ ✺ ✺ ✺ ✺

The following morning Meg stood beside her luggage in the midst of her family at the San Francisco train station. The sound of steam building in the locomotive engine filled the air. People, dressed warmly against the January chill, hustled along the crowded walkways between tracks. Porters—some black and some Chinese—pushed carts of luggage along briskly. Everyone seemed to hurry.

Meg felt the urgency inside herself. The past twenty-four hours had flashed by like a one-reel movie. She recalled expressions on the faces of friends and family, short bits of distracted conversations. Her blood fizzed in her veins. Del needed her. She needed to get away!

Aunt Fleur and Uncle Clarence rushed up in the bleak early-morning light. "Oh, we're in time!" Aunt Fleur stood on tiptoe embracing Meg. "I brought you the letter of introduction to my cousin Emilie. If you need anything, just call on her. I wish you would stay with her. I telegraphed, and she'd love to have you—"

"I'll be happier at a hotel." Meg smiled to soften her refusal.

"Oh, these modern girls!" Aunt Fleur, still a pretty brunette at forty, exclaimed. "Cecy, I can't get used to girls rushing off places without chaperones. I'm afraid we're quite old-fashioned now." She affectionately tucked her arm into the crook of Cecy's elbow.

Meg's father pulled her close. He whispered fiercely into her ear, "I don't want you to go. I wouldn't let you go if there were any other way!"

"I'll be fine," Meg assured him. He was so dear, so handsome, so good. He'd always made her feel proud he was her father. But she'd gone to France. She could face New Orleans alone.

"I'll be praying every minute, and I'll come as soon as I can leave your stepmother—"

"I'll be back before you know it." She spoke these words with another smile, but she didn't feel any confidence in them. After helping Del, she might go back to New York City. She hadn't felt quite so desperate there.

She itched to be on the train and away, but leaving proved hard. She hugged her parents tightly, communicating her love for them without words, then did likewise with her honorary aunt and uncle. Sweet Kai Lin and her husband moved forward, bowing and somber. Meg bent to kiss their infant in Kai Lin's arms. This child alone gave her hope that she might once again feel like herself.

The strident train whistle and the conductor's "All aboard!" released Meg from the parting. She ran up the metal steps, following the black porter who carried her bags. When she reached her Pullman compartment, she looked out the window and saw her stepmother and Aunt Fleur nestled in the midst of the two families.

Smiling wryly, Meg waved to them as the train pulled out. With her straight, thick brown hair cut in a Dutch Boy with heavy bangs and her unexciting brown eyes, Meg always felt her lack of beauty when compared to her mother and aunt. Cecy and Aunt Fleur had been San Francisco belles in 1906—Cecy, an auburn beauty, and Fleur, a devastating brunette. The two women, though attractively dressed, still kept their skirt hems barely above their ankles, and neither had yet parted with their old-fashioned long hair and large hats. Meg heard Aunt Fleur's words again: "these modern girls."

Meg dragged off her close-fitting cloche hat and ruffled her short, bobbed hair. A French officer in Paris had once told Meg she was more than a beauty; she was a striking woman with an air of mystery. Since he'd been trying unsuccessfully to seduce her at the time, she hadn't taken him seriously. How shocked her mother and Aunt Fleur would be if she told them that story! Since her return from France, the gulf between her and her parents left her feeling isolated and alone.

Sighing, she crossed her silk-stockinged legs and leaned back into the seat, accustoming herself to the rhythm of the rails again. She swung her ankle to the increasing clickety-clack of the metal wheels speeding away from San Francisco—her hometown, where she no longer felt at home.

※ ※ ※ ※ ※

Dismal rain ran down the train window as Meg arrived just after dawn in New Orleans. The old city looked gray, dilapidated, and depressing to her. The porter knocked and entered. Meg rose and opened her purse. With a smile, she handed him three dollar bills. "One is for you. One for James in the dining car. One for the redcap to take my bags."

"Thank you, Miss. I'll take care of it." A sincere smile split his dark face in two.

She tugged her ruby-red cloche hat over her hair, then glanced at her compact. She powdered her nose and put on fresh lip rouge. "Make sure I get an honest cabby too."

"You'll have the best in New Orleans, Miss." The way he pronounced the city's name, it sounded like "Nawlins."

Meg left her tiny compartment, feeling crumpled and grimy after two days and two nights in the swaying car. *If I could only sleep.*

A short time later she stepped out of a yellow cab in front of the hotel Aunt Fleur had recommended. Under her black umbrella, Meg scooted through the pouring rain into the imposing white frame building with ornate black wrought-iron balconies. Once inside, she folded her drenched umbrella and let the stream of water drain down its point. Damp and drowning in fatigue, she trudged to the desk and placed a hand on its smooth wood.

A clerk behind the desk approached her. "May I help you?" he asked in a thick Southern accent.

"I'd like a room with a bath please."

The clerk's mouth primmed up. "Will your husband be joinin' you?"

"I'm single." She sighed. "Where is your guest register? I've been on a train for two days."

"You are travelin' alone?" His tone was icy.

Meg finally looked the man directly in the face. It was a very plain, but frosty, face. "What is the problem?"

He cleared his throat. "Here at Hotel Monteleone, we are not in the habit of registerin' young *painted* females without escort." He folded his hands on the polished oak counter.

Good grief! Young painted female because she powdered her nose and rouged her lips!

Meg mockingly folded her hands just the same way he had. "Please ask the manager to give me a moment of his valuable time."

The clerk began to object.

From under the low brim of her hat, Meg stared him down.

After a moment of silent struggle, he shrugged. Within a few seconds, Meg was ushered into the manager's office. The impeccably groomed manager stood just within the door, as though poised to give her a quick denial. Meg brushed past him and sat nonchalantly in the commodious dark green leather chair in front of the mahogany desk. Forced to give ground, the manager seated himself and eyed her grimly.

Meg sat back and gave the man a sophisticated smile. "Your desk clerk has extremely outdated notions about women who wear makeup and travel alone."

"Our policy has always been not to allow unattended young women—"

"Are you saying you think I'm a prostitute?" Meg's incisive tone contrasted with the garbled reply the manager stuttered out.

Meg opened her red leather bag and pulled out a letter, which she opened and handed to him. "This is a letter of introduction from my Aunt Fleur." She said no more, but watched the manager as he read. The change in his expression would have been amusing if Meg had been in the mood to be amused. She wasn't.

Without a word, she retrieved the letter and stood. Soon, the manager himself escorted her into a large luxurious room. She nodded his dismissal and then locked the door behind him and the bellman.

Undressing as she went, she made her way across the thick maroon carpet and headed straight for the rose-and-white bathroom's claw-foot tub. She twisted its ornate brass knobs. Hot water pounded against the white porcelain bottom. She dropped in paper-packaged bath salts. Steam rose. She shed her black silk teddy and slid into the fragrant, frothy bubbles. Lavender! She breathed in the soothing floral scent.

Yet despite the restorative waters, bitterness welled up as a sour taste in her mouth. She closed her eyes. "They really know how to make a lady feel welcome in New Orleans. I can't wait to meet the parish attorney. He'll be a treat, no doubt." She closed her eyes, letting the hot water relax her stiff muscles. "Del, why did you have to come here? I told you to stay in Paris."

※ ※ ※ ※ ※

After trying to eat a breakfast of overcooked eggs, spicy sausage, and something lumpy and white called "grits" in the hotel dining room, Meg took the short taxi ride to the court-house. She'd chosen to wear black except for her red cloche, handbag, and heels. She'd also worn her ruby earrings and soli-taire ring. A discreet show of wealth might make her path to Del easier.

Still under a black umbrella, she mounted the courthouse's worn marble steps as the insistent rain pounded down. Her stomach tightened with her grim mood, but outwardly she maintained her habitual mask: calm, in control—so at variance with the restless, dissatisfied feeling she strove against every wak-ing hour.

She made a quick perusal of the list of names and offices on the board and then walked up another flight of marble stairs to enter the parish attorney's office.

Standing behind his desk, a pale young man with freckles and prominent ears greeted her.

"I'd like to see Mr. St. Clair," she said as she handed the young man her gilt-edged card. She waited patiently while he took it in. Overhead, one lone lamp dangled from the high white ceiling and cast a ghostly glow over the darkly paneled outer office. The door to the inner office opened. She glanced up.

St. Clair, tall with black hair and a rakishly handsome face, stood before her. She studied him in a calculating manner. What kind of man was he? He'd telegraphed, but would he help her or not?

He paused, returning her scrutiny. He held her card. "Miss Wagstaff," he read from it. "How may I help you?"

She longed to say, "Just give me Del DuBois and I'll go away and leave you alone." But, of course, that was impossible. She had to play out her role, just as she had in France. "I've come to inquire about Delman DuBois. What is the status of his case?" To her own ears, her voice sounded too careless.

"Delman DuBois?" No recognition touched his cool gray eyes.

"Yes, you sent my father a telegram?" She watched the man's face. He had a small red scar along his jaw.

A crease appeared between his jet black eyebrows.

"Lincoln Wagstaff, San Francisco," she prompted.

"Sorry, I don't—"

Fury flamed through her. She stepped forward. "Do you have so many murders in New Orleans that you can't remember the names of the suspects?"

He scowled at her. "*Oh,* that telegram I sent for the piano player who robbed and shot his boss."

"*No!*" With her index finger, she prodded him right beneath the knot of his black tie. "The *innocent* piano player *you* have falsely charged."

He caught her hand and gripped it.

Her gloved hand tingled within his grasp. She blushed hotly and tried to pull herself free.

He held tight.

Scorching him with a glance, she tugged once more.

He released her. "Miss," he said in a low voice, "I don't understand your interest in this case. I thought that telegram went to Delman's people, a colored family. You obviously aren't family."

Arrogant . . . Several more descriptive terms in French raced through her mind. She wanted to shock him with the truth— that, though they were of different races, Del was like a brother to her, that he was probably worth ten Gabriel St. Clairs!

But she held it in. The truth could be of no interest to this insufferable Southern gentleman. Didn't antebellum males go out with the bustle? "Del's grandmother raised me." She forced out the words. "When she died, my father became Del's guardian."

Her explanation appeared to take the edge off his opposition. "Why didn't you say that in the beginning?"

Because I thought you were smart enough to recognize the name of the man to whom you sent a telegram three days ago. My mistake. "Would you please tell me the status of his case?" Meg asked in a measured tone.

"Where is your father?"

"What?" Had the man's brain stopped working?

"I sent that telegram to your father."

He's still sparring with me. Why? Was it just because she was a woman, or something else? "And my father sent *me* to see what Del needed to get this matter cleared up. Now what is the status of Del's case *please?*"

"I'll give you a list of local attorneys—"

"Thank you,"—she held onto the shreds of her frayed temper—"but *why* won't you tell me what's taken place in the three days since the telegram?"

"Criminal law is no fit topic for a lady."

Meg stared at him. "I can't believe you said that with a straight face."

She finally nicked him.

He flushed red.

Pent-up words flowed out of her lips. "Haven't you heard down here in Dixie that the Nineteenth Amendment is about to become law? I will be a voting citizen soon. Furthermore, for your information, I've been accepted at Stanford University law school for the fall term. If I intend to be a lawyer, law is a fit topic for me. *Now,* I'd like to know the status of Del's case. I'd like to visit him and then hire local counsel." Tempted to hit him with her dripping umbrella, she stared at him, daring him to insult her again.

"I'll give you that list of local attorneys." With a hard jaw, he met her stare.

CHAPTER 2

In the world you will have tribulation.
John 16:33, NKJV

MEG STARED AT ST. CLAIR. "Why are you behaving this way?"

"In what way? Your old nurse's grandson needs legal counsel, and that's the only help I can give you."

"You're being helpful?" She thought she'd talked to stubborn men before. More furious words bubbled in her throat. Realizing animosity wouldn't get her anywhere, she held them back and substituted, "Fine."

"Won't you come into my office then and wait while I make out the list myself?" He nodded once to his secretary, then pushed his door open wider and ushered her into his neat, masculine office.

With a great deal of unnecessary ceremony, he took her black umbrella and damp coat and seated her in a comfortable dark leather chair. If his former behavior hadn't shown his lack of respect for her as a woman, this wouldn't have offended her. But as it was, she suffered this behavior, which she considered insulting and demeaning, without a word. She felt like a kettle just starting to boil, but Del was depending on her to get this misunderstanding straightened out. This man was the prosecuting attorney. She couldn't indulge herself further by telling him off, even though he so richly deserved it. Perhaps, she conceded, he might merely be treating her as he had been taught. But how could such a young, twentieth-century man act like a Neanderthal?

He'd never have survived in France. The rigid ones always cracked, then broke.

As he quickly wrote out the list, he kept up, in a rich Southern accent, a soothing flow of inconsequential chatter. Meg commented appropriately but doubted he would have noticed if she'd remained silent—or even disappeared.

The self-absorbed Southern gentleman—handsome, sleekly-tailored, and completely maddening. She wanted to ask him if he understood the Fourteenth and Fifteenth Amendments and especially the Nineteenth, which would grant women the vote and was so close to passage. As a lawyer, he must have at least read them. The poor man didn't realize he was a relic, the last of a dying breed. Deciding to view him as a museum exhibit made it possible for Meg to sit quietly and just observe.

Standing, St. Clair handed her a half-sheet of yellow paper. She rose and accepted it. Even though her hands were gloved, the brush of his strong fingers on hers set a tingling racing through her palms. Had he done that on purpose? Did he have enough nerve to flirt with her?

If so, she might as well use whatever means she could, even feminine wiles. She smiled up at him demurely from under her fluttering lashes. If she flirted with him, would he actually think his gentlemanly behavior had reminded her of "her place"?

She glanced at the paper. Only four names and addresses had been jotted down. "I didn't realize there would be so few lawyers in New Orleans."

"I'm afraid very few lawyers will be interested in such a cut-and-dried case."

"Especially for a black man?" she asked disingenuously, smothering her irritation at his prejudgment of Del's case.

He nodded. For a moment, he looked as though he might say more. He obviously changed his mind and went to open the door for her.

Burning with unspoken outrage, she allowed him to show her out with every courtly courtesy. When he shut the door firmly behind her, she murmured, "You'll rue this day, Gabriel St. Clair." She marched down the hall to the ornate staircase. As she descended the marble steps, she struggled to turn her anger into action. She needed a cool head to think how to get Del out of this scrape with the law. How had Del gotten into this fix? Helplessness and the frustration it caused clustered around her heart, threatening her peace of mind. After France, why had Del insisted on coming here?

Outside, she rode away in a black-and-white taxi. Rain pounded on the metal roof. When the taxi passed the building marked Jail, tears of frustration stung her eyes. She hated to think of Del, so alive, so good, being caged up away from his music. *Del, he wouldn't tell me anything. He wouldn't even let me see you. What am I going to do?*

In the distance, above the two-story buildings that crowded each other along the narrow streets, an imposing cathedral spire caught her eye. The lure of the old comfort of religion, of faith, ensnared her. She tapped the cabby's shoulder and directed him to take her there. Out of the taxi, she hurried into the shadowed church.

The sound of the splashing rain on stone steps lingered by the open double doors. Farther inside, however, the French colonial church was quiet. Meg closed her eyes, letting the peace of the cathedral seep inside her heart. She felt transported back to France, where every city and even some villages boasted a medieval church. How many times, either in the midst of battle or on leave, had she stolen into the back of a church and listened to the murmur of prayers and felt warmed by the glow of candles?

The churches in France had been different from her home church—completely foreign. But that hadn't put her off. She had been half a world away from San Francisco. Of course, the churches would be unfamiliar.

Sliding into a rear pew, she knelt on the padded kneeler. Closing her eyes, she bent her head to the top of the worn wooden seat in front of her. She wanted to pray for Del, to ask God for guidance. She couldn't. All her life, she'd been taught to pray. But now, inside, she felt parched, empty.

Why pray? Rain falls on the just and the unjust here in New Orleans as it had in France. She remembered two soldiers standing in a city square: one was taken, killed by exploded shrapnel; the other was left, stunned and alone.

Now, instead of prayer, snatches of sermons, hymns, and memory verses surged and rolled in Meg like the dark sea at Cherbourg: Oh, God, my God, why hast thou forsaken me? Vanity, vanity, all is . . .

Outside, the rain cascaded in gray sheets. Barely any daylight glowed into the cavernous church. Why couldn't the storm pass? A little sunshine might help her hope.

Stop! Stop this, she told herself. *Del's counting on me. If I can't get this cleared up, his life could hang in the balance. No time for angst, Meg. Time for action.* She sat back in the pew, wiped her eyes, and drew in a few deep breaths. Two black-robed nuns entered and rustled about at the front. Their white wimples glimmered in the murky light.

Meg opened her purse and drew out the yellow paper. St. Clair had told her to go to one of the lawyers on this list. However, he'd made his stance against Del clear, so she couldn't trust the man. Using his list would be the last thing she did. She glanced at the names. They might be the worst lawyers in New Orleans!

In order to find a lawyer, to find out what was happening to Del, she'd have to go where lawyers were, see them in action. She stood and walked swiftly out into the dreary street. The rain had softened to a mist. Jackson Square, a city park surrounded by a black wrought-iron fence, lay before her. At the far end, she glimpsed street vendors standing under dripping awnings. The French Market that Fleur had spoken of must lie there beside the river. But Meg had no time for those things today. Hailing another taxi, she ordered, "Take me to the county . . . I mean, parish courthouse please."

✹ ✹ ✹ ✹ ✹

"Marie didn't die." Gabe couldn't get Paul's letter out of his mind. The bleak sky outside the courtroom resulted in almost no natural light coming through the tall windows. Someone coughed. From the high ceiling dangled lonely globes of light in the austere white plaster and polished oak room. The only colors—royal blue, red, white, and gold—in the long room were the three flags in front, the Louisiana flag, the U.S., and the Confederate.

Gabe felt as if he were waiting in a funeral parlor. He'd opened the letter right after that Yankee woman left. Why hadn't Paul written sooner? *Marie! Oh, Marie!*

"All rise," the bailiff called, bringing Gabe back to his surroundings. Just another numbing, mundane day of prosecuting duties, initial appearances where he announced charges against prisoners. Petty theft, prostitution, first-degree murder . . . *I shouldn't have left France.*

Ignoring his unsettled feelings, Gabe put this internal argument aside as white-haired and black-robed Judge Simon LeGrand gaveled the court back into session.

Gabe efficiently stated charges, first against a thin man who had been caught pickpocketing, then against a black prostitute in a wrinkled blue dress who had strayed from the Storyville red-light district. Both in turn pleaded not guilty, and bail was set. Then Delman DuBois was brought out and led to the desk facing the judge's bench. Someone behind Gabe let out a shocked gasp.

Gabe glanced around, then looked at the prisoner more closely. Three days had improved the boy's appearance, though a white bandage stood out starkly on his dark forehead.

Remembrance of the Yankee woman's arresting face intruded on his confused thoughts. Miss Wagstaff would be worth a second look if a man could overlook her naggy voice. Still, what kind of man sent his young daughter alone to take care of a murder charge?

·"You weren't much kinder," Gabe's conscience prodded him. "Why wouldn't you tell her that Delman's initial appearance was before the court today?"

Because it would only upset her. Even I was disgusted by his battered face. I couldn't expose a lady to something like that.

"You mean you felt guilty, not disgusted, don't you? A bound prisoner had been beaten," his conscience pressed harder.

I can't be held responsible for others' crimes. Worse happened in France! I sent the telegram, checked to make sure the boy received a clean bed and medical attention. I can't change the way things are. I'm just the prosecutor.

The Yankee woman's extraordinary face, framed by that ridiculous scrap of a hat and full bangs, flashed through his mind again like a red flag waving to irritate him.

The ancient judge straightened a few papers in front of him with clawlike, blue-veined hands. "What are the charges against the prisoner?"

Gabe replied, "Theft and murder in the first degree."

"How do you plead, Delman DuBois?" The judge peered down at the prisoner.

"Not guilty, Your Honor." Delman stood tall in spite of his rumpled clothing.

"To both charges?" the judge prompted.

"Yes, Your Honor," the prisoner's voice sounded defiant, but hollow.

Then Gabe noticed the judge's gaze straying from both him and the prisoner to a point behind them. Unwilling to behave unprofessionally by twisting his neck around, Gabe waited in a silence that settled over the courtroom as everyone wondered what had caught the judge's attention.

"Miss," the judge asked in a polite tone, "is there a reason for your standing in the aisle of my courtroom?"

"Yes, Your Honor."

It couldn't be. Gabe stiffened as he recognized that Yankee woman's voice. She had nerve, he'd give her that! Gabe forced himself to keep his eyes on the judge; he wouldn't allow her audacity to draw him into ungentlemanly behavior. Why did this woman have to push her way where she didn't belong . . . and today of all days.

"Would you care to give the court your reason?" the judge continued with exaggerated courtesy.

"If I may."

Her sweeter-than-sugar tone aggravated Gabe. She hadn't sounded that way in his office. She might fool this old judge, but not him.

"You may if you'll do so quickly." The judge motioned for her to come forward.

Her high heels clicked on the hardwood floor. Each tap made Gabe's irritation mount. "Thank you, Your Honor. I just wanted to let Del know that I'm here to help him—"

"Meg!" Delman swung around.

She hurried down the aisle past St. Clair.

In the stark courtroom, Gabe took in the sight of her. Tall, slender, dressed in daring high fashion—all in black, with long silk-stockinged legs. Red hat, red purse and shoes, and rouged lips, she flaunted herself like an exotic tropical bird.

She reached for Delman's hands.

His wrists were shackled, but he caught her hands in his and bent his head over them. "Thank God, you've come," he murmured.

Gabe averted his eyes, uncomfortable by the show of emotion inappropriate between them—and in a courtroom no less.

Seeing Del's battered face more closely evidently shocked her. "What did they do to you?" With this question, she cast a blistering glance at St. Clair.

Gabe wanted to clear himself of her suspicion, but what did it matter what some Yankee thought anyway? She had no business standing in judgment over him. He had more important things, matters of life and death, on his mind. Marie's sweet face slipped through his thoughts, disrupting his concentration. How had she survived?

"Counselor, would you explain what happened to the prisoner?" The judge stared pointedly at Gabe.

Holding tightly onto his self-control, Gabe gave a cramped smile. "Delman resisted arrest."

The prisoner straightened up and let go of the lady's hands. She stared at St. Clair and, in a quiet voice directed to him alone, demanded, "Is this why you wouldn't tell me about the status of Del's case?"

Before Gabe could reply, the judge asked, "Mr. St. Clair, do you know this young lady?"

"Yes, Your Honor. She visited my office this morning. I gave her a list of lawyers who might represent Delman." Men went to court, not ladies. And her showing up here now shouted an immodesty that no real lady would ever display. Another wild flapper.

The judge asked her what her relationship was to the prisoner. She gave the judge the same answer she'd given St. Clair.

The judge looked sympathetic. "Young lady, we can't hold up this proceeding any longer."

"I'm sorry, Your Honor. But could I ask one question please?"

Her flustered expression was very convincing. St. Clair gripped the back of the chair next to him, fighting the urge to hurry her out into the hall and give her a piece of his mind.

The judge nodded, obviously enjoying a lovely distraction in a boring, gray day.

She tilted her head shyly. "Is this a case where bail would be possible? Bail is the right term, isn't it, Your Honor?"

Her bewildered tone didn't fool Gabe. A woman who said she'd applied to law school knew something about bail.

"Mr. St. Clair," the judge asked patiently, "has the defendant obtained counsel?"

"Your honor," Gabe replied in a measured tone, "I wrote her a list of names—"

"Yes, he did, but I'm a stranger here," the woman interjected, sounding earnest. "How do I know how to judge which one to hire?"

Her helpless-sounding explanation made Gabe clench his jaw so he wouldn't let a rash word slip. This judge was a stickler for decorum. And obviously he was also a sucker for a well-turned ankle, which this woman definitely, unfortunately, possessed.

The judge spoke again, "It would have been better if a male member of your family had come, Miss."

My thoughts exactly, Judge. Gabe shook his head fractionally.

"My father couldn't leave my stepmother. She's at the end of a very difficult confinement."

"That is unfortunate. But the question of bail will have to be postponed until Delman has obtained counsel. Mr. St. Clair, I will order a continuance for this case for two days while this little lady seeks counsel for him."

"Thank you so much." Her voice dripped with honeyed relief. "Your honor, are prisoners allowed visitors?"

"You'll have to talk to the bailiff about that, Miss."

"Thank you again." She touched the prisoner's shoulder, then he was led away. Gabe watched her as she sauntered to the back of the courtroom to sit down again. As she passed him, the blasted woman had the nerve to smile sweetly at him.

Gabe continued his duties in the courtroom. All the while he felt her eyes burning into the back of this head. Women and law didn't mix. She'd just proven that.

But the question lingered inside him—what was he going to do about Marie?

✻ ✻ ✻ ✻ ✻

Shaking inside with outrage, Meg remained for nearly a half hour observing St. Clair, who would be prosecuting Del; then she made her way out of the courtroom. In the hallway, she asked the bailiff about visiting Del. He told her she could see him at the jail the next day at four in the afternoon. She walked out to the street. The rain had stopped, but dismal clouds obscured the late afternoon sky.

Seeing the evidence of the abuse Del had suffered had more than shocked her. Now in addition to justice, she wanted revenge. Her father had never sheltered her from the nasty side of life. At fifteen, she'd started doing interviews for her father's issues magazine, the *Cause Celebre*—talking to abused orphans, striking workers outside factories, suffragettes, children picking fruit twelve hours a day for pennies. Then in France she'd witnessed wholesale carnage and unimaginable suffering—too horrible to put into words. But this was Del—her lifelong friend, nearly a brother, and one of the finest men she knew. At the very least, she'd yearned to slap the prosecuting attorney's smug, Southern face.

Another taxi took her to the telegraph office where she struggled to suppress her anger enough to sound confident in a message to her father: "Dear Father, arrived safely. Stop. Spoke to parish attorney. Stop. Have seen Del. Stop. In process hiring counsel. Stop. Love to all, Meg."

Soon she returned to her fern-laced hotel lobby and requested her key. An envelope awaited her, a pink gardenia-scented one. Upstairs in her room, she slit it open with her nail file. It was an invitation to dine with Aunt Fleur's cousin, Emilie. Meg tossed it onto the soft bed and lay down. Dinner? She should be starving, but all she wanted was to storm the parish jail, free Del, and shake off the must and mold of this dreadful town.

"Get a grip," she told herself firmly. Today she'd learned Del's situation was more serious than she'd thought. The only way she could help Del was by arming herself with all the information she could find, not only about law but about this city as well. She needed to know where the power lay here, and who had clean hands. *I'm a stranger here.* But Fleur's Cousin Emilie could introduce her to people of influence. She saw now that she'd need influence to free Del. He didn't merely face a false charge; he faced unabashed racial prejudice, perhaps hatred.

She phoned Emilie, who was just thrilled that Meg was in town, couldn't wait to meet her, and who would send her car to pick Meg up at 7:30 P.M.

✻ ✻ ✻ ✻ ✻

The evening mist masked the moon and stars. Dressed in a sleek ebony wrap, Meg stepped out of Cousin Emilie's car. Feeling nearly invisible in the gloom, she nodded her thanks to the Negro chauffeur and was greeted at the door by a white-haired black butler in tails. She'd guessed correctly then—this would be a formal dinner. A footman received her evening cape, and she was announced to a drawing room dotted with about ten people. The ivory-and-green room had a faded elegance. She guessed that much of the graceful empire furniture with its glowing patina was original to the house, probably dating back to the Louisiana Purchase and before. Meg was reminded of a French chateau she'd once been invited to during leave in the south of France.

Cousin Emilie, a petite graying widow, came forward with arms outstretched. "Meg, honey, we are so happy you could join us. Fleur has often mentioned you in her letters over the years. How is our dearest Fleur? How I would love to see her."

After embracing Emilie in return, Meg smiled and murmured polite responses, all the while being drawn to a grouping of chairs around a fireplace. A generous fire flickered behind a brass screen and chased away the damp chill of the January night. Emilie seemed honestly glad to see her, and that soothed Meg's frayed nerves. Maybe she would find help for Del here.

Emilie introduced the assembled party—starting with her daughter, son-in-law, and her teenage granddaughter, Maisy. The three women showed a family resemblance to Fleur—all petite, attractive brunettes. But a branch of the family must also be fair. A stylish blonde cousin, Dulcine Fourchette, about Meg's age, had also been invited. Dulcine affected the pouty look of film star Mary Pickford, a look that was all the rage.

Then Meg was introduced to the other guests. Her interest perked up. They were Mr. and Mrs. Sands St. Clair and their teenaged daughter. Mr. St. Clair, still a handsome man with graying temples, sat in a wheelchair. His wife sat beside him. Plump and pretty in a china-doll way, she was dressed very conservatively. St. Clair? Could they be related to Gabriel St. Clair?

Meg didn't ask. Saying the man's name out loud would necessitate explaining how she had met him. She didn't think, at this moment, she could be civil about Gabriel St. Clair, and this was a polite occasion. Besides, she hadn't gathered enough facts to come up with a strategy to free Del. On no account did she want to make the wrong impression or to embarrass Aunt Fleur with any lapse of decorum. She banked the fire in the pit of her stomach. Meg needed these people and what she could learn from them. Taking the place Emilie indicated, Meg lounged back against a wicker chair and smiled politely.

"I just love your dress, Miss Wagstaff," Emilie's granddaughter, Maisy, gushed.

"Thank you. I brought it back from Paris." Meg had chosen to wear a black silk Charmeuse that skimmed over her slender form. Meg noted the cousin, Dulcine, surreptitiously evaluating, weighing, and measuring her.

So Meg reciprocated. Dulcine, who still wore her long blonde hair pulled low in a neat bun, obviously realized her fair beauty called for pastels. She wore blue satin with a peplum waistline and a modest longer skirt. Did Dulcine think Meg intended to rival her in this social setting? How amusing. Meg couldn't resist teasing her along. Meg crossed her legs and managed to let her slim skirt slide a bit higher toward her knee.

"You've been to Paris?" Maisy asked with excitement lighting her eyes.

"Yes." The girl's innocent reaction made Meg feel at least a century old. She folded her arms as though protecting herself from the past.

"Don't be so modest!" Emilie exclaimed. "Meg spent almost two years in France. She was one of our brave young American women who worked at YMCA canteens sustaining our gallant doughboys!"

Both young girls in the room looked at Meg as though she'd just been crowned queen. Their reaction contrasted sharply with Dulcine's and Mrs. St. Clair's. The latter frowned deeply and cast a worried glance at her young daughter. Meg was used to this reaction.

Don't worry, madam, your innocent daughter is safe from me. I won't lure her into disaster with exciting tales of France. The war is over. An unidentifiable emotion, something akin to fear and grief, washed through Meg. She smiled, masking it.

The raven-haired young St. Clair girl, appropriately named Belle, breathed, "How exciting that must have been."

No, never. Why did young women still react like this? Hadn't enough truth about the war reached the States? "Sometimes the work got a little too exciting," Meg commented dryly and forced another deceptive smile. "You can't believe what it was like being one of only three women when a hundred soldiers came to dance. Sometimes I changed partners ten times during one song. I wore out several pair of shoes just dancing!"

Her two young admirers looked a bit daunted.

"My, that *does* sound like a sacrifice," Dulcine slipped in coolly.

"You're too modest, Meg." Emilie made a deprecating motion with her hand. "Why, Fleur wrote me that you were injured at the Somme."

Meg smiled and swung her leg slightly. Her pointed-toe pump cast a shadow on the wall. She pushed away her dark memories of the Somme.

"You were?" Belle squealed. "How?"

"Belle," Mrs. St. Clair admonished, "Miss Wagstaff is a lady, and a lady never discusses physical problems."

"Well," Maisy announced, "you don't look like being in Paris hurt you at all. You've got the goods! Your dress makes us all look frumpy by comparison—"

Dulcine shot a razor-sharp glance at Meg.

"Oh, no! You look lovely." Meg went on nonchalantly, "Most of us bought Parisian designs to help the designers get back on their feet. The war decimated the French economy."

"That was indeed charitable of you," Sands St. Clair put in.

Meg caught the hint of irony in his tone and laughed. "And, of course, the temptation to come home with the thoroughly modern look was irresistible."

"Personally," Mrs. St. Clair said with a disapproving moue, "I don't understand what the Paris designers are thinking. The new fashion is no fashion at all! How much skill does it take to drop a sack on a woman?"

Meg could detect all too clearly the likeness in outdated ideas between the prosecuting attorney and this woman.

"Mother!" Her lovely daughter, with her long black hair coiled at her nape, blushed with embarrassment. "Miss Wagstaff will think us dreadfully old-fashioned."

Meg laughed again. "My father wasn't too happy with my new look either. My skirts are too short!" She smiled warmly at the little brunette.

"I think it's the cat's meow!"

Dulcine chuckled in a superior manner, which made Meg wonder—was this woman one of those who couldn't abide any other eligible females in her territory? How tiresome.

The butler entered and announced dinner was served. Cousin Emilie led them to the dining room, and Meg was given the place of honor next to her hostess. Glancing about the table, Meg noted one seat still unoccupied and wondered briefly who might be missing. This day of extreme emotions had begun to tell on her. She wished she felt sharper mentally. With so much on her mind, how would she continue polite conversation?

"Everyone, enjoy the wine." Emilie lifted her glass to salute her guests. "That dreadful Prohibition is only weeks away."

Meg raised her glass to her hostess but didn't take a sip. She viewed the coming Prohibition with mixed feelings. Her own European experience had also affected how she viewed the amendment. She wondered if it could work out as the temperance workers anticipated.

"Emilie," Sands St. Clair spoke up, "you needn't fear losing your right to drink your own wine in your own home. Prohibition only regulates the sale and distribution of liquor."

"But my wine cellar cannot hold a lifetime supply!" Emilie countered.

"Those foolish Yankees, pushing such a ridiculous law down our throats," Mrs. St. Clair said with a frown. "Why can't they understand that dinner without wine is like a rose without its fragrance?"

A murmur of agreement flowed around Meg. This woman who evidently wanted no change in the still-new century just had to be the mother of the Neanderthal Meg had met this morning. The connection was absolutely certain in her mind now.

"It is a foolish law," Sands said with quiet authority. "How the U.S. government expects to enforce this law considering the vast borders of our country and without spending money on a sizable enforcement fleet is beyond me. It is not only a foolish law; it is bad law."

"You speak like a lawyer," Meg commented, surreptitiously evaluating him.

"Until my riding accident before the war, I had an active law practice."

Meg nodded in a sympathetic way. "My father, though a teetotaler himself, has said the same thing, sir. He says bad laws make honest men criminals and lawbreakers rich."

"Well said," Sands agreed.

"What brings you to New Orleans?" Mrs. St. Clair asked, striving to sound interested.

From the dining room doorway, the black butler announced: "Mr. Gabriel St. Clair."

Hearing the name brought Meg instantly alive. She, along with everyone else, looked toward St. Clair, who strode in wearing impeccable evening dress. The phrase *devastatingly handsome* slipped through Meg's mind. He looked like a Spanish noble-man from a Renaissance painting: olive skin, black hair, high cheekbones, and a look of insufferable superiority. He bowed over his hostess's hand, then glanced up.

Concealing the shiver of recognition that trembled through her, Meg smiled and lifted her water glass to him, then took a sip. Round three was about to begin.

CHAPTER 3

Don't be impatient.
Psalm 27:14, TLB

Meg forced herself to smile urbanely while inside she flared with animosity. That man! Of all the people in New Orleans, she'd have to eat dinner with Gabriel St. Clair!

"Gabriel, dear," his mother called for his attention.

He turned and bestowed a light kiss on her pale, unrouged cheek.

"How dreadful you had to work late again, son."

"I'm sorry. It couldn't be helped. I'll make it up to you and Emilie." He gave his hostess a dazzling smile.

Meg waited for him to recognize her. What would his reaction be?

From her place at the head of the long damask-covered table, Emilie waved gaily to him. "Oh Gabriel, I must present to you Miss Meg Wagstaff from San Francisco."

St. Clair turned to her politely. Meg read no sign of recognition on his face. What? He wouldn't deny meeting her earlier, would he?

But unbelievably, he greeted her as though he'd never seen her before, then took the vacant mahogany chair beside his mother. His refusal to acknowledge that they had met earlier stumped her. What was he about?

"Gabe," his sister claimed his attention, "Miss Wagstaff was in France!"

"Very interesting," was his only comment as he leaned toward his mother in conversation.

Meg watched Dulcine greet him. Meg sensed the other woman's interest in him, although outwardly the young blonde showed no particular partiality for him. *Dulcine, you're welcome to him.*

Amid a discreet rustle of linen and with quiet commands from the butler, the footmen served the first course, stuffed crab. St. Clair continued to behave as though they had never met. He chatted with his mother and Dulcine and teased his sister about a beau sending her a nosegay. His behavior made no sense, but if he intended his denial to put her at a disadvantage, he'd failed. Meg wasn't about to let one irritating lawyer fluster her.

She toyed with the idea of embarrassing him by recounting his refusal to help her, but she couldn't put her hostess in an awkward position, and in the end, it would do Del more harm than good.

The dinner proceeded uneventfully. The highly polished silver gleamed in the candlelight. The gilt-edged china was obviously old, but treasured. Emilie certainly knew how to set the mood of elegance and ease, and Meg's own deep fatigue threatened to take the edge off her alertness. She pondered the enigma of Gabriel St. Clair. Was she nettled by him because she resented men who refused to see women as equals? Had he refused to recognize her because he feared looking bad over mishandling Del's case? Or was this another high-handed I'll-put-you-in-your-place tactic?

Finally, Meg decided to stir the simmering situation and see what floated to the top. She leaned against the table. "Mr. St. Clair?"

Both men looked at her.

She smiled. "Yes, I might as well address this to both of you. I'm looking for a good defense lawyer." She observed St. Clair closely, but he didn't show a flicker of recognition.

"Why do you need a defense lawyer?" The senior St. Clair asked, appraising her with a sharp glance.

Emilie replied before Meg could, "That's why I invited you, Sands. I thought you and your son might advise her. She's come to get her old nurse's grandson out of some trouble here."

Watching St. Clair from under her straight bangs, Meg nodded. "Yes, after being mustered out of the infantry, Del decided to come here to learn more about New Orleans jazz. You see, he's a very accomplished pianist."

Mrs. St. Clair shook her head and murmured in a disapproving tone, "That awful jazz."

Ignoring this, Meg leaned forward, folding her hands under her chin. "He's been arrested for robbing and murdering his boss at the nightclub where he played."

Dulcine paused with her fork above her plate and smiled archly. "Not a very appetizing dinner topic, Miss Wagstaff."

"No, indeed," Mrs. St. Clair agreed.

"I agree, but I need to find Del counsel. He's obviously been framed, and I need someone who can prove that in a court of law."

A lull settled over the table as though everyone waited for a response to Meg's statement.

"A most unfortunate incident," Sands murmured. "Are you positive he's innocent?"

His question didn't anger Meg. He didn't speak condescendingly. "Del is no murderer. We grew up in the same house. He isn't capable of dishonesty."

Sands accepted her answer by nodding.

Gabriel St. Clair leaned back in his chair and challenged her with his glance. The flickering shadows of the candlelight wavered over the contours of his face, giving him a mysterious quality. Meg felt the pull toward him from deep inside her. She resisted it. He was just the kind of man she couldn't respect. He had no social conscience.

"What if you're wrong? Do you know what evidence there is against him?"

His blunt words weren't unexpected, but they hit Meg hard anyway.

His mother spoke up, obviously to divert the conversation. "Perhaps you could call on Gabriel tomorrow, Miss Wagstaff, for advice. Now let's talk about the social season. After all, this is Belle's year to come out. I can't believe my little girl is all grown up."

Maisy, Emilie's granddaughter, exclaimed, "Miss Wagstaff, you've come to New Orleans at just the right time. It's Carnival!"

"Carnival?" Meg continued the exchange in spite of her concentration on the young attorney.

Maisy added enthusiastically, "Carnival starts each year with January's Twelfth Night Ball and ends the night before Ash Wednesday. That's Mardi Gras!"

Emilie smiled. "Yes, you must come to our cocktail party tomorrow evening. I'm one of the first hostesses in New Orleans to give one! A pox on Prohibition! In spite of it, from now until Mardi Gras, it's just one gala after another!"

The facts of the New Orleans social season were of no interest to Meg, but she made a polite rejoinder. With any luck, she and Del would be long gone before Mardi Gras. Out of the corner of her eye, she noted Belle's young face. The girl looked close to tears. Why would talk of parties depress a young debutante?

Like a high sandbar in the Mississippi, Meg sat back and observed the remainder of the evening flow by—taking in Emilie's gardenia perfume, the sweet chocolate mousse, the easy conversation of long-time friends. Beneath her unruffled surface, however, dangerous currents swirled and eddied.

Inwardly, she fretted over coming up with a plan for tomorrow. She had to find a willing and competent lawyer, then visit

Del at the jail. Recalling the image of his mangled face, she gripped the curved arms of her chair. She had to find some hope to give him.

✻ ✻ ✻ ✻ ✻

Later, at Emilie's request, St. Clair offered the Yankee woman his arm and escorted her to his Franklin Touring Car to drop her at her hotel. The hour was quite late. The air was thick and chill. As he helped her into the passenger seat, he watched his parents' car as their chauffeur drove them away.

His sister's underlying unhappiness had been evident to him also. Why couldn't she just enjoy her first season? With one last wave to his hostess, he started his car and turned down the short lane to the street. He predicted the ride wouldn't be a quiet one, not with the Yankee in his car. He glanced at her from the corner of his eye.

Beside him, she leaned back against the seat indolently. Her sensuous posture mocked him. "So, why didn't you want anyone to know that we had met earlier?"

Her mocking tone scraped his taut nerves to the breaking point. He answered bluntly, "I have better manners than to discuss legal business at dinner. Ladies aren't interested in law."

She had the nerve to chuckle. "Where do you get these Gothic notions?"

He tamped down his rising irritation. Even though this woman had popped up three times in his day, she wouldn't last in New Orleans for long. She'd find out all too soon she couldn't wrap every man she met around her little finger, even with her "come-hither" look. "My mother has always requested that my father not discuss legal matters at dinner."

"Why doesn't that surprise me?" The ivory lace of her collar shone in the darkness, casting faint light onto her face.

Her implied criticism galled him. "My mother is a wonderful woman—"

"Your mother is a wonderful *nineteenth-century* woman." Languidly, she pushed her bobbed hair behind her ear.

40

Her presence worked on him even as he resisted it. He forced himself to concentrate on their dispute, not her obvious appeal. "Well, isn't your mother?"

"Heavens, no."

"I don't expect you to understand our ways," he asserted.

"Yes, I'm just a Yankee." She stretched like a cat. "Now, I don't believe your first answer to my question. Why didn't you let on that we had met earlier?"

He gave no answer. When he'd entered Emilie's dining room, the sight of Miss Meg Wagstaff had driven a stake into the possibility of the soothing meal with old friends he'd anticipated. He hated to admit to himself how much this woman had bothered him—in his office and later in court. Then to find her at the table in the midst of friends . . .

He'd really been through too much today: Reading Paul's disturbing letter about Marie, then tedious hours of courtroom detail and duty. Finally, he'd spent more than an hour trying to get a phone call through to the American Embassy in Paris without any luck.

Meg lifted her fingers through her bangs. "You're angry with me because I wouldn't do what you told me to do."

His exasperation burst. "You are the type of modern woman I dislike the most," he bit out. "You say you are the equal of men, but you don't hesitate to use feminine wiles to get your own way."

"Oh, you're making me feel so ashamed," she taunted him as she angled her body toward him, using all her feminine attraction to mock him. "If you're honest with yourself, you'll recall I was frank with you until you began acting like a medieval lord. If you don't fight fair, I don't feel compelled to either."

Her comment rankled him. How dare she tell him how he should behave? "You don't know what you're talking about." *You don't know me at all!*

She sniffed audibly.

"That boy is guilty. The evidence proves that."

"Boy?" she retorted. "Del's a man, a good man, and he's innocent. You and your vicious police have made a mistake. All I need is a good lawyer to prove it."

"Fine. Some people have to learn everything the hard way." *And you're lucky you're in New Orleans. In France, that meant dying.*

Then his mind whispered, *Marie didn't die.* And that was the only thing that really mattered.

❋ ❋ ❋ ❋ ❋

Today Meg would finally get to visit Del—if she survived the search for a lawyer to represent him. It was early afternoon as she sat in another law office and smiled painfully at the secretary, the fourth one she'd met that day. "Mr. Gibbon's name was given to me by Mr. Gabriel St. Clair. I need to hire a lawyer for a friend."

This lawyer was the last one on the St. Clair list. A night of worry had brought her no new ideas on how to find counsel for Del. She had to get a lawyer, and St. Clair had given her a list of four. Though outdated and narrow, he might be honest. If nothing else, she would eliminate the four names he'd suggested, then go on.

The secretary showed her into the lawyer's office. A white-haired man stood to greet her. Would this man take on Del's case? Facing Del today without a lawyer would crush them both.

She sat down and smiled. "I'm interested in hiring an attorney to represent a friend of mine."

"This is about that black boy charged with murdering Mitch Kennedy?" the man asked briskly.

She stiffened. "Yes, how did you know?"

"Got a call from a friend. Said a Yankee woman stopped in his office this morning."

This frankness threw Meg off her stride. "Oh?"

"I'm afraid I'll have to give you the same answer he did. I just don't have the time to take on another case right now."

The room felt as though it was growing warmer, much warmer. Meg stood up abruptly, afraid she might begin to cry. "Thank you for your time."

Outdoors again, she stood on the street corner, wondering what she could do now. The judge's continuance gave her only today and tomorrow to obtain counsel for Del. She needed a lawyer to plead for bail. How could she give Del hope if she couldn't even hire a lawyer for him?

She knew a great deal about law, but not Louisiana law, and she wasn't qualified to practice yet. She would be no help to Del without a New Orleans lawyer. Maybe her first thought had been correct and St. Clair's list was exactly the men she should not be applying to. This thought fired her frustration twice as hot as the day before. Hiring counsel shouldn't be so hard. Del's arrest had just been a dreadful mistake. A good lawyer could unravel it, and she and Del could get out of New Orleans as soon as possible.

She marched back inside the same office building she'd just left. She scanned the list of lawyers and notaries public on it. She had learned that Louisiana law was similar to English common law in criminal cases, but much different in civil law, which was patterned after the Napoleonic Code. Therefore she ignored the notaries listed and chose the next lawyer, one who hadn't been recommended by St. Clair.

An hour and two more rejections later, she walked across the narrow street and into the first law office there. This office held no secretary. A very young lawyer greeted her himself.

She noted interest flare in the man's eyes. Using her most convincing helpless-female tactics, she told him she was a stranger in New Orleans and needed legal advice.

"Please, Miss, do take a seat. Now how may I help you?"

"I have a friend who needs a lawyer."

"What is the charge against him?"

Meg was so weary of explaining, but she had to keep trying. Some lawyer in this city would accept Del's case. She kept her eyes downcast demurely. "It's a rather serious charge."

"Yes?"

"I'm afraid it's murder."

"You mean that black boy?" The young man's tone hardened.

"Yes, Del DuBois." She looked him directly in the eye.

"That's not the kind of case I'm interested in—" He stood up.

"But—"

"I'm sorry—" He took her by the arm.

"But—"

The man literally hurried her out of his office. Meg had never felt like a Typhoid Mary before, and it wasn't a pleasant experience.

What was going on here? First, she'd thought St. Clair had given her a list of the worst attorneys; then she decided to try his list. Finally, she'd gone hunting her own and been turned down by everyone she asked. This shouldn't be so hard. Was it Del's race? Was it the crime he was charged with—a black man killing a white man? *What am I missing?*

✻ ✻ ✻ ✻ ✻

Dread gnawed at Meg's empty stomach. When she left for France in 1917, she had gone overseas plump. But she had come home without a spare ounce of fat. Hunger still touched her, but food never seemed to be what she needed to satisfy her. She barely ate at all these days.

Now, as she walked down the dingy corridor with others who had come to visit a friend or a relative at the Orleans jail, she was glad her stomach was empty. The odor of disinfectant, body odor, and cheap perfume sickened her.

How could she face Del and tell him she had failed? Her knees weakened.

Following the bailiff's instructions from the day before, she had arrived at the parish jail at quarter to four. Now, along with the others, she halted and listened to the deputy's gruff practiced speech: "When you enter the room, go to the table of the prisoner you wish to visit. Do not touch the prisoner at any time.

Sit down and put your hands on the table. Keep them there or you'll be asked to leave. Are there any questions?"

Aware of covert glances from the other visitors, Meg stared at him silently like everyone else. She felt like replying to the unasked question that hung in the air around her, "I don't belong here and neither does Del."

The deputy went on, "Very well. Follow me. You will be allowed in one at a time." He unlocked the door and began letting them in one by one, asking for the name of the inmate from each.

Meg's turn came. She murmured Del's name.

The deputy touched her arm, halting her. "Who?"

She repeated Del's name.

The man stared at her hard. His expression made the hair on the back of her neck prickle. "You'll be sittin' on the colored side of the room."

She nodded, then stepped into the room. Everyone watched her as she crossed from the area of white inmates to the black. Jim Crow lived in jail too. Why hadn't that occurred to her before?

As she negotiated a path around the many square wooden tables, her heart beat in her ears like the bass drum in a marching band. She sat down, placed her hands on the scarred tabletop, then looked at Del.

The swelling had gone down from the day before, but Del still looked wounded, haggard. She longed to take him out of here to a doctor, a hot bath, and a good meal.

"Meg." He nodded to her, then attacked without preamble. "Why didn't your father come? I didn't want to put you through this . . ."

"He couldn't leave Cecy so near the end of her pregnancy."

Del nodded, but his expression stayed stormy.

Meg understood a little of his frustration. Even under normal circumstances, he hated waiting. Now he had to wait, powerless to get this sorted out. She wanted to touch his hand, to tell him she was taking care of everything, but she could do neither.

Besides, pointing up his helplessness would only make him feel more desperate. Her own failure caught in her throat.

After studying Del's battered face, she asked, "Tell me what happened. How did you get mixed up in this?"

He hung his head. "You were right. I should have stayed in Paris. But I couldn't reconcile myself to leaving my own country like that, and I thought I could lose myself in playing jazz here." He sighed. "I was wrong. This was the last place on earth I should have come."

"Because of the racial unrest?" Fear crouched inside her.

"Yes. The KKK is riding high in the South. Black men serving in the war and returning home in uniform has upset the racial apple cart. We need to be reminded of *our place*. But the KKK didn't get me arrested."

"Who did?" Her mouth was dry.

He paused. "I had decided to head north to Chicago. That's where everyone's going—Kid Ory, Jelly Roll Morton, Louis Armstrong. Jazz was born here, but the music is too free to prosper here. At least now. In Chicago and New York, they're paying big bucks and even recording good bands. A few guys decided to head north with me. The boss didn't like it."

Del never could leave anything alone. She pursed her lips. "He's the man you're supposed to have robbed and—"

"And killed?" he supplied. "Yes, the four of us should have just left, but he was holding back our last two weeks pay. We couldn't leave without it. So I asked him for it. He gave me the runaround. We had words."

The last three words were spoken with deadly emphasis. Meg cringed inwardly. *Oh, Del, the crusader and defender! Couldn't you for once have avoided confrontation?*

"What happened then?"

"In the early hours of the next morning, the police broke down my door, found cash and a gun under my bed, and arrested me." He fell silent momentarily. "Somebody must have put something in my last drink. I remember being really tired when I got to my room, and I fell asleep immediately. When the police questioned me, I couldn't react. It was like swimming up from deep water."

An awful dread sparked in Meg's middle. "You were drugged and someone planted the evidence in your room while you slept?"

"That, or they planted it before I got there, but I didn't notice. I was just so sleepy."

Meg gazed at him. Del's words had changed everything. This wasn't just a mistake. If Del had it right, someone had set him up. Ice slid through her veins. *Oh, Del!* A silent moan snaked through her. How could she tell him she hadn't even found him a lawyer?

And what if she couldn't get a lawyer? Would she have to stand alone and help him the best she could? She needed more information. Maybe a good private investigator could help her. Del wouldn't want her dealing with a private eye. Too often in the past, Del had tried to protect her from the truth. He didn't want her to worry about him, and he might hold back facts she needed now for the same reason.

She looked at him narrowly. She'd try to get enough information out of him now to get an investigator started with. "Who were you playing with?" she asked, watching Del intently.

"Tommy Willis, LaVerne Mason, Pete Brown. Why?"

"Are they still here, and free?"

"Yes."

"Where were you playing?" she asked off-handedly.

"A hole-in-the-wall in Storyville."

"Storyville?" she asked.

"Yes. It was the district for legal prostitution before the war. But the police don't make much of an effort, even now, to stop it if the girls stay in Storyville. It's where all the clubs are."

Recalling the prostitute in court the day before, Meg nodded. "What's the club's name?"

"Penny Candy . . ." He paused to give her a worried look. "Meg, you stay out of there."

"Del, I need to talk to people—"

He cut her off. "Meg, I don't even want you here in New Orleans."

"What?"

He appeared to struggle with himself. "Get me a lawyer, and then get out of this town."

"Why do you say that?" His words struck her as fatalistic, not like Del at all. "You know I can't—"

"That's the way I want it." He spoke emphatically, "Just get someone to represent me, then go home."

"No, I won't leave until you're free." She stared at him. "Leaving you would be the last thing I'd do."

He scowled. "Meg, I know the Wagstaffs are a family of reformers. But this is New Orleans. It's a dirty city. Just give me a fighting chance. That's all I can hope for."

His plea struck a raw nerve. How could she tell him that so far she hadn't even gotten him that fighting chance? "Del—"

"And this city won't tolerate anyone who crosses the color line. Do you understand me?"

She gripped the edge of the rough table. She'd already crossed that line when she'd walked to this table. "They all seem to buy my story that I'm concerned because you're the grand-son of my old nurse. It's true—"

"That may be. But if you show too much concern for me, it will get you into trouble." His voice became rough. "I mean it."

A kaleidoscope of images from their shared childhood swirled through her mind. She and Del had been raised in the same home. Meg's father and stepmother had raised him as their son. All through their life together, their contrasting colors had perplexed Meg. Why did the surface of their skin make such a vast difference to people? No answer had ever satisfied her. "We've dealt with this our whole lives, Del. Why do you want to let it separate us now?"

"You're alone. I can't protect you."

This sounded like the Del she knew. "I can take care of myself. I got through a war, if you recall."

"We both did." He gave her grim smile. "But both of us know it was by the skin of our teeth."

"That's the only way anyone comes through a war." She lifted her chin bravely.

The deputy's nasal voice cut through the buzz of voices. "Time's up. Everyone, stay seated. I'll dismiss you table by table. Stay seated and await my order."

Meg suddenly felt close to tears. They'd only had minutes together. She hadn't told him about not being able to find a lawyer. The deputy started going from table to table, tapping visitors one by one, signaling them to leave.

"I'll come tomorrow," she said. Surely she'd have a lawyer by then. She'd call her father. Maybe he'd found some link to an attorney here.

"No, don't. Coming every day is too much. You came to my appearance, and now today. Don't come tomorrow. I'll see you in court with my lawyer."

Meg felt the tap on her shoulder.

"Ma'am, stand up, fold your hands together, and walk to the door."

She wanted to drag Del from his chair and make a run for it, but she obeyed the deputy. Leaving Del in this dreadful place squeezed her heart, making it hard to breathe. Again she wished she possessed enough faith to pray for Del, but again she couldn't bring herself to pray. Why had God made the world this way? Her white skin and her family's money always protected her, but Del always stood defenseless before the world. Now neither their money nor influence could shield him. It wasn't fair! *Del, I won't let you down! And I won't leave you to face this alone! What do I care what these people think?*

As Del watched Meg go, he wondered if he should have whispered what he feared had caused all this. He closed his eyes. When he opened them, she was gone. A feeling of impotence gripped him. He was helpless to protect her, and he knew she, unfortunately, could be depended upon to stir up the delta muck. *Meg, be careful please.*

*　*　*　*　*

Feeling like an empty shell, Meg stepped out of the cab and walked up to Cousin Emilie's door for the cocktail party. Tonight the large house was ablaze with lights. Laughter and the hum of voices greeted Meg as she let the footmen take her cape. The butler showed her to the door of the drawing room. Some of the furniture must have been removed to make space for the people in evening dress who stood around talking to each other with cocktails in hand.

"Meg, honey!" Her hostess greeted her warmly. "You must have a Sazerac. Our Sazerac days are nearly done."

Meg took the chilled glass and sniffed the scent of lemon on its rim. She took one sip and savored its anise bite. "Very distinctive." Drinking wine in France had been natural. The drinking water had been unsafe, and wine had been plentiful, even in wartime. But now she was stateside, and in a few weeks, Prohibition would be the law of the land. The Sazerac held no attraction for her.

What's more, tonight she had to keep a clear head and try to find someone who knew a lawyer who could help Del. So when Emilie wasn't looking, Meg poured most of the drink into a potted fern. Since an empty glass would call for refilling, she'd hold a partially filled glass as protection.

Cousin Emilie led her around the room, introducing her to the other guests. All were dressed to go to the opera following the party—silks, velvets, and satins glowed in the light of the electric sconces. The men looked like stuffed penguins in their black-and-white tuxes. *Among these there must be lawyers,* Meg thought, *and there must be at least one attorney in New Orleans who would represent Del. One of these people might know him.*

From across the room, Meg glimpsed Dulcine. The blonde wore a rose jersey dress that fit tight at the waist, then flowed to the floor. A scooped neckline revealed creamy white skin. Dulcine was flirting with two successful-looking men, but Meg noted that Dulcine's glance darted back to the doorway often. Was she looking for Gabriel St. Clair, or someone else?

Meg was curious to find out if Dulcine favored St. Clair over the others or had she seemed so possessive of him the previous night merely because he'd been the only eligible man present. Dulcine's type of woman, a man-trap, always intrigued Meg.

"Good evening, Miss Wagstaff."

Meg looked around and found the senior St. Clair in his wheelchair. "The same to you, sir."

"Are you an opera lover?" he asked.

Loud laughter made her bend over to answer him. "I am, but I'm not attending tonight. I've got too much on my mind."

"Who did you find to represent that young jazz musician?"

"No one. I talked to more than a half dozen attorneys today, and no one was interested." She tried to keep her voice unperturbed. Not easy to do.

"That's unfortunate."

Meg saw Dulcine glance over, then fix her gaze on the drawing room doorway.

St. Clair spoke, "My son has arrived."

Meg nodded, watching Dulcine turn away slightly as though masking her obvious interest in the young lawyer.

Meg glanced up at St. Clair when he approached his father. She felt wicked. Suddenly she wanted to irritate someone in New Orleans, this city that had wronged Del. And she especially wanted to disconcert this tall, dark, handsome Neanderthal.

"Gabriel," she said warmly and loud enough for Dulcine to hear, "we meet again." She coyly offered him her hand and drew as closely to him as the outer limit of good manners allowed her. The scent of sandalwood hovered around him.

"Miss Wagstaff," he said woodenly. He shook her hand and tried to let go.

She kept his fingers in her grasp. "I've just enjoyed my first New Orleans Sazerac."

He nodded and gently pulled against her hold on him.

She gripped his hand more tightly. "Oh, Dulcine!" she exclaimed. "Where did you come from?" Only then did she let go of Gabriel's hand.

Directing a stormy look at Meg, Gabe then bowed to Dulcine.

Meg smiled. So the pretty Dulcine wanted Gabriel St. Clair. *He's yours, my dear. I wouldn't take him gift-wrapped.* She murmured a polite nothing and drifted away from them.

"Miss Wagstaff, please let me know whom you engage in your friend's case," Sands St. Clair said as she departed.

She nodded mechanically while she made her way to another cluster of people. For the next half hour, she went from group to group, chatting. In each group, she let it be known she was seeking a lawyer for a friend.

Finally, Meg had made it around the room. Not one person had taken the bait, though two of the men had been identified to her as lawyers. What should she do?

Meg set her glass on a tray by the door and walked the hallway to the room where ladies could freshen themselves. Stepping inside, she heard someone crying. She found Belle St. Clair weeping in front of the mirrored vanity.

The girl jumped up. "Oh!"

"My dear, what's wrong?" Meg asked.

"No . . . thing," the girl stammered.

Meg shook her head, not accepting this obviously false answer.

Belle's pretty face crumpled. "Oh, I just want to die."

CHAPTER 4

Provoke not your children to wrath.
Ephesians 6:4, KJV

FOR ONE MOMENT, MEG CONSIDered the idea of offering to summon Belle's mother. With Del in jeopardy, she had too much on her mind. Could she deal with any more? But she squashed this selfishness. If any girl needed a friend, Mrs. St. Clair's daughter needed one indeed. Meg crossed the room and took both Belle's soft hands in hers. "What ever has happened to you?"

Belle's tears increased, flowing down her flushed cheeks. The poor girl couldn't even speak.

"You've got to get yourself under control." Meg tried to keep her tone sympathetic. But what problem could this innocent have? A spat with a friend? "Someone else might come in."

This last phrase appeared to reach Belle. She began to draw in deep breaths.

Meg took her lace hankie and dabbed the girl's pretty face dry. "There now." But Belle still showed telltale signs of tears— reddened eyes and a pink nose. That wouldn't do. "Wait here. I'll ask the butler for a room where we can go to talk privately. I'll say you are indisposed."

Biting her lower lip, Belle nodded, then swallowed another sob.

Within minutes, Emilie's butler ushered them to a cozy den on the first floor. Meg thanked him as he closed the door behind himself. By the fireplace where low, orange flames flickered, Meg sat down on a chair and motioned Belle to sit opposite her. The damp delta January had chilled the evening. The warmth was welcome. "Now, what has upset you?"

"I'm a thankless daughter," Belle replied morosely, twisting her damp handkerchief.

Meg didn't know whether to curse in exasperation or chuckle. She considered the debutante. The resemblance between Belle and her brother showed in the girl's raven black hair coiled at her nape and her perfect olive skin. Even weeping, she made an attractive picture in her elegant, white satin dress. "What have you done to cause your mother to say that?"

"I . . . I don't want a season." Belle lowered her head and continued twisting the scrap of white lace within her fingers.

"What?"

Belle repeated her words.

Meg turned this over in her mind. This was more than a spat with a friend. "I missed mine too," Meg answered in a light tone, afraid of fostering more tears. "Why don't you want one?"

Belle gazed at Meg, her soft chin trembling. "You didn't have a season?"

"No, I went to Europe instead." Saying it aloud to this young girl made Meg wonder the extent of the anxiety her parents must have experienced when permitting her to travel, alone, to another continent and in time of war.

"Oh. But I can't go to Europe—"

Meg interrupted, "Tell me what you would rather be doing."

"I . . . I'd rather stay in high school and graduate in the spring." Her arms resting limply in her lap, Belle stared at the toes of her white satin slippers.

"What?" Was that all? "Why can't you?"

Belle explained with an earnest expression, "Because women in my mother's family *always* have a season at seventeen, and make a brilliant marriage——"

Meg interposed, "And they don't finish high school?"

Belle nodded with a frown.

Meg pondered this repressive attitude, which definitely fit what she'd seen of Belle's mother. She voiced the first suggestion that came to mind, "Why don't you have your season next year, after you've graduated?"

"I told you——"

Meg held up one hand. "You don't understand me. I want you to explain to me *why* what other women in your family have done *in the past* has anything to do with you. You're not British royalty! I mean, what could your mother do to you if you just continued going to school?"

Belle stared at her as though Meg spoke a foreign language.

"I wouldn't suggest you disobey your parents if you were planning to . . . say . . . elope with someone unsuitable or run away with the circus." Meg chuckled. "But what is unreasonable about your wanting to graduate from high school?"

Belle blinked. "Mother says men don't want overly educated women for wives."

Meg gave a crack of laughter. "Maybe in the Dark Ages, but this is the twentieth century! High school isn't that much education. I plan to attend law school this coming fall. That certainly won't put off the kind of man I intend to wed!"

Belle gaped at her, then looked down and fussed with the folds in her skirt, shimmering pale in the low light. "What if I want more than high school too?"

Meg sighed. "Just tell me what you want—plainly."

After a second's hesitation, Belle lifted her chin. "I want to go to college, Newcomb College here in New Orleans."

Meg wondered why any mother would object to such innocuous plans. But she had been raised by progressive parents who had assumed she would have a career. She reminded herself that this attitude still proved advanced for the times. "Go on."

"Then I'd . . . I'd like to train to be a nurse." Belle stared at Meg, half-defiant, half-scared.

Meg nodded. "Why not?"

Belle blurted out, "Mother says it is beyond unladylike. She absolutely forbids me even to think of such thing!"

Meg smiled ruefully at the foolishness of that instruction. What an unwise woman!

Belle reacted defensively to the smile. "Your parents let you skip your season and go to France! You can't understand how difficult it is for me to go against my mother's wishes."

"That's not why I smiled, Belle. My family is quite different from yours, no doubt. But you've only quoted what your mother thinks. What does your father say?"

"My father?" Belle sounded stupefied.

"Yes, what does your father say? Does he object to your pursuing an education?"

Belle looked puzzled, a line creasing her forehead. "I never thought of asking him."

"You didn't?"

"No." Belle went on explaining, "When I ask him about things, he always says, 'What does your mother say?'"

This view of Belle's family gave Meg pause. Did Belle live in such a closed-minded home?

"Do you really think he might let me go back to school?"

"I think it's worth a try. Your father seems to be intelligent and reasonable." *Unlike your mother.*

Staring at the fireplace, Belle pondered this obviously new idea. "I'll try it."

"Good." Meg tried to imbue her voice with optimism.

"What if he says no, too?"

Meg stood up. She had pressing goals to accomplish tonight. Belle must take her life into her own hands or suffer the consequences. "I have a feeling he might surprise you. But be sure to tell him everything—high school, college, and nurse's training. I think he will take you more seriously if you let him know all your ambitions."

"Take me seriously?" Belle grumbled. "No one takes me seriously."

"That means you have some work to do." Unfortunately, Meg suspected Belle's older brother would be no ally to his young sister. Not Mr. Antebellum.

Belle rose, smiling uncertainly. "May I sit with you at the opera?"

"Sorry. I'm not attending the opera tonight." Now that this young girl's problem had been dealt with, Meg champed at the bit to be off. "I have another place to visit tonight."

"Where?"

"It's called Penny Candy." Meg slipped out her white gold compact. Opening it, she studied her reflection. She fluffed her bangs and freshened her scarlet lip rouge.

Wordlessly, Belle requested Meg's compact and examined herself, frowned, then handed it back. "That's a funny name. I've never heard of it."

Meg slipped the compact into her black beaded bag, then led the young woman from the den. "Let me know what your father says."

"I will, and thank you. You've been so kind."

Meg smiled and went off to bid her hostess good night.

※ ※ ※ ※ ※

Storyville differed from Emilie's cocktail party as hell differed from heaven. The murky atmosphere of Storyville, a neighborhood in the hip pocket of the French Quarter, reminded Meg of the notorious Barbary Coast at home. Black prostitutes dressed in skimpy bits of shiny red, blue, or gold lingered at each street lamp. On the narrow lane, a sign over a doorway read "Penny Candy." Meg shivered with vague fear. "This is the place, driver. How much do I owe you?"

"Miss, are you sure dis be where you're wantin' to go?"

She handed him a silver half-dollar. She'd asked herself the same question. If Del's life didn't depend on it, she would never come to a club like this unescorted. But she had no choice. "Yes."

Still, he hesitated. "I see swells come down here after society parties, but ladies don't come here without no gentlemum." He took the half-dollar and handed her thirty-five cents in change.

"I won't be staying long. I just need to meet a few musicians, then I'll head home. Keep the change."

"Thank you, Miss. If you be thinkin' to stay just awhile, I'll stay in de area and come back around a few times."

"Fine, but don't feel compelled to pass up fares for me. So far, the nicest people I've met in New Orleans are the cabbies."

The man chuckled and thanked her again.

Meg clutched her purse as she got out. She couldn't let anyone snatch it tonight, not with what she had in it. She walked directly into Penny Candy. The rich jazz enveloped Meg, making her blood spring to life and surge through her veins. She nodded to the club bouncer and strolled past him.

Pausing, she let her eyes adjust to the dark interior. A haze of cigarette smoke hung overhead. Candles on the table glowed as points of light dotting the crowded room. The club had a tiny, jammed dance floor where couples, many in the latest evening dress, danced the new fox-trot. On a low stage, three black musicians—a pianist, a coronet player, and saxophonist—blasted out the jumpy rhythm Meg had learned to love from Del.

She chose a small empty table and perched on a hard café chair. A waiter stepped to her side. "What will it be, lady? Bourbon or gin?"

A card on the table announced: "No cover. Minimum: three drinks." She didn't want to order a drink, but to sit in the chair she had to pay for at least three. "Bourbon."

He nodded and left.

She eased back. Soon the waiter set a short glass of amber bourbon in front of her. She paid him, then motioned him to lean closer. "When the musicians take a break, I'd like to buy them whatever they choose." This ploy gave her a cover to explain speaking to them. She didn't want to rouse any suspicions about her interest in the three black musicians.

He nodded and left.

Meg looked at her drink, then slid it away. Being in a club once more swirled through her feelings like a breeze stirring dry leaves. Closing her eyes, she allowed the music to take her back to Paris, to the little clubs on the Left Bank. In 1918, James Reese Europe's American Marching Band had taken France by storm. American jazz had become the rage. Off-duty military musicians and civilian Americans who had traveled to Europe in spite of the threat of German U-boats were welcomed with open arms.

Jazz's syncopated beat and lively songs had overpowered war-torn France's pervasive misery, pain, and loss. Listening to ragtime and blues let one forget . . .

Colin took her hand in his, then he kissed it lightly. "I don't know why you've come all this way, my dear. But I'm so glad you did."

Meg straightened up, her heart racing. The memory had been vivid, undiluted by time. She had felt his caress!

She nearly reached for the glass of bourbon. No. Drowning pain in alcohol never worked. She'd seen too many soldiers in France try it and sink into utter disintegration. She had to forget her private sorrow and brace herself. Del's life depended on her!

The song ended. Meg clapped, adding her praise to the thundering applause. The couples drifted from the dance floor. The band bowed. Meg noted her waiter delivering a tray of drinks to the band, then gesturing toward her.

Her pulse beating a rapid six-eight rhythm, she rose and approached the musicians.

"Thank you, Miss," the saxophonist said amid the raucous voices.

"Don't mention it." She raised her voice over the noise, "I'm Meg Wagstaff, Del DuBois' friend."

All three of the men regarded her, then introduced themselves—Tommy was the saxophonist; LaVerne, the horn-player; and Pete on the piano.

Meg observed them for any reaction, any hint of their thoughts. They all appeared guarded, their eyes sliding away from hers. What were they wary of? "I visited Del yesterday. He gave me your names. I thought you might be able to give me more information about what happened to him."

No one answered her. She noticed, from the corner of her eye, a young black woman, wearing a stylish red dress and standing alone, staring at her from the edge of the dance floor. Or was it Meg's imagination?

The continued silence of the three men began to irk Meg. Perhaps reminding them that Del had been willing to stick his neck out for them might prompt them to help her. "Del explained that you four had intended to go up North together."

LaVerne, a tall serious-looking man, spoke up, "Del's a great guy. We told him we'd hitchhike north or ride the rails. Not to make a big deal—"

"It wasn't fair to hold up our wages, but Mitch would have paid us eventually," Tommy who had a round, boyish face put in.

Fretting at their caginess, she moved closer to them to make certain they'd hear her. "Do you have any idea of who might have set Del up? Did Mitch have any enemies?" She itched to shake them. *Help me! Del needs friends. What are you holding back and why?*

"Everyone's got enemies, Miss," LaVerne said. "We don't know nothin' about what happened to Mitch or why Del had the cash and gun in his room—"

"Good evenin'." A tall thirtyish man wearing evening dress drew alongside Meg. Near the end of her rail journey from California, Meg had glimpsed alligators slither in and out the swamps or bayous near New Orleans. This man moved like an alligator sliding into the water to watch and wait for prey. He smiled at her. "May I help you?"

Meg gave him a measuring look, hoping to repel him. "I was just complimenting the band." The slender black girl in red focused her whole attention on Meg now.

"I'm happy you're pleased, Miss." He turned to the musicians. "You boys, finish those drinks. Your break is about up."

"Yes, sir, Mr. Corelli," Pete, the thinnest of the three musicians, spoke for the first time. The others obeyed the man who obviously managed the club.

Meg's stifled her irritation and hid it under a coy smile. "Yes, I'm ready to hear some more great jazz." Trying to look unconcerned, she turned and sauntered toward her table.

"Miss Wagstaff," Corelli said behind her.

He knew her name? Or had he just overhead her say it to the band? Uncertain, she ignored him and sat down at her table again.

"Miss Wagstaff," he repeated.

She looked up at him. Who was he? And why did she interest him? "Were you speaking to me?"

"Yes."

"I didn't know anyone here knew my name." She fixed him with an unwavering gaze. What explanation would he give?

He gave her a reassuring smile, like a French merchant about to cheat her. "A lady as beautiful as you"—he paused to kiss his fingertips—"can't remain anonymous long."

She nodded coolly, but his words and manner sent a zigzag of gooseflesh up her spine. What did he want?

Without an invitation, Corelli sat down on the other empty chair at her table.

She bit back, *Who invited you to sit down?* She needed information, and she needed to keep this man thinking she was no threat to whatever he was about. She'd simper like a helpless female and see what developed. Her timing lagged a bit, but she managed to give him a sweeter-than-sugar smile. "How kind of you to join me."

"A pretty lady like you shouldn't be spendin' tonight alone." He leered at her.

Do you know anything, Mr. Smooth-as-Snakeskin? His presence made her nerves jump. "You know who I am then?"

"Yes, you're that Yankee woman who came to hire a lawyer for Del DuBois."

His knowing this proved he hadn't merely overheard her giving her name. That struck her as ominous. Evidently she'd been under observation, but by whom? She tried to think—what would a helpless female say to this? She tilted her head and sobered her face. "You must be upset over losing Mitch Kennedy," she made her voice sympathetic. "My condolences on your loss."

He frowned at her.

Good. She'd thrown him a curveball. She ran her fingertip around the smooth rim of her bourbon glass. "Del was saddened by Mr. Kennedy's death as well."

"His murder, don't you mean?" He lifted one eyebrow.

Meg ignored this and went on in a sensitive tone, "How long had you and Mr. Kennedy been partners?"

Corelli surged forward on his chair. "Kennedy and I were never partners."

She'd nicked him! "Oh? You seem to be the owner. You're the manager then?"

He glared in aggravation, his chin jutting forward. "You misunderstand. I am the *new* owner."

She let her mouth open. "I hadn't realized probate moved that swiftly in Louisiana. My, that is impressive."

"I didn't have to bother with probate." Something had caught his notice. He suddenly became distracted. "Mitch sold to me before he died."

"That made everything so much . . . easier for you, didn't it?" Meg slipped in.

"You've got that right." Corelli shot his cuffs and straightened his black tie. Someone at the bar had his attention now. Corelli rose. "You'll excuse me, please."

Meg nodded graciously. Toying with her glass of bourbon, she observed her unwanted companion talk to a short, bald man at the bar. The short man lifted his hand. Even in low light, the diamond solitaire on his pinkie finger flashed. Both he and Corelli glanced in her direction. As though she didn't notice, she kept her attention toward the band, which was playing once again.

Out of the corner of her eye, Meg observed the young woman in the red dress hesitate along the nearby wall only ten feet from Meg. Meg kept up the appearance of watching the musicians in the band, who had begun to play "Bunch O' Blues."

Meg wondered if she should make some motion or nod toward the woman. Who was she, and why did she seem to want to talk to Meg?

Suddenly the black girl's face widened with shock. She turned swiftly away—

A hand clamped hard on Meg's shoulder.

Meg jumped and reached into her purse.

"You are a complete idiot." Gabriel St. Clair, still in evening attire, sat down on the chair opposite her.

Meg's stomach clenched. Jolted from fear to anger so quickly, she felt ill. "What are you doing here?"

"I came to ask you the same question," he said with a belligerent expression.

She sent him a withering glare. This was just what she didn't need—to be seen with the parish attorney! "I am not accountable to you. Now, go away. You're spoiling my enjoyment of the jazz."

"You spoiled my enjoyment of the opera! At the intermission, Belle asked me where Penny Candy was—said that you had gone there instead of the opera—"

"I was in the mood for jazz, not opera. Why is that any of your business?" His elegant appearance stood out in sharp contrast to the drab men around them. Corelli quite obviously attempted to cut a figure like St. Clair, but seeing St. Clair here proved Corelli had failed miserably.

Right now, St. Clair looked like he could have cheerfully strangled her. "This is no place for a lady. Chivalry demanded that I protect you from your own folly."

"Folly! What a delightfully old-fashioned word. It suits you." Nothing more could be accomplished tonight—thanks to St. Clair! She stood up. "Let's leave."

Startled, he rose also. "What? You mean you are not going to argue with me and insist on staying?"

"There's no reason for me to stay now. You've ruined my evening." *And my plans.* Having a parish prosecutor sitting at her table would scare away anyone who might want to talk to her. The lovely, young black woman in red had disappeared.

"Then we're even." He trailed her as Meg led him through the maze of tables. Behind them, LaVerne was squeezing off high notes on his horn in a haunting solo. The melody put her own frustration and worry into sound.

Outside the door, Meg paused. The young black woman had preceded her outside and now stood across the street with two other women under a street lamp.

Meg tightened her grip on her bag. Its beads prickled her palms, which itched to push this oh-so-proper gentleman out of her affairs. With St. Clair at her elbow, she didn't dare try to make contact with the girl. Meg raised her voice. "Did you bring your car or do we need a taxi? I'm staying at the Monteleone."

"I know where you're staying," St. Clair growled. "I took you home last night, if you remember." With the wave of an arm, he hailed a taxi.

Just as she slid into the cab, she snapped, "I can go home alone. You don't have to accompany me."

He shoved in beside her, his solid form forcing her to make room for him on the seat. "I'm going to make sure . . . *very* sure you go to your room and stay there for the night." He gave the hotel name to the cabby.

St. Clair sitting so close made her intensely aware of him— his clean scent, his broad shoulders, his masculine arrogance, all under the civilized mask of evening attire. "How are you going to make sure I stay there?" Meg goaded him. "Going to sit outside my door all night?"

"No, I'm going to remind you that your behavior in New Orleans reflects on Emilie and her cousin, Fleur Fourchette Bower. I don't care if *you're* bent on social ruin, but I do care about Emilie and the Fourchette family."

Meg bit her lower lip. She hadn't thought of that tonight. She glanced over tentatively.

"You probably didn't know," he admitted grudgingly. "Penny Candy is one of the most notorious clubs in Storyville. *Anything* could happen to you there."

Did he think her a complete fool? "I don't think so." She slid an ivory-handled derringer from her purse. The gun weighed heavy and cold in her hand.

In the faint light, St. Clair looked shocked. "Put that away," he hissed. "I don't know what you're about, but I can see you're a danger to yourself."

Slipping the gun back into her black bag, she chuckled to irritate him. She'd gotten the exact response she'd wanted. Oh-so-proper Gabriel St. Clair invited her to be audacious. "Is that the best you can do?"

"I have said all I'm going to say. It's obvious that you have no common sense or any sense of decorum—"

"I'm not interested in being decorous." His censure galled her, and she couldn't hold back any longer. "I'm interested in finding out the truth about why Del has been falsely arrested. I'll do anything, go anywhere necessary, to see him free again."

"He's guilty. And you're out of your depth."

Blistering words smoldered inside her, but she didn't bother to answer. Why waste words on him? The man had behaved as maddening as a foul-tempered mule since their first words.

They reached her hotel. Instead of leaving it at that, he escorted her inside. Striding ahead of him as though he weren't near, she did her best to ignore him. But his powerful presence made this impossible.

Eyeing St. Clair over her shoulder, the night desk clerk handed her a key and a yellow envelope. "This telegram came for you earlier in the evening."

She accepted it with a serenity she didn't feel. "Thank you." She had already received a reply to her first telegram to her father. Had something happened to her stepmother or Kai Lin's baby?

"Good night, Mr. St. Clair." Without a backward glance, she hurried to the staircase, glad to be free of him.

"Don't mention it, Miss Wagstaff." His voice dripped with sarcasm. "See you in court."

Meg gritted her teeth. His reminding her that tomorrow she had to face Del in court without a lawyer to represent him was just what she would expect from St. Clair. She would best this man if it was the last thing she did!

CHAPTER 5

Seek, and you shall find.
Matthew 7:7, NASB

"GOOD MORNING, FATHER and Gabe." With thin morning light behind her, Belle sat down in her usual place at the breakfast table. She wore an unusual expression on her pretty face.

Gabe stared at his younger sister and wondered why she was dressed in a red cashmere sweater and plaid wool skirt, an outfit she had formerly reserved for school. Gabe took a drink of coffee, hoping it would brace him for the day. When would he get a decent night's sleep? His mother hadn't come down this morning, and he hadn't expected Belle either. "You're up early. You were out until 2:00 A.M. at that post-opera party. Why aren't you still in bed?

Belle lifted a cup of coffee to her lips. It shook a bit. "I am a bit tired, but I wanted to ask you to give me a ride to school." Her chin quivered with the final two words.

Gabe set down his cup. Coffee splashed over the rim and onto the white tablecloth.

Before Gabe could say anything, his father inquired, "You're going to school today, Belle?"

She lowered her tired eyes and in a subdued voice, said, "Yes, Father, I'd like to."

"But you quit school before Christmas!" Gabe objected.

Belle didn't answer, merely traced the pansy pattern around her china saucer.

"This is your season, your Carnival! You can't go out all night every night and go to school every day!" Gabe declared.

Father touched Gabe's sleeve and shook his head.

Gabe closed his mouth, though objections multiplied in his mind.

"Why don't you tell us what you're thinking, my dear? I know I'm interested." Father's tone remained gentle.

Belle glanced up tentatively. Her gaze flickered from her father to Gabe, then back. "I've made a decision."

Gabe detected an unaccountable anxiety in her brown eyes.

"Yes?" Father encouraged.

"I decided I want to reenter school and graduate in spring." These words brought a rosy blush to her cheeks, but Belle continued to face the two men, her expression defiant. "Then I want to enter Newcomb in the fall."

"What!" Gabe couldn't help himself.

"This is very sudden," Father commented.

"No, it isn't." Belle's jaw line and tone firmed. "I've wanted this for a long time."

"But what do you need a college education for?" Gabe asked dismissively. "You're just going to be a wife and mother."

Bristling, Belle threw him a disgusted look. "I'm only seventeen. I don't want to be *just* a wife and mother yet."

"What do you plan to do after college, Belle?" Father asked, still calm.

Belle drew herself up and took a deep breath. "I'd like to train to be a nurse."

Gabe couldn't believe his ears. "My sister is not going to work as a nurse! No *lady* becomes a nurse!"

Leaning forward, Belle propped a hand on her hip. "What about that French nurse who helped you recover after you were shot down in the south of France? You said *she* was a lady! She saved your life!"

"That was in the middle of a war! She had no choice but to come to the aid of her country!" Speaking of Lenore cost him. When would he get a chance to call Paul again? He had to talk to him!

Father cleared his throat. "Son, this is really between Belle and me."

"You can't mean you're going to listen to this . . . this nonsense!" Gabe flung up a hand. He tried to imagine his sister going to college. This completely unforeseen idea made him eye her with uncertainty. In a world run mad, timeless New Orleans—where nothing ever changed—had become his anchor.

Father ignored him. "Belle, your mother has her heart set on your taking part in this year's Carnival as a debutante. You've had dresses made—"

"I know. I do want to attend some parties, some balls. But do I have to go out every night? Couldn't I just attend a few each week? I don't want to stop my education. I have wanted to attend Newcomb College ever since I visited there with my freshman class." Belle's expression begged for understanding.

"Why didn't you say something then?" Father asked.

Belle's eyes flashed with pent-up resentment. "I *did*. Mother said it was out of the question!"

"I see." Father looked grim. "What caused you to decide to talk to me now?"

Though addressing their father, Belle's gaze met Gabe's. "Last night I felt so miserable that I went to Emilie's powder room and broke into tears."

This surprised Gabe. His sister didn't cry easily.

"Miss Wagstaff came in and found me." His sister's voice softened.

Gabe's temper flared. *I might have known!*

"She took me to the den and helped me stop crying. I was so distraught."

"What did Miss Wagstaff suggest you do?" Father asked.

Gabe didn't have to ask! *Rebellion* was that woman's middle name.

"She told me I should talk to you, that you seemed to be a reasonable man, and intelligent too."

Gabe could just imagine Miss Wagstaff's opinion of him!

"I'm flattered." Father smiled.

"She didn't have a season at all." Belle rushed on, "She went to Europe instead."

"I'm not surprised," Gabe snapped.

"That's not fair, Gabe!" Belle exclaimed. "You wrote about the American girls who worked at the YMCA canteens, how brave and good they were! Miss Wagstaff was even wounded! How can you forget so easily?"

Gabe grimaced, disgusted with himself. "You're right. I did forget. It's just . . ." He passed a hand over his forehead. "You can't know how unreal the war seems to me now. It's like some . . ." He didn't want to say "like a ghastly nightmare." He didn't want to shatter Belle's innocent illusions.

But out of that ghastly nightmare he'd gotten Marie, Lenore. *I must call Paul!* Glancing at his watch, he rose. "I've got to be off."

Half-rising, Belle cast a worried glance to her brother, then her father. "Will you give me a ride to school, Gabe? May I go, Father?"

Gabe started a denial.

His father cut him off, "I've decided to go into town today. I'll drop you at school and explain to the principal that you'll be reentering—"

"Oh, Father, thank you!" Ecstatic, Belle jumped up and hugged his neck.

Gabe watched his sister and wondered what his mother would say. He didn't like the idea of that Wagstaff woman abetting his sister in flouting their mother. But it wasn't for him to correct his father. Belle, a nurse! What next? But he only said, "I'll see you this evening then."

"Goodbye, Gabe!" his sister called after him cheerfully.

"I may see you downtown later, son."

Gabe paused. His father didn't venture downtown often. Gabe thought since his father could no longer practice law, being around the courthouse depressed him. "Did you want to meet for lunch? I won't be free today." With any luck, he'd be talking to Paul in Paris.

"That's fine. Just go about your business. If our paths cross, they cross."

"Well . . ." He left as Belle began serving herself a generous breakfast of scrambled eggs, sausage, and grits. If he didn't reach Paul at lunch, he'd try again after the 3:00 P.M. recess. He'd surely get a Paris telephone operator eventually, and Paul would have to show up at the hospital sometime.

❉ ❉ ❉ ❉ ❉

Last night's telegram had told Meg that her stepmother was on complete bed rest now until the baby would be born next month. Now, after awaking from a sleepless night and choking down two bites of scorched toast and a cup of coffee, Meg stared at the back of the cabby's black curly head. Frustration frothed inside her. She wanted to scream and pound the seat in front of her.

At 9:00 A.M. sharp, she had begun another round of visits to law offices to hire a lawyer for Del. Two hours and four lawyers later, she still had found no one to help her. Two had refused to take Del's case. One had named his price, which she was certain was about one hundred times the going rate. The fourth she had rejected. The man had been as stupid as an ox and twice as ugly. The latter didn't bother her but the former did.

She stared out the window at another misty Delta morning. "Cabby, I don't suppose there are any Negro lawyers in New Orleans?"

"I never seen one, Miss."

Perhaps in New York City or Chicago, but not New Orleans, definitely not here. Perhaps it was time to try her second option. If she couldn't hire a lawyer, maybe she could start gathering evidence. She heaved a sigh. "Do you know of any private investigators?"

"Yes, Miss. A couple of them has offices on Charles Street."

"Take me to one please." Chilled, she pulled her thick, black tweed cardigan closer around her.

"Yes, Miss." He drove her away.

Soon she walked into an upstairs office, gave her name to the receptionist, and was promptly ushered into the inner office.

A polished-looking man shook the black-gloved hand she offered him. "Berkeley James, at your service, Miss. How may I help you?"

Arranging her close-fitting black-and-white tweed skirt, Meg sat in the chair he indicated. "I'd like to hire a private investigator to look into the murder of Mitch Kennedy, a local club owner."

"Mitch Kennedy?"

With a sad smile designed to pique his sympathy, she chose her words with care: "Yes, I'm a family friend of the man who's been arrested for the crime."

🦋 🦋 🦋 🦋 🦋

With a heavy heart, Meg concealed her total dejection. As she dragged her feet—one, then the other—up the steps of the courthouse after a hasty, too-spicy lunch, the sensation of doom permeated her every fiber. She'd failed. Del had no lawyer. Even the private investigator had turned her down. He specialized in cases of trailing unfaithful spouses, not violent crime. She didn't blame him.

God, why is this happening? Del's been through so much. We both have. What's going to happen? Do you have a point? Or am I just talking to cosmic emptiness? Are you there?

Why didn't the faith learned from her father feel real after France? Why had God deserted her? Meg forced back tears of frustration.

She had to show Del a brave face. They'd survived an earth-quake and a war, now this—and they'd once again be con-fronting it alone. Somehow, some way, she'd get Del set free. Clinging to this vow, she entered the formidable courthouse, now a fortress in her mind, where her best friend in the world was held against both their wills. She climbed more marble steps to the courtroom.

Inside, she made her way to the front row of the viewing section. St. Clair sat facing forward. An image of him in evening dress spun through her mind like a movie. His meddling still irked her. A man that annoying should look like trouble—not a matinee idol.

Now sitting right behind where Del would sit alone, with-out counsel, she briefly entertained the idea of putting up bail and helping Del flee the county. *What's happening to me? Am I coming unglued?*

Gabe glanced out of the corner of his eye and watched Meg Wagstaff take a seat on the defendant's side of the room. She car-ried herself erect and with confidence. Giving nothing away, she looked neither triumphant nor downcast.

As usual, she was dressed fashionably in sleek black. The small ruby studs in her earlobes called his attention to her pale cheek and creamy neck. Though not beautiful, she was the kind of woman one couldn't ignore.

Pulling himself back to business, he tried once more to read her profile, but he couldn't. Had she actually found someone to represent Delman, or not?

"All rise."

Everyone stood as the judge in his black robes, stark against the pasty white of his face, entered. A group of rumpled pris-oners, all keeping their eyes down, were herded in and slumped down on a low backless bench along the wall.

Gabe covertly studied Delman. Still swollen, one of his eyes resembled a mere slit, but he no longer wore a bandage to cover the crudely stitched gash on his forehead. Unlike the others, he sat stiffly, like a man nursing broken ribs.

Silently, Gabe cursed Rooney's clumsy brutality. If the policeman didn't stop this, he'd be forced to speak to the chief of police. This wasn't Bolshevik Russia. Even blacks had some rights in America.

From the side wall, Delman lifted his eyes, glanced at the judge, then over the rest of those in the courtroom. For a fraction of a second, Del and Gabe's gazes met. The contempt in the prisoner's eyes sent a shock wave through Gabe. Then Delman looked to Meg. He didn't appear surprised that she sat alone. Had Delman accepted his fate? Was his contempt a reaction to this fact?

The judge tapped his gavel, silencing murmurs throughout the room. Everyone sat down with much shuffling of feet and creaking of the old wooden pews. "The court will now entertain a discussion of bail for Delman Caleb DuBois."

The businesslike bailiff called Delman to the bar. Delman stood and hobbled in his shackles to the defendant's table. He stood with his back to Meg.

"Delman, have you secured counsel?" the judge asked.

Meg stood up. "Your Honor—"

Delman cleared his throat. "I have counsel, Your Honor, but—"

The double oak doors at the rear of the courtroom pushed open with a bump and a swish of air. Gabe turned to see his family's chauffeur carrying his father inside. "Dad?" Caught off guard, Gabe stepped into the aisle. "What are you doing here?"

"I'm here to represent my client." His father gave an unruffled smile.

Gabe gaped at him.

Coming behind his father, another bailiff pushed his father's empty wheelchair, one wheel squeaking in a turning rhythm. The three of them reached Delman's side. The chauffeur settled Sands in his wheelchair. In deference to the court, he then pulled off his cap and retired to the rear of the courtroom.

Sands thanked the bailiff, then turned his attention to the judge. "Please forgive my tardiness, Your Honor. Getting me up all those stairs took my man a little longer than we expected."

The old judge's thin, deeply lined face lifted into a brief smile. "Sands, you're a sight for sore eyes. But don't be late again."

Sands bowed his pepper-and-salt head as though accepting his reprimand. "I assure you, it won't happen again."

"I take it that this means you have taken Delman as your client." The judge sent a sharp glance at the two of them.

"I have, Your Honor." Sands nodded.

Meg gave a little gasp.

Gabe clenched his jaw. His father wasn't well enough to be in court! Over his shoulder, he glared at the Yankee woman. This had to be her doing somehow.

"This is an interesting situation," the judge commented. "I'm confronted for the first time by two lawyers with the same last name. This could be awkward." The judge regarded them with a stern expression. "Since I have known both of you for years, I will simplify matters by calling you—respectfully—by your given names."

Sands nodded.

Gabe nodded, then proceeded with the bail hearing. Gabe's words came out harsher than he intended: "Your Honor, the parish asks that bail be denied. Delman DuBois has no family or other strong ties to New Orleans. There is the possibility of flight."

Judge LeGrand nodded. "Sands?"

"Your Honor, my client has never been in trouble before. He is an honorably discharged soldier. He has no desire to leave New Orleans until his honest name has been absolutely cleared of all wrongdoing."

"That sounds very good," the judge replied, "but this is murder in the first degree. The prosecutor is correct. Bail denied." The judge tapped his gavel once. "Next case, bailiff."

Gabe had no time to question his father. This morning he had asked himself, *What next?* Now he'd gotten his answer. He'd have to do something to counter that woman's effect on his family. He was beginning to think Meg would be a good name for a hurricane.

Listening to the bailiff call another name as his father rolled his squeaking wheelchair to the back of the courtroom, Gabe muttered a few choice words with which he'd like to favor Miss Wagstaff. The next thing he knew his mother might decide to run for mayor!

Leaning forward, Meg touched Del's sleeve as he turned to follow the policeman.

"Do what my lawyer says. Be careful," Del muttered, then he was separated from her. The policeman led him toward a side door and out.

Meg stepped into the aisle and hurried to catch up to Sands. She knew what she'd seen. She just didn't believe it. How? What? Why? Questions, surprise, gratitude danced through her. What she'd just witnessed seemed like a magician's act! She slipped out the door behind him.

Just outside the courtroom door, Sands awaited her, his chauffeur at his side. "Miss Wagstaff, are you free for a brief consultation?"

"When?" She felt winded, as though she'd run a mile.

"Now. It's just routine really. I just want to get the facts you've put together."

"Yes." Meg nodded, trying to catch her breath. Sands taking the case was like an answer to prayer. *Dear God, have you heard me?*

"Then come with me. We'll discuss this at my office at home."

CHAPTER 6

Blessed are those who keep justice.
Psalm 106:3, NKJV

GABE SENSED THE OMINOUS hush like a suffocating mist gathered in around the four of them—his parents, his sister, and himself. After serving the chocolate-rum mousse, the St. Clair butler signaled the footman to leave. "That will be all," Gabe's father said. The butler bowed and left. Though the rich aromas of chocolate and rum hung over the dining table, no one picked up a dessert spoon.

Dinner had been a stilted meal full of pregnant pauses and reproachful glances. Who would open the discussion? Gabe's own taut nerves revved like a motor racing.

"I would be pleased, Sands, if you would tell me why our daughter returned to high school this morning." His mother's voice, though low, vibrated with outrage.

His father nodded.

Gabe couldn't help himself. The ragged edges of his own discontent goaded him to speak. "And I'd be interested in knowing why you were in *my* court today?"

"*Your* court?" Father gave him a quizzing glance. "I thought it was Simon LeGrand's court, not yours."

Gabe flushed. "You know what I mean."

"I don't!" his mother exclaimed. "Is that where you went this morning? Is that why that Yankee girl was in the office with you? Why were you in court today, Sands?"

Father took a relaxed sip of café au lait. "This family has been operating on two assumptions—two disastrously incorrect ones, I might add. Today I realized that, and things have changed."

"What assumptions?" Mother stared at her husband.

Father stirred his coffee as though taking time to choose his words with care. "The first assumption was that Belle wanted to quit school and get married this year."

Mother's soft chin went up. "That *is* the truth. I've waited all my life to see Belle have her season—"

"I'm going to have a season, Mother," Belle put in.

Color flooded her mother's lovely face. "Belle—"

"Celestia," Father interrupted, "why didn't you tell me Belle wanted to go to Newcomb?"

Mother waved her delicate hands. "That was just a girl's foolishness. A woman doesn't need an education. It could ruin her chances to make a match. Do you want people to think Belle is bookish?"

"That wouldn't bother me a bit," Father returned.

Mother looked nonplussed at this startling sentiment.

"Belle, tell your mother what your plans are," Father continued.

Belle looked uncertain, then drew herself up. "I plan to graduate from high school in the spring. During Carnival, I'll attend a couple of balls each week—"

Mother trembled with her upset. "No—"

"Let her speak," Father said.

Belle eyed her mother with uneasiness. "Then in the fall, I will enter Newcomb. If I do well in college, I plan to go on to nurse's training—"

"Over my lifeless body!" Tears started in Mother's eyes. "Sugar, you can't be serious! Ladies don't become nurses!" Her voice quavered, "That's for poor, ugly women who can't find husbands—"

"Celestia, please let our daughter finish."

Mother visibly grappled with her upset. "I can't believe this. You are encouraging our daughter in such folly."

Belle spoke in a coaxing tone, "I can marry after nurse's training, Mother. It's not that I don't ever want to marry. I just don't want to marry now."

Mother's lips quivered. "And what true gentleman wants a nurse for a wife, may I ask?" She lowered her voice. "I lacked only two months of turning eighteen when I married your father. Why is that wrong for my daughter?"

Father reached over and placed a hand on hers. "That was in another century, ma cher."

"It was only twenty-eight years ago!" Mother declared, looking only into Father's eyes.

"And that means you're a woman in the prime of your life. I don't see you as a grandmother yet. Do you? Have I told you lately that you are more lovely now then you were at seventeen?"

This flattery obviously disconcerted Mother. Father never said such things in front of them. Gabe watched the exchange of glances between his parents. He thought of Marie. Would his mother welcome her?

Father spoke gently, "Ma cher, it is unreasonable to think that Belle's life would imitate yours exactly. Too much has changed in our world. I courted you in a horse and buggy. Our son grew up to fly in the air. There are dirigibles, movies, phonographs—"

"Those are just things. People are the same!" Mother interrupted.

"Are they? Maybe in some ways. But our daughter was born in this century. I think she is better in tune with her own generation. How do we know the changes she will face in the coming years? Do you want our daughter to be in the vanguard or be a relic from the past?"

Mother opened her mouth, then closed it.

"Father!" Belle gazed at him with wide eyes. "You do understand!"

"A little. Just *un peu.*" He sipped his coffee again.

Mother frowned. "How will I face our friends? I can't tell them my daughter is going to college!"

"If you say it with pride, you may be surprised, cherie." Father gave her one of his twinkling smiles, something Gabe hadn't seen in ages.

The smile acted on Mother also, but she still looked dubious. Shaking her head, she sighed. "I can't believe this."

Gabe agreed. Thinking of his sister as a college girl, then a nurse, seemed incredible. What had been going through his sister's mind? He'd been gone for two years. When he'd returned, she had been all grown up. *Maybe I should have talked to her more since I came home.*

"Father, what was the second wrong assumption?" Belle asked. "I need to get up to my room. I have double homework tonight because I don't want to miss the Jupiter Ball tomorrow night."

Mother gave a little moan.

"Mother, I'm not the only girl who's planning on going to Newcomb! Martine Leon and Nadine Roberts are enrolling too." Belle turned her attention to Father. "Now, back to the subject. Does the second assumption have to do with your going to court today?"

Looking grave, Father nodded. "I'm afraid we all have assumed that my injury had ended my law career. It hasn't."

Gabe objected, "You're not well enough—"

"Are you my doctor?" Father's tone stiffened.

Mother echoed Gabe's sentiment, "Dr. Sankey said you are able to go back to work?"

Father picked up his spoon. "He's been suggesting it for months."

"He has?" Mother looked startled.

"I'll never walk again. I will continue having my headaches. But nothing has impaired my reason or my memory." Father took a spoonful of the mousse.

Gabe still resisted the idea. After the riding accident, his father had been bedridden for months. At first, just seeing him in a wheelchair had been a joy. "What if a headache incapacitates you when you're due in court?"

"Most of the judges in Orleans Parish would give me a continuance if that should occur, don't you agree?"

Gabe nodded, but grudgingly. His father had an impeccable reputation. Knowing his father would never use his headaches as a ploy, most judges would grant him a continuance.

Father caught Gabe's eye. "And since you decided not to come into practice with me, I may take in another young lawyer. Then I would have someone to cover for me, if necessary."

Gabe stared at him. For more than two years, Gabe had considered his father on the shelf. He'd given up hope of practicing law with his father and had taken the position with the parish. "I see."

"I realize it will be peculiar to face each other on opposite sides at court—"

Peculiar didn't say the half of it, Gabe thought.

"What?" Mother demanded.

"I'm defending Miss Wagstaff's friend, Del DuBois—"

"Hey, that's Jake!" Belle leaped up and kissed her father. "Miss Wagstaff has needed someone like you to help her!"

Mother shook her head sternly. "Belle, please watch your language. A lady doesn't use slang."

Gabe still couldn't accept the changes. His father wasn't well enough to practice law. Belle was too young to make such momentous decisions. That Wagstaff woman's influence was changing, hurting, his family.

Mother gave a sour expression. "I might have known that wild San Francisco flapper would be at the bottom of all this."

Exactly, Mother.

❉ ❉ ❉ ❉ ❉

Later that evening, Gabe sat alone in his home office. Only the desk lamp shone in the dark room. He had tried three more times since 10:00 A.M. to get a telephone connection to the Paris hospital where Paul now worked. He'd failed. His call to the still-ravaged city hadn't been important enough to get through. Official government calls had priority, relief organizations . . .

He rubbed his forehead. Then taking out a sheet of onion-skin paper, he began his reply.

> Dear Paul,
>
> Your news took me by surprise. Please do all you can to bring Marie to Paris to you. Yes, I want her. With all my heart. I would never have left France if I'd known she'd survived the bombardment.
>
> By wire I will set up an account at the Bank St. George that will have funds sufficient to bring Marie with a companion from Paris to New Orleans. I will specify that you or Jean can draw funds. Please wire me as soon as you know anything. I have tried to call your hospital without success. *Merci, mon ami.*
>
> Yours,
> Gabriel

He sealed the envelope and slipped it into his briefcase. He would send a duplicate telegram tomorrow. One or both would reach Paul. The agony of loss plunged its sharp, poisoned claws into him. Bowing his head, he grimaced with pain. "God, help him find her. Don't let anything happen to her. She's so sweet, such an innocent. Protect her. Bring her safe to me. I have no right to ask you anything. I ask for her sake. Please . . ."

Hot tears flooded his cheeks, and a sob forced its way through him. "Oh, God . . . God . . ."

❉ ❉ ❉ ❉ ❉

The strains of jazz, "High Society Blues," floated from Clairborne House on the cool evening breeze. The Jupier Ball had begun. Carnival unleashed. The day had been unusual—crisp and clear—and the night had followed suit. Stars gleamed and twinkled around the full moon.

Belle, on Gabe's arm, stared at the bright round orb. "What a luscious moon," she murmured. Ahead of them, their mother, in a wispy gray gown, walked beside her father, who was being pushed along the walk by their chauffeur.

With a heart of lead, Gabe squeezed his sister's arm in response. All day long he'd thought about the conversation the evening before and the letter and telegram he'd written. Del's battered face and Meg Wagstaff's tart, rebellious expression at Penny Candy had intruded too. How had life suddenly become so complicated? Miss Meg Wagstaff had acted as a catalyst, an unlucky one. He had to speak to that woman and convince her to stop interfering with his family.

Inside the airy foyer they were welcomed and relieved of their wraps, then they drifted into the luxurious wine-red and gold ballroom. Without realizing it at first, Gabe scanned the large filled room for Meg. He spotted her across the room chatting within a circle of gentlemen. He stiffened with disapproval.

"She's not what I'd call pretty," his sister teased close to his ear. "But she does know how to catch a man's interest."

He glanced at his sister and made a face at her.

"Hi, Belle." A young man approached. "You're a regular baby vamp tonight."

Belle giggled. "Oh, Corby, you're the cat's pajamas yourself!"

Gabe kept his amusement to himself, but he didn't think he'd call anyone a "baby vamp" tonight!

Pretty indeed in her pink satin, Belle drifted away with Corby toward the younger set.

Gabe glanced around the room again. Miss Wagstaff certainly did know how to catch a man's eye. The black beaded evening dress she wore flowed over her slender form to her ankles. In front, the elegant high neckline and long formfitting sleeves gave the dress a modest appearance. Only when she turned did it become apparent that it was not as demure as it seemed. She wore a backless evening gown—wide open at her shoulders, it came to a V just above her derriere. That others noticed her was obvious. All over the ballroom, heads turned to catch a glimpse of her elegant spine, then looked away.

Gabe hoped this shocking display would give his father something to think about. Would he still think this Yankee woman was someone he wanted his innocent daughter imitating?

The band at the end of the room stopped playing for one of their breaks.

"Good evening, Gabriel."

He glanced down at Dulcine Fourchette. He bowed.

"I see you were taking in the view," she murmured cryptically.

He didn't pretend to misunderstand her. "Evidently, we're not quite up to the new Parisienne styles."

She gave a mirthless laugh. "I hope my cousin, Maisy, isn't going to try to mimic her. Whenever Miss Wagstaff is present, Maisy watches her every move."

"I'm sorry to hear that," Gabe said.

"I'm sure your sister is much less easily led."

Gabe hoped Dulcine's opinion proved correct.

The band began a waltz, "The Blue Danube." Gabe lifted Dulcine's wrist to read her dance card that dangled from a golden cord there. "Excellent. I see that I'm down for this waltz."

"Are you? Did you write with invisible ink?"

He laughed as he drew her to the dance floor and pulled her into his arms. Dulcine gazed up at him as they circled the floor. Her rapt gaze soothed his ruffled nerves like honeyed balm. She was a pretty girl, and the light blue gown she wore brought out the blue in her eyes. Her form was soft and pliant in his arms. For a second, behind Dulcine, he caught a glimpse of his mother's face. She was beaming. He knew she approved of Dulcine as a potential bride for him.

Inside, he faltered, then gathered his composure. Matrimony did not appeal to him. Too much had happened in France. He'd thought it was behind him, but now he knew it wasn't. If Paul didn't locate Marie, he'd have to go back to France himself.

Gabe glanced as Corby Ferrand waltzed by with Meg in his arms. As he whirled Meg around floor, Corby's hand pressed the bare skin at the small of the woman's back. For an instant, Gabe felt Meg's warm flesh under his own palm. The sensation jolted through him like fire. Immodest flapper!

"Corby," Dulcine chuckled, "looks as though he's won a horse race."

Gabe tried to push Miss Wagstaff out of his mind. Displaying all the knightly courtesy he'd been raised to show a lady, Gabe danced the rest of the waltz with Dulcine. But he couldn't concentrate on her. His unruly eyes kept tracking the shocking brunette and the creamy skin down her slender spine. Vixen.

Unfortunately, when the waltz ended, Gabe and Dulcine found themselves right next to Corby and Meg.

"Dulcine," Corby said politely, "is there any room left for me on your dance card?"

Dulcine pouted prettily. "You shouldn't wait so long to ask. It would serve you right if I didn't." She glanced at her card. "I still have the two-step open."

"Fill in my name." Corby grinned.

While this exchange took place, Gabe locked gazes with Meg. The band began playing the lively new fox-trot.

"Thank you for a lovely waltz, Gabriel." Dulcine touched his arm.

"I beg your pardon?" Gabe glanced at her. "Oh, you're welcome. My pleasure." His gaze drifted back to Meg, then back to his partner.

Dulcine was frowning.

Another man came up and claimed Dulcine, who left Gabe's side with a backward glance. Corby thanked Meg for the dance and went off in search of his next partner.

Gabe was vaguely aware that couples formed around him and Meg, then moved in four-four time to the music. His eyes lingered on the lady in front of him. His thoughts scattered. He could only breathe in her rich French perfume and take in the elegance of her form.

Meg grinned. She put her hand on Gabe's shoulder and took his other hand in hers. "Start dancing. People are beginning to stare."

His face burned, but he took her into his embrace and began to dance woodenly. He couldn't understand why he'd become mesmerized like that just standing beside her.

"It's my elemental appeal." She made her voice sultry and low. "I can't help myself. In an evening gown—I'm a siren."

"You're something all right. And pardon me, but I think you left half your gown at home."

"Which half would that be?" She mimicked his Southern drawl.

He ignored her comment. "Evidently the gentlemen here haven't fallen for your elemental appeal. You had space on your dance card."

"What dance card?" She wiggled her wrist. "Are you seeing things now?"

He noted then that she didn't have one dangling from her wrist. "Why not?"

"Do you mean why shouldn't you see things?" she asked tartly. "Or why don't I have a dance card?"

He glared at her.

Meg shrugged. "It's simple. I'm not a debutante, so I don't need a dance card."

"That's right." Her nonchalant dismissal of custom angered him. "You so kindly told my sister you went to Europe instead of having your debut."

Her expressive face slid into melancholy. "It's not something I would recommend to her."

This brought him up short. "Those are the first sensible words I've heard from your mouth."

She stared at his face as though reading it. "You went too?"

He nodded, then pulled her in tighter to him. They danced, focused on each other. Her skin against his palm warmed him. Her fragrance took him back to Paris, to crowded cafés where he had grabbed a few moments of relief from memories of the war.

He read deep loneliness in her eyes. The same loneliness he carried inside himself every day. He wanted to ask her, "When did the despair hit you? When did you realize you'd forgotten why you came? Who did you lose in France?"

Though she spoke no word, she answered him. He glimpsed understanding in her. A flicker of warmth flared in his heart. Perhaps if he spoke to her of Marie and Lenore, she would understand, not judge him.

The fox-trot ended. Shaken, he still couldn't pull himself together or release his hold on her. Slipping out of his embrace, she linked her arm in his. "We're going to get refreshments. We need them."

He let her direct his steps to a love seat beside a lush potted palm where they sipped tangy punch. Slowly, he surfaced from his preoccupation as from a daydream. "Sorry," he muttered. "I've been under a great deal of pressure."

She nodded. "Me too."

This brought all his grievances to a quick boil again. His lips straightened into a line. "How did you persuade my father to represent Delman?"

"I had nothing to do with it. Anyway, don't you think you should discuss that with your father?"

"I can't. We are representing the opposing sides in Delman's murder case."

"I heard that," she said with a flippant lift in her voice.

"You've had quite an effect on my family. You've inspired my sister to become a nurse—of all things!"

She smiled thinly. "When you were seventeen, did your mother tell you to get married and outline what you should do for the rest of your life?"

"Of course not—"

"Then why don't you think your sister has a right to her own decisions, her own life?"

"It's not the same. She is a woman."

"Yes, she is a woman! And she deserves the same freedom as you."

He glared at her.

As though in deep thought, she sipped her punch. "Your sister has depths you haven't even begun to comprehend. I think that must be the way between older and younger siblings. I have an adopted brother who just started high school this year. When I left for France, he was just a boy. I came home and found him on the threshold of manhood. I didn't know how to talk to him." She sighed.

Again, her mood touched a similar wound deep inside him. Since the war, he'd felt separated from home and family, even as he sat among them.

Still, he resisted her ideas. "Your brother starting high school is natural, but I don't see any happy endings here. Belle may fail to make a good match because she won't make as big a splash at Carnival as mother intended." He ignored Meg's attempt to speak. "And my father's health will suffer because of his taking Delman's case."

Meg saw where his words were leading. For an instant, she contemplated slapping him for his stubbornness. Had he learned no wisdom in France? Then she decided on a better punishment.

His impetuous words flowed on, "And your friend will—"

"Oh, Gabriel! The things you say!" she exclaimed teasingly. She let a deliciously outrageous laugh ripple out of her. Then she leaned forward and kissed him lightly on his parted lips.

He wanted to kill her. She read it from his expression. To keep others from reading it also, she kept her face just in front of his. "If you keep spewing nonsense, I'll only behave more shockingly."

He seethed visibly. "No Southern lady would behave as you have!"

"If being a lady means behaving as though I agree with all the nonsense you spout, I don't want to be one. You are quite sure you know exactly the lives your sister and father should lead. But you wouldn't, *haven't*, submitted to anyone telling you what life *you* should lead, have you?"

"The cases are not the same," he bit out.

"Oh?" She gave him a scathing glance. "I suppose you've never heard—Do unto others as you would have them do unto you?"

He scowled at her.

"Don't worry. Dulcine is on her way to rescue you from this notorious Yankee. I wonder if she will deign to kiss lips I've kissed. Oh dear. I may have ruined all your chances!"

She sprang up to greet Dulcine and her escort, who eyed Meg uncertainly. "Dulcine! Thank you for bringing me another dance partner." She took the startled gentleman's arm and sauntered off with him in tow.

Fuming, Gabe stood.

"Gabriel," Dulcine's voice had lost its usual liquid charm, "it's time you took me down for the buffet."

Unsettled, he began to agree, then something caught his eye. A uniformed police officer had entered the ballroom and approached his father. "Dulcine, I'm sorry. I must see what's happened."

"Of course. I hope it's nothing serious." Worry in her voice, Dulcine released his arm.

He nodded, then slid between the dancers to reach his father across the room. The officer had just straightened up.

"Father, what is it?" Gabe murmured, aware all eyes—though discreet—must be on them.

"Gabe, an attempt has been made on my client's life."

"What?" Gabe understood the words, but he stared at his father with disbelief.

"Get Miss Wagstaff." His father glanced at the officer. "All three of us will come down—"

"Rooney said that wasn't neces—"

Gabe cut him off. "We're coming."

CHAPTER 7

A man's heart plans his way,
but the LORD directs his steps.
Proverbs 16:9, KJV

GABE, WITH MEG WAGSTAFF AT his side, pushed his father's wheelchair down the stark stone-and-mortar hallway to the jail infirmary. Leaving the Jupiter Ball, where laughter and music reigned, for this dark, sad place struck him with blinding force.

At the doorway, he let the lady—as out of place in her black evening gown as he was in his tux—precede him into the cell-like room. She, in turn, held the barred door open for him while he entered behind his father's chair. In the hallway, the family chauffeur waited, his hat in his hand.

The room, small and painted stark white, looked clinical but shabby, with three cots along one wall. The overpowering smell of pine cleaner made Gabe queasy. Rooney leaned negligently against the rear wall. The doctor who tended prisoners stood with his back to Gabe, blocking Gabe's view of the patient who lay on the middle cot.

"What did you bring that d——— Yankee woman here for?" Rooney barked.

Gabe froze Rooney with a look. "Keep a civil tongue in your head in the presence of a lady."

Rooney glared back but said nothing more.

Out of the corner of his eye, Gabe watched Miss Wagstaff. She'd frozen just inside the door, staring at what she could see of Del beyond the doctor.

Gabe moved closer to the doctor. He must see for himself how bad this was. Delman was his responsibility, and he'd failed to keep him safe. "How is he, doctor?"

The man turned his head slightly. "He was stabbed in the shoulder. But in spite of a few cracked ribs, he was able to defend himself, and it didn't go deep enough to touch his lung. Evidently, he was a greater challenge than his assailant thought."

"Who was his assailant?" Father demanded.

"His cellmate," Rooney replied, sounding unconcerned.

This wasn't uncommon, but something just didn't seem right about tonight. "What was his motive?" Gabe asked.

Rooney snorted. "Who knows? Maybe he said somethin'. You know how these people are."

Gabe longed to shake Rooney. Didn't the man care about the figure he was making of himself—especially in front of Gabe's father. Had Rooney forgotten what a stickler his father was about his clients, their rights and protection?

The Wagstaff woman approached the doctor. "May I see him please?"

"Meg?" Delman's thin voice whispered.

She moved to the other side of the cot opposite the doctor. "Del, can you hear me?"

"Yes," Del said in a dry, gravely voice.

The doctor stepped back, allowing Gabe a better glimpse of Del.

Meg took Del's hand in hers. "How did it happen?"

"Jumped me," Del muttered.

Meg looked up at the physician. "What have you done?"

"I sewed up his shoulder. The blade didn't go deep, but he did lose blood, and he'll be laid up for a week or two. Fortunately, he's young and strong."

Gabe's sense of responsibility weighed him down even more. "Where is his cellmate?"

"Delman knocked him unconscious. Fortunately, the guard heard the fracas. He separated them and confiscated the homemade knife."

Meg looked faint. "How did he make a knife in jail?"

Rooney scowled. "Maybe stole a butter knife, figured how to sharpen it. Who knows? These people knife each other. They don't know any better—"

In a flash, Meg faced him. *"Who are you?"*

Rooney pulled himself up, smirking. "I'm Rooney. Deputy to the chief of police."

"You?" The unbelieving tone she used made Rooney flush. He took a step toward her.

Gabe moved to step between them. With a look, he warned Rooney back.

The lady stepped to Gabe's side, her hands balled into fists. "Let me give you a piece of advice, Mr. Rooney. My parents are very prominent in San Francisco. If anything further happens to Del, I repeat *anything,* my family and all its resources will come down on you. You'll feel it, Mr. Rooney, and you'll rue the day you ever heard the Wagstaff name."

Rooney gave her an ugly look. "Don't threaten me—"

"Rooney!" Father called him to account. "You've already been warned about your behavior in the presence of a lady. Don't think this wheelchair makes a difference. The only part of me that is crippled is my legs."

Gabe glared at Rooney and recalled that years ago his first impression of the man had been never to turn his back to him.

Father rolled closer to Rooney. "Don't think just because I've been out of commission for a few years that I can't shake things up as I did before. You know my reputation. My contacts reach to the state house."

Rooney opened his mouth, then shut it.

Father fixed the man with a hard stare. "Now, this is what I am going to do to insure my client's safety. After tonight in the infirmary, I want him moved to a cell by himself, and I'll be hiring an around-the-clock, private guard—"

"You can't do that!" Rooney shouted.

Father held up his hand. In an ominously quiet voice, he warned, "Rooney, you know I can."

Relief trickled through Gabe. He had rarely witnessed his father wield his influence to such an extent. Was his father justified? Was this more than an undisciplined prisoner? Gabe couldn't quite believe it.

Rooney's jaw worked. His eyes blazed, but he said nothing.

"I'll take that as an affirmative. Now, show me to the nearest phone." Father turned the chair himself. "Son, please stay with Miss Wagstaff while I contact the man I want to come stay the night with Del."

Gabe nodded. He didn't want this case tainted by further brutality either.

Rooney slammed the door behind himself. Father, being pushed by the chauffeur, went to make the call. The doctor departed too.

With everyone gone, Gabe withdrew to stand near the door. Miss Wagstaff's visible distress made him uncomfortable. Yet how could he, her legal adversary, ease her pain?

She drew closer to Del, then stroked his cheek. "Oh, Del"— her voice trembled with unshed tears—"if I could only take you home—" A sob stopped her voice.

"I'll . . . be—"

"No, you won't be all right. Not here!" She dropped to her knees, her elegant gown pooling on the stone floor. "Not ever! I have to get you acquitted of this murder and back to San Francisco." Tears spilled down her cheeks. She bent her head near Del's. "I can't stand to see you here . . . like this."

Gabe stood removed from the tableau. The woman's grief and tenderness toward the colored man jarred him.

With effort, Delman lifted his hand and patted her shoulder. "Meg, Meggie, don't cry."

Then Gabe recognized the tone in Delman's voice. It was the same he would have used to comfort Belle. Miss Wagstaff had said she'd been raised by Delman's grandmother. Evidently they had grown up relating as closely as brother and sister, a situation that shouldn't have been allowed to continue. The distance between the races, between them, should have increased as they grew into adults.

Meg lifted her head. "We've come through so much together—"

Delman rumbled, sounding weak, "Don't worry, Meggie. Mr. St. Clair knows what he's doing. You listen to him."

Meg nodded and wiped her moist cheek with her hand. "I will, Del. I will."

The woman's easy acceptance of Delman's instructions aggravated Gabe. Why couldn't she heed him like that when he tried to talk sense into her?

"How is Cecy's pregnancy going?" Delman asked in a comforting tone.

"She's on bed rest, but the doctor is still hopeful she'll deliver safely."

"I wish . . . I wish I could see them again."

The tone Delman used told Gabe clearly that the man thought he wouldn't see them again in this life. He probably was right. Gabe didn't see Delman beating the murder charge.

"You will." Meg smoothed the covers around Delman's shoulders. "It won't be long, and we'll be away from this dreadful place."

Delman nodded.

Gabe's father reentered the room. Gabe turned to him.

Father looked up at him. "Will you drive Miss Wagstaff home?"

"No! I—" she objected, rising.

Father held up a hand to halt her. "I'm staying to give definite instructions to the man I have called. Del will be quite safe with me and my man until then."

"Meg," Del murmured, reminding her of her promise.

She nodded, bent to touch his cheek, then stood.

Uneasy at this, Gabe spoke up, "I'll take Miss Wagstaff to her hotel, then return to help you."

Father shook his head. "No, I'll be fine. One of the jail guards will carry up my chair, or my man can make two trips. I want Miss Wagstaff safely in her hotel."

"Certainly." Gabe stepped forward. "Come, Miss Wagstaff, I'll take you home."

She nodded, but reluctantly. She made one final adjustment to Delman's blankets.

Turning the situation over in his mind, Gabe led her from the room, down the corridors, and outside into the cool, fresh air. He walked beside her to the car and helped her in.

As he drove away, a peculiar restlessness gripped Gabe, giving him an acute sensitivity to the silent, serious woman beside him. She struck him as much different than she had when he had driven her home from Emilie's dinner party. He didn't know what to say to her now. As before, she reclined like a sleek cat on the car seat. Her perfume, something rich and exotic, wafted toward him.

Even in repose, the woman beside him emanated a dangerous attraction. She had called it "her elemental appeal," but did she have any idea of its potency? At first glance, her backless evening gown had appeared to be what had drawn men to her. That was an illusion. If Meg Wagstaff had worn a dowdy gown appropriate to a middle-aged spinster, she still would have garnered admirers. Her attraction wasn't in her clothing or features.

So much of Meg Wagstaff lay beneath the surface, an enigmatic personality with rich layers of the woman inside wrapped in an elegant form. This held her secret allure.

It wasn't the first time he'd experienced this in a woman. Lenore had been the first. He recalled that awful dawn when he'd become aware of Lenore in her nursing uniform beside his cot. In that moment of acute awareness, the force of her personality had burst over him, drawing him to her once and forever.

At the memory, Gabe's pulse quickened. A peculiar mix of discontent and awareness keyed him up. The woman beside him stirred too. Moonlight illuminated dozens of the dark but glossy beads on her gown. She turned toward him, her pale skin glowing against the night. Her scarlet lips drew his attention. She had teased him with a kiss earlier. What would her lips taste of now—if he kissed her for true?

But the image of her stroking the black man's cheek had burned itself onto his brain. It bothered him. Why? Was it just the crossing of the color line, or more personal? Had he wished it had been his cheek?

She broke the silence. "That Rooney isn't to be trusted."

Gabe longed to disagree, but words of denial caught in his throat. He'd never trusted the man, and he trusted him less now. Rooney's swaggering attitude had increased recently. Why?

"I see." Her tone pronounced her understanding of Gabe's dilemma. "Doesn't it strike you as ominous that Del was attacked?"

"These things happen," he said tightly. It was true. Fights in the jail were commonplace.

"Especially around a man like Rooney." She paused. "Why would someone want to silence Del?"

Gabe wouldn't follow her down this path. No one had tried to silence Del. This stabbing was merely an unfortunate coincidence, nothing more. He voiced none of these. Fatigue weighed him down. The events of the evening gripped him still. He couldn't face returning to the ball or going home. He also didn't want to be separated from this woman—although why this was so eluded him. He wanted her with him now—that much was clear. Suddenly he knew his destination. "Are you going to be all right?"

She turned her head toward him. "Why do you ask?"

He shrugged. He wanted to take her to a spot he'd become familiar with while a student at Tulane. "I can't go back to the ball. Not now. But I don't want to go home."

Meg instantly agreed with him. Tears were still so close and her nerves jumped in her hollow stomach. Facing all the frivolity and partying was unthinkable. Yet going back to her solitary hotel room to watch the hours inch by till morning. . . . She covered her burning eyes with her hands. "Where did you want to go?"

"I was thinking of going to Alice's."

"Alice's?"

"It's a little café in Tchoupitoulas Street. Alice caters to late-night diners. We'd be early."

Food held no attraction for her, even as her stomach ached with emptiness. So tired, she simply spoke her thoughts, "I haven't eaten all day. I still don't have an appetite, but I'll go with you. I can't go back to the hotel. I'm so tired, but I couldn't sleep."

"Good."

As he drove, Meg watched the light from the full moon flicker over St. Clair's somber face. Gabriel St. Clair possessed that born-to-privilege arrogance that had never failed to irritate her. She'd dealt with it in others since she was a child. Being raised by wealthy, but progressive, parents had given Meg a kind of double life, a double vision.

She'd grown up in a mansion on Nob Hill, but when she was thirteen, she had picked melons with migrant workers. That week had been the preparation for her first article for *Cause Celebre,* her father's muckraking journal. All her life, she had moved in two separate worlds: San Francisco society and the everyday world—the world where people weren't born with silver spoons in their *houses,* much less their mouths.

She glanced at St. Clair again. Tonight he'd revealed something she hadn't thought possible. "You said you were in France?"

"I don't talk about that."

Her mouth dropped open. *What nonsense!* "Why?"

"Why talk about it? It's over, and war stories bore people."

She imagined his mother had given him this advice. It sounded just like her, like telling Meg not to discuss law at dinner. Why wouldn't she be expected to tell her son to forget the horror of France? How could she stop him from letting go of what he'd suffered? It was sad, more than sad.

Tonight, seeing Del wounded had taken the insides out of her. She'd nearly crumbled. But this man, her adversary, had come to her aid by calling Rooney to account twice. She had tossed the Golden Rule into his face earlier. Now she regretted it. In protecting her, Gabriel St. Clair might have been merely following his gentleman's code, but his eyes had told her a different story. He had been upset and uncertain about Rooney. And like Del, he had served, suffered in France.

Not one man, not even Sergeant York, could return from the Great War without dragging sacks of pain along home. Gabe couldn't be the one exception. She hadn't met any.

Could that be what made this man so quick to jam people into pigeonholes they didn't fit? Did that explain why he was so averse to change? Had so much altered inside him that the outside world must stay the same or his world might career out of control?

She understood that feeling. She'd experienced it on three occasions during her life: her mother's death, the 1906 earthquake, and the day . . .

Her mind stuttered on this thought and wouldn't go on. The third shattering loss still throbbed too fresh, too raw.

She glanced at Gabe. A question to ask him popped into her mind. Would she, could she ask it?

He parked the car on the narrow street across from a brightly lit café. Coming around, he helped her out and across the street. In spite of her wrap, she shivered in the wintry night. Inside, the black-and-white round clock on the wall told her the new day had already begun.

The restaurant was long and narrow with rough brown-red brick walls. A long counter with round, red-leather-covered stools ran along one wall. The other wall was lined with a half-dozen booths, and down the middle of the café was a line of small square tables. Everything was clean, but obviously not brand new. The café's cozy atmosphere smoothed Meg's frayed nerves.

Gabriel led her to a booth at the rear. He paused beside her. "Shall I help you with your wrap?"

Inwardly, she grinned at his proper tone. His own ideas of propriety forced him to request to help her off with her wrap. But his disapproval of her backless gown made him hesitate to "expose" her here. "You may help me off with it, then drape it over my shoulders."

He looked relieved. "As you wish."

This courtesy performed. They sat down opposite each other in the oak-paneled, high-backed booth. A tall, slender black woman dressed in a neat, stylish black dress with white, lace-edged collar and cuffs approached them with menus. "Evenin', Mr. St. Clair."

"Good evening, Dottie."

"Coffee?" She handed them the small white menus.

Gabe nodded, but Meg looked up and smiled. "I think tea might settle my stomach better. Please bring cream and sugar too."

Dottie nodded and left them.

"Alice's biscuits and red-eye gravy is excellent," Gabe offered.

The thought of red-eye gravy nearly wiped out Meg's already-touchy appetite. "I think I might be able to eat some dry toast and poached eggs."

Glancing up from the menu, Gabe looked at her. "You should eat more."

Meg sighed. "I lost my appetite in France." Would he react to her mention of Europe?

He grunted and held up the menu, shielding his face from her.

What are you hiding, Gabriel?

When Dottie returned with their beverages, Gabe gave their orders and she departed.

Holding the warm, white china mug in her hands made Meg realize how chilled she had become by the cold. Looking up, she found her companion gazing at her. She grinned. "After earlier events, I didn't expect that you and I would be breaking bread together tonight."

As soon as the words escaped her mouth, she regretted them. "Sorry. I didn't mean that the way it sounded. I think it might be good for both of us if we discovered a neutral topic. Can you think of one?" She sipped her sweet creamy tea.

He shook his head. "I'm sorry, but I don't know what you are interested in."

"What interests me?" she mused. "I'm interested in buying a car."

In the act of lifting his coffee cup to his lips, he paused. "A car?"

She nodded. "Yes, I'm beginning to know my way around New Orleans, and I'd like to have my own car while I'm here. Can you recommend a good dealership?"

"You drive?"

"Yes." She grinned. "Is this another touchy subject?"

"No." He sipped his coffee. "You might try Abbott Automobile on Baronne Street. They advertise that they are the oldest automobile dealer in the South."

"Thank you." *A straightforward answer from St. Clair! Progress!*

"You mentioned you have an adopted brother?"

A safe topic indeed, Mr. St. Clair. "Yes, Shadrach. His parents died in the 1906 earthquake."

"Any other siblings?"

"Just the one who is about to be born to my stepmother." She took a full swallow of the soothing orange pekoe tea.

"I see." He frowned. "There is one thing tonight I wish you hadn't said."

"What's that?" Would he say something to spoil their truce?

"The part about your parents' prominence and their implied wealth. Was it true?"

She nodded. "What's your concern?"

"Possibility of kidnapping. Wealth is . . . unusual here. Many people have genteel fortunes in New Orleans, but—"

"Like your family?"

"Like my family," he agreed. "But you implied great wealth. That, plus the fact you don't have any family ties here, might make you a prized target."

"I hadn't thought of that. I thought, well, I wasn't really thinking just then," she admitted. "I was reacting to the situation."

"What do you mean?"

"Rooney is a bully, and I wanted to intimidate him. I suppose subconsciously I chose my family's power as the biggest club I could shake in his face."

"I don't think . . . I don't know . . . ," his voice petered out. "I'm tired."

More than tired, exhausted. For the first time, she noticed the gray shadows under his eyes. *Do you sleep at night, Gabriel? Or do you dream of the whine and pounding of exploding shells?* If she asked this question, would he answer?

At least she'd faced the reason her days passed in deep, lonely mourning.

Dottie brought Gabe his biscuits and gravy and Meg's dry toast and poached eggs. The white plate with the yellow yolks with firm whites and golden toast looked like an advertisement in a magazine. Meg sighed deeply. "That looks delicious."

Dottie gave her an inquiring look. "Eggs and toast?"

"Just what my stomach ordered. Thank you."

Meg and Gabe ate in silence, not an angry one—nor was it stilted or uncomfortable. They were merely two hungry people eating a welcome meal.

Meg felt as though her stomach had earlier collapsed in on itself and now began to expand. Dottie brought more hot tea and coffee. Other diners filtered in. A pleasant hum of voices and the clinking of china filled the air around her.

Swallowing a bite of toast, she relaxed against the cool, high back of the booth. Replete. "Ambrosia," she sighed. For many minutes, her eyes drank in Gabriel. As she savored the last cup of tea, and he the last cup of coffee, their booth became an island of peace. She ate, and the simple food satisfied her, a sensation she hadn't experienced for months. She lingered as long as she could.

But finally at her nod, he rose and helped her into her wrap again. Aware of his hands through the warm fabric, she wondered how it would feel to have Gabriel's arms around her for more than a fox-trot. He led her outside.

In the darkness of the frosty January night, she clung to his arm and leaned into his strength. For a few moments, she allowed herself the illusion that she was protected and loved. Heady feelings.

The short drive passed too quickly. He helped her out at the entrance of her hotel. At the curb, she paused beside him and asked the question that had been on her mind all through their meal, "What was her name?"

"What?"

She repeated.

He scowled at her.

She walked past him, then turned back. "His name was Colin."

CHAPTER 8

A merry heart does good, like medicine.
Proverbs 17:22, NKJV

THE NEXT AFTERNOON, GABE raced up the second flight of marble stairs to the courtroom. Wiring money to France had proved more complicated than he had anticipated. Overhead, above the double doors, the implacable courthouse clock read 1:06 P.M. Six minutes late for Simon LeGrand's court. Drat! Gabe took a deep breath and entered.

In his black robe, Judge LeGrand sat, his chin down vulturelike, in the absolutely silent but palpably edgy courtroom. "Mr. Gabriel St. Clair, how kind of you to be only seven minutes late."

Sliding through the worn oak gate, Gabe tucked himself behind his desk. Now wasn't the time to argue over a one-minute discrepancy. "I apologize, Your Honor. It won't happen again."

The steely glance the judge gave him made it clear Gabe had better be as good as his word.

The judge frowned, making his skin on either side of his pinched mouth droop like parallel commas. "Gabriel, are you ready to proceed with the pretrial hearing for Delman DuBois?"

"Yes, Your Honor. The parish believes it has enough evidence to go to trial." Gabe's unruly mind had trouble settling into the courtroom routine. Instead, it taunted him, *What was last night's attack on Del evidence of?*

Judge LeGrand turned his gaze to Gabe's father.

Sands returned it. "I don't think the prosecution has enough evidence to connect my client to the death of Mr. Mitch Kennedy."

The judge glanced to Gabe. "Are you of that opinion, Gabriel?"

"As I said, the parish is ready to begin its case."

"Sands, I notice your client is not beside you. Why is that?"

"Your Honor, my client is unable to appear in court today due to injuries he suffered in his cell last night."

"Injuries?" The judge fingered the gavel in front of him, not looking at Sands.

"Yes, his cellmate stabbed him."

LeGrand didn't react visibly to this news, but continued, "Gabriel, were you aware of this?"

Gabe nodded. "Yes, sir." An understatement. The scene he'd been a part of in the jail's infirmary last night lingered in his mind, replaying over and over. Why had Rooney been so surly?

Gabe's father said, "I believe it is impossible for us to proceed without the defendant."

"When will the defendant be able to appear to face the charges, Sands?" The judge folded his gaunt wrists one over the other.

Sands replied, "The doctor said my client would be incapacitated for a week or two."

The judge turned to Gabe. "Is that your understanding, counselor?"

"Yes, Your Honor. The prosecution has no objection to a continuance until the defendant is well enough to appear in court." In fact, the prosecution had no choice. This case was beginning to taste bitter in Gabe's mouth.

"Very well. The court grants a continuance of two weeks. Next case, bailiff."

Gabe's father reversed his wheelchair, nodded to Gabe, then pushed himself to the gate where his chauffeur waited.

The sight of his father in the courtroom still struck Gabe as unreal. But since the advent of Miss Wagstaff into his life and the arrival of Paul's letter, reality had tilted off center.

That isn't true, Gabe confessed to himself. Reality, his old reality, had vanished soon after he arrived in France, and it hadn't yet returned. He kept telling himself it was just a matter of time. But was it? Would things here ever be the same? And what of Marie?

Last night at Alice's, he'd almost spilled everything about Lenore and Marie to Meg Wagstaff. But he'd known her for such a brief time, and she remained unpredictable. Why hadn't she come to court today? Where was she, and what was she stirring up?

※ ※ ※ ※ ※

Wrapped in her thick cardigan, Meg, chilled, wandered through the open-air stalls at the French Market. Only a mission of importance to Del's case would have dragged her here at the same time Sands was facing Gabriel in court. Laid out on great marble slabs were fish of every hue possible—gray, pink, silver— waiting to be purchased. Over tiny stoves standing on tripods, black women with colorful tignons—handkerchiefs wrapped and tied around their hair—cooked fried oysters and fish.

The pushing and shoving of the shoppers, the loud voices, the odor of fish and frying oil made Meg gag as though a ball had lodged in her throat. Meg paused and bought a steaming cup of café *au lait.* Maybe it would settle her stomach and her nerves. And the heat from the stove warmed her cold toes.

"You want to buy crab, lady?" The next vendor asked, holding up a frantic live crab in one hand, waving it inches from her face.

"No, thank you." Holding her cup close so the aroma of coffee, not fish, filled her nose, she turned a watchful eye on the crowd milling around her and haggling in loud voices and flamboyant gestures with the vendors. A hundred voices called out their wares: "Chicken! *Poulet!* Sweet ham! *Jambon!* Turtle! Turtle eggs! Grouper!"

The frying oysters and fish looked tempting, but her empty stomach felt like a tightly knotted drawstring purse. The pleasant memory of the simple meal of eggs and toast taunted her. Last night, in spite of what had happened to Del, she'd been able to eat; then she had slept soundly through the night and into the morning. The maid, coming in to clean Meg's room, had finally awakened her.

When Meg had dressed and gone down for a late brunch, she'd received a note from the desk clerk. Meg had it in her pocket now. The note had said simply: "Meet me at the French Market near the fish stalls after lunch." No signature.

The note had wiped out her appetite. She'd sat down in the hotel lobby staring at the unfolded paper in her limp hand.

Who wanted to talk to her, and why? Was this some trick? Would it put her in danger? Last night Gabe had mentioned kidnapping, so before coming, Meg had slipped her derringer into her sweater's large pocket where it would be within easy reach.

Surely, she couldn't be in any jeopardy if she stayed in plain sight and in the midst of so many witnesses. No one could lure her out of the market to the nearby river's edge unless she did something stupid. She wouldn't leave the safety of this public market, no matter what. But even permitting this line of thought made her glance over her shoulder. *Stop that! Don't be ridiculous!*

A navy-uniformed policeman strolled by whistling—as if on cue to reassure her that help was at hand. Seeing him brought Del to mind. How was he? She must get permission somehow to visit him again soon. Right now, Sands was in court asking for a continuance. Would it be granted? One would think so, but her short stay in New Orleans had already proved that unusual things happened here—daily. Meg finished her coffee and began strolling again, trying to appear nonchalant.

More than an hour later by her watch, she wondered if the note had merely been a prank or a ruse. Why would someone think it amusing to lure her here? And why would someone particularly want her here? What, after all, could happen to her at the French Market?

"Meg," a low voice spoke beside her ear.

With a jolt, Meg halted, turning her head. Standing beside her was the pretty girl who'd worn a red dress at Penny Candy. "You know my name?" The raucous voices all around them protected Meg from being overheard.

"Yes, you're Meg, Del's friend. He showed me your photograph once."

Meg nodded. "Who are you?"

"I'm LaRae. Del and me . . . we was close. He was gonna take me to Chicago with him. I can sing . . . a little."

Meg wondered why Del hadn't mentioned LaRae. She was even prettier in daylight, but so very young. Was she even seventeen? Would Del be interested in someone seventeen? It didn't fit. "Del didn't tell me—"

"He wouldn't say nothin'. He try to protec' me."

"Protect you from what?" *This doesn't make sense!*

LaRae shook her head. "I can't tell you that. It would only get you in more danger than you're already in."

"*I'm* in danger?"

"Yes'm. Don't ever come to the Penny Candy again. That's what I come to say. Don't come back." Her large, dark eyes scanned the market as the girl edged away.

Meg caught her arm. "Please, won't you tell me what you know?"

"I can't . . . I mean, I don't known nothin' more than Del. Leave New Orleans."

Meg tried to hold on to the young woman, but LaRae pulled away and disappeared between two stalls, heading toward the riverside. Meg began to follow her, then froze in place. *Could this girl be the bait in a kidnapping attempt?*

Fear rumbled through her like unexpected thunder. Her heart pounding in her ears, Meg couldn't breathe in the midst of the crush of people. She pressed her folded hands against her lips. *What should I do?*

Jostled from behind, she spun around, thrusting her hand into her pocket.

"Pardon, Miss." A shopper bowed his head in apology.

Grasping the cold metal in her pocket, Meg shivered. She pushed her way through the throng, then out onto the *banquette,* the sidewalk. She scanned the old city square, Jackson Square, just opposite her. Beyond the grassy park, surrounded by the black wrought-iron fence, two old buildings—the gray and brooding St. Louis Cathedral and the Spanish government building, the Cabildo—loomed up, forbidding in the gray afternoon. A tall, well-dressed man with his profile to her stood just inside the entrance to the park and caught her notice. Was that Corelli? Unfamiliar indecision paralyzed her where she stood. She stared across the way, trying to think. What should she do? Where should she go? No, it couldn't be. The idea that she was being watched sent icy tentacles up her spine. *My mind is running wild!*

I'm just rattled. Del stabbed and now LaRae . . .

A cab pulled up. "Taxi, Miss?" the driver called politely.

Reacting to the request, Meg moved toward the taxi, then halted. What if this taxi driver had been paid to whisk her away from the French Market? She shook her head at him and stumbled backwards.

Seeking cover in the jammed marketplace, she pushed back inside. She leaned against a rough wooden signpost. Moments passed while she tried to pull herself together. Her stubborn pulse raced, unchecked. She trembled with fear and it disgusted her. Out of habit, she found herself praying, but without any actual hope she would be heard. *Dear God, guide me. I'm all alone. What danger lurks here in this old city?*

When she could, she threaded her way back out to the curb. She'd choose a taxi to head for her hotel. Walking to the corner, she hailed a cabby. She slipped into the rear seat and gave the driver the name of her hotel.

As it pulled away from the curb, she thought she glimpsed Pete Brown, the piano player at the Penny Candy. He was staring at her. Was it really him? And did he want to talk to her too? Did he have some information about the murder? She waved a hand. The man turned away, pulling up his shabby collar. Was his being here just coincidence?

Or was it really Pete Brown? Was her mind beginning to let her down? How long could a person go barely sleeping, barely eating, before one caved in, fell apart?

I'm not imagining things. LaRae had obviously been frightened. That much had been real. Did she have good reason to be? Evidently, whoever killed Mitch Kennedy didn't want Meg helping get Del acquitted. LaRae must know who that is. Or was LaRae just very frightened?

Only one fact was clear in Meg's mind—LaRae had definitely scared her. The corollary to that being, she wouldn't mention this in her next telegram to her father.

✳ ✳ ✳ ✳ ✳

At half-past eleven that evening, still unnerved by LaRae's warning, Meg sauntered—with paper-thin bravado—into Antoine's and gave her card of invitation to the maître d'. He bowed and motioned her on. The lower floor of the distinguished French restaurant, opened since the 1840s, provided the setting for another Carnival occasion, the Ball of Pandora.

Meg had used the name of the ball to come up with an easy costume for the masquerade. The hotel manager had recommended one of the hotel maids who sewed and altered clothing. One evening and the costume had been delivered. Dressed in the style of ancient Greece, Meg wore a flowing costume of fine white linen and leather sandals. Under one arm, she carried a small box of ornately carved wood, Pandora's box.

The irony of her costume was not wasted on Meg. When she arrived in New Orleans, she had opened Pandora's box. LaRae's assignation today had prompted Meg to go over and examine every minute she'd spent that night at the Penny Candy. First of all, Del's three friends—or associates—had looked at her with ill-concealed alarm.

Then after LaRae had evidently recognized Meg from the photograph Del had shown the girl, LaRae stared at her as if Meg had horns. What's more, Corelli had already known her name and had been eager to intimidate her and send her on her way. That night Meg had passed it all off—except for wanting to meet LaRae. But had Corelli also been subtly trying to unnerve her, to scare her off? But how was he involved? Had he killed Mitch to get Penny Candy?

Did LaRae know something dangerous about why Del had been framed for murder? The girl must, or why would she warn Meg to leave New Orleans?

As these thoughts buzzed around like angry wasps, Meg greeted her hostess, Mrs. Edward Larocque, and thanked her for the invitation. The lady and her husband, dressed as a Mandarin couple, made her welcome. They'd invited her so that in tomorrow's *Picayune* society column, Meg's name—a lady from San Francisco—and Meg's father's journal could be mentioned. Inviting Meg had become New Orleans' pleasure!

Tonight Meg had nearly sent her regrets. But if she were being watched, attending the ball would lull her enemies into thinking she was just another society damsel without a brain— while at the same time, giving her an opportunity to talk with Sands St. Clair without arousing the least suspicion that she was contributing anything to Del's defense. She hated the fear that caused her to take what may be ridiculous precautions, but Del's life hung in the balance. Last night had reemphasized that awful fact.

The ball was already in full swing. The restaurant had been decorated in amber-and-green silk and fresh garlands of glossy green smilax. Entire walls had been decked with glazed amber paper. Wall sconces were shaded with amber silk and draped with more greenery. Amber lanterns hung from the ceiling. Along the walls, garden benches were nestled among a profusion of potted palms. Either the latest *trés chic* colors were amber and green, or the exotic combination must be Mrs. Larocque's favorite colors. As striking as the visual art were the rich buttery and spicy scents of French cooking in the air. These tantalizing fragrances took her back to the outdoor cafés along the Champs Élysées.

Finding an empty bench against the wall, Meg laid her wood box beside her, then sat back to enjoy the colorful costumes and let them distract her. Her unruly mind, however, drew her back to the French Market. Perhaps Sands would shed light on LaRae's warning. But she didn't want Gabriel to hear of it. He might mention it inadvertently, and someone might learn of LaRae's speaking to her.

Mitch Kennedy had been murdered. Del had been attacked. She couldn't dismiss LaRae's warning and the danger it represented.

Meg gazed at the festive party-goers. Fortunately, no one wore masks at masquerades anymore. Meg couldn't have dealt with that kind of uncertainty tonight. She needed something to put her back on an even keel. Life, once more, had become deadly serious, just as it had in France. *God, are you there? Reach down and help me recover. I need to know your love exists.*

Idly gazing, Meg surprised herself by recognizing many faces. Without realizing it, she had become familiar with New Orleans society. Now the cream of that society paraded in front of her. She watched Spanish dancers in flamenco costumes as well as eighteenth-century French nobles—ladies in wide brocade skirts and white powdered wigs of towering curls and men in pastel silk stockings and satin knee britches.

Others sported new innovative costumes. A tall lady—draped in green cloth with a silvery cast and on her head, a flowing headdress of sparkling rhinestones—impersonated a fountain. Another lady was dressed in stuffed red silk as a red balloon while another was a peacock. Meg noticed that Corby Ferrand, the young man whom Belle seemed to favor, wore a black-and-white-striped prison costume. Where was Belle?

"Good evening, Miss Wagstaff," a cloying voice said beside her.

Meg turned to see Dulcine. "What a lovely costume," Meg said automatically.

The blonde wore an antebellum dress with a hooped skirt of ruffled blue tarleton, and on her head she wore a picture hat tied with a wide, matching bow under her chin. "This dress belonged to my great-grandmother, the first Dulcine."

"Really?" Meg lifted one eyebrow. This Southern lady's affected speech could get on one's nerves.

"May I sit beside you?"

Meg gave the blond a dubious once-over. "If you can."

Dulcine settled cautiously on the edge of the bench. A hoop skirt could be tricky. If Dulcine weren't careful, her dress could fly up in front—no doubt revealing ruffled pantaloons, probably also worn by the first Dulcine. Imagining Dulcine in that fix amused Meg, but she suppressed her grin.

"I take it that you are dressed as Pandora?" Dulcine looked down her nose at Meg.

Meg picked up her prop. "Should I open my box?"

"I think you already have."

Meg couldn't think what the woman meant specifically. "Oh?"

"I hear that you persuaded Mr. St. Clair to allow his daughter to return to high school—"

What business is that of yours? "I must protest," Meg imitated Dulcine's oh-so-proper sickeningly sweet tone. "I did nothing but soothe Belle's nerves and suggest she discuss the matter with her father."

Dulcine pursed her pouty mouth. "Be that as it may, your influence has encouraged my cousin, Maisy, to also reenter high school—"

"Now that is shockin'!" Meg added Dulcine's Southern accent to her imitation of the blonde's over-bred speaking style.

"What will New Orleans do with so many fair and educated ladies! It is mindboggling!"

Dulcine glared at her. "I might have expected you to behave in this way—"

"You expected me to behave just like this, didn't you? Why? So you can tell everyone—behind my back—how unmannerly I am?" Meg fixed Dulcine with a hard stare.

"What an unpleasant remark." Dulcine stood up abruptly, causing her skirt to sway and billow precariously.

"Be careful, Miss Fourchette, or you'll embarrass yourself!"

Without a backwards glance, Dulcine sashayed away, her nose in the air.

Meg chuckled. But instantly came the backlash. Her amusement burst like soap bubbles. The contrast between her inner worry and her jovial setting made it difficult to behave naturally. Dulcine's spitefulness distressed Meg. She couldn't breath. The pain pressed down on her. *Can't the sadness end? Wasn't France enough? My heart is weary unto death, O, God.*

In the early hours at Alice's, she had felt this relentless vise that crushed her heart loosen. What a blessed relief that had been. But meeting LaRae had brought the pain surging back. *How am I to go on? Will this agony never end?*

"My sweet Meg," Colin whispered, *his tender lips grazing her ear. "Let us be happy while we can."*

Meg closed her eyes and leaned back against the wall. *Too short! Our time together was too brief!*

"Good evening, Miss Wagstaff."

Meg opened her eyes and gasped. Hiding her turmoil, she exclaimed, "Belle, what a delightful costume!"

Belle blushed. "Do you think so?" The debutante had come dressed as a powder puff in sheered pink satin and swansdown. A hoop high around her shoulders continued down and all around stretching the pink satin in a full circle. Belle wore pink silk stockings and pink gloves up the length of her arms. On her head she wore a tight matching silk cap that covered her hair completely.

"It's the most imaginative costume here!"

"Thank you—"

"You're the bees knees!" Corby Ferrand, in prison stripes and a flamboyant mustache, appeared at Belle's elbow. Spying Meg, Corby cleared his throat. "I mean, Miss St. Clair, could you find room for me on your dance card?"

Belle blushed even more, becoming as rosy as her costume. "I would be honored, sir."

The friendly convict puffed out his chest and offered Belle his arm. "May I escort you to the punch bowl?"

Beaming, Belle nodded, and Corby led her away.

Meg saw Gabriel watching the scene from across the room where he stood beside his parents. Picking up her box, Meg arose and crossed to join him. After his sharing Alice's with her, she couldn't view him in exactly the same light as before. He was old-fashioned and never questioned his own arrogant belief in his superiority as a white male. But last night she'd glimpsed the man hidden under that staid facade.

Still, she must keep any hint of LaRae and her warning from him. Gabriel St. Clair was the prosecution. She must not forget that fact merely because she'd eaten a delicious late-night supper with him in blessed peace.

He exchanged polite greetings with her. "Your costume suits you."

Outwardly composed, Meg nodded her thanks. Gabriel was dressed as a gentleman from the time of the Louisiana Purchase. He wore a high white collar; a short, fitted black coat with tails; and form-fitting, buff-colored knit breeches. The outfit showed off his athletic form and broad shoulders. Awareness of him skittered through Meg. She recalled leaning close to him last night, feeling his warmth and strength.

"Yours suits you too." Before he could reply, she turned to his father. "I received your message at my hotel. I'm glad Del's continuance was granted."

"Simon LeGrand is a stickler in court, but he is a reasonable man. I told you I didn't doubt I could get the continuance." Sands had come attired in regular evening dress.

Meg stepped close to him and bent to whisper into his ear, "I need to tell you something."

"After dinner," he replied.

Dressed all in lavender with a tall pointed hat like a medieval lady in a fairy tale book, Mrs. St. Clair frowned. "I don't like Belle's outfit this year. Little Bo Peep would have been charming on her. But she said it was out-of-date. A powder puff! She doesn't even wear powder!"

Meg wondered if the woman were really saying this to Meg herself. Did she think Meg had suggested Belle's costume? No doubt Mrs. St. Clair yearned to tell Meg to stay away from Belle, that she exerted a bad influence on her daughter. What a tiresome woman. Change had come with the war, but not everyone had faced that fact yet, especially those who didn't want to bend.

For a moment, a longing to sit and chat with her own stepmother, Cecy, broke open inside Meg like the first finger of dawn piercing a dark horizon. When Meg had been home in San Francisco, she had avoided being alone with the young, beautiful stepmother who had raised her after Del's grandmother had died in the earthquake. Now Meg regretted this. Cecy would have been so kind, so understanding.

She was nothing like Mrs. St. Clair, who seemed petty. How did a woman turn out like Mrs. St. Clair—only concerned about society and appearances? Homesickness, an emotion Meg hadn't felt since her first trans-Atlantic voyage, swamped her.

With a coy smile and a come-hither expression, Dulcine floated by in her antebellum gown. Meg expected Gabriel to follow her. The thought brought a distinct tug to Meg's midsection. But Gabriel stayed at Meg's side. Why? She glanced at him. Had he begun to take Dulcine's true measure?

"Doesn't Dulcine look lovely?" Mrs. St. Clair cooed.

"Very," Sands said.

"Yes, she does," Gabriel agreed, but he still didn't budge. Instead, he turned to Meg, "Miss Wagstaff, may I escort you to dinner? I see our hostess leading the way."

Meg stared at him. "If you wish." *But why?*

Taking his arm, Meg let herself escape into this moment of nearness. Maybe she could recapture some of the peace they'd shared in the early morning hours. She glanced at him as he led her to the dining tables. His short, raven hair still showed a tendency to wave around his ears. Meg imagined her fingers tracing the patterns of those silky, close-cropped curls.

When they were far enough away from Gabriel's mother, Meg decided to tease him. She murmured, "I'm certain your mother would prefer you escort Miss Fourchette."

"I'm old enough to make my own decisions."

Looking up at him, she studied his gray eyes, so soulful. Then she tilted her head, inquiring. "I agree. But are you escorting me to point this out to your mother?"

"I wanted to take this opportunity to repeat to you what I told my father just before we came tonight."

"Yes?" *Had he decided to doubt Rooney and really investigate the evidence against Del?*

Gabriel looked her in the eye. "I'm glad my father took Del's case."

Midstride, she halted, taken by surprise. "You are?"

"I am." He took her arm and led her to where long tables set for dinner awaited them.

"Why?" Meg wondered what had brought about this change of heart. The first day Sands had returned to the practice of law in court, Gabriel St. Clair had looked ready to froth at the mouth.

"Because I believe every citizen should be represented in court if he faces a capital crime."

"Is that all?" More lay behind his declaration. Had he begun to notice there was more to Kennedy's death than an argument over money?

He frowned. "Does there need to be a further reason?"

"I suppose not. I was hoping you might have begun to doubt Del's guilt."

"I am the prosecutor. Del has been charged with murder and has been imprisoned. It is my duty to prosecute him to the full extent of law—"

"And to the best of your ability?"

He gave a slight nod. "We understand each other then?"

"We do," she agreed. With this admission, he had proved himself a man who might need to be persuaded to look at the truth, but he was able to face the truth when he found it. The words they exchanged had been formal, but Meg didn't miss their importance. *Admitting this cost you, Gabriel St. Clair. I honor you for it, but you're still my opponent. I'll get Del acquitted in spite of you.*

Meg located her name card on the table and sat down, greeting Emilie and her son-in-law, one on either side of her. After helping Meg with her chair, Gabriel bowed to Meg and drifted away to find his place. Meg forced herself not to follow him with her gaze.

After dinner, Meg danced with Belle's young beau, Corby, then Emilie's son-in-law, biding her time till she could speak to Sands privately. Finally, she gravitated toward the older gentleman and sat down beside him under a palm and the abundant glossy green smilax garland. "Alone at last," Meg murmured.

For a change of pace, the band began to play the rollicking Virginia Reel and one of the musicians took the role of "caller." Dulcine and Belle had switched places. Corby partnered Dulcine while Gabe went through the lively steps with his sister.

Sands grinned. "What do you have to tell me?"

"When I went to Penny Candy, I noticed a pretty young black woman who looked as though she wanted to talk to me. When your son escorted me outside to take me back to my hotel, I purposely said my hotel's name loudly so she would know where to find me."

"How did she know who you were?"

"Del had shown her a photograph of me."

"I see. Did she find you?" Sands glanced at the dancing.

In the center of the room, the dancers laughed and called encouragement to each other as they tried to follow the caller. With her eyes, Meg followed the twists and turns of the dance. The smaller-than-usual dance floor put the wall decorations at risk. One garland hung askew already. Meg brought her attention back to the conversation. "She got a note to me early today, asking me to meet her at the fish house at the French Market after lunch. So I went."

"I wish you would have consulted me——"

"I woke late and you were due in court. I was going to such a public place, I knew I would be safe." Meg paused. Still dancing, Gabriel laughed. Belle shook her head good-naturedly at him. "Besides, I took my derringer in my pocket."

"Heavens." Sands grimaced ruefully. "Modern women. Well, did she come?"

Meg nodded. "She told me to leave New Orleans."

"For what reason?"

"She said I was in danger."

"What kind? From whom?" Sands demanded in an undertone.

"That's all she would say."

"Really? Think back. Tell me everything she said."

Meg closed her eyes, concentrating against the rollicking tune of the Virginia Reel. "She told me her name—LaRae. She said she was a close friend of Del, that I should never go to Penny Candy again, and that I should leave New Orleans."

"That's all?"

"Essentially." The dancers began to swing their partners round and round.

Sands frowned. "Did you see anyone else you knew?"

"I thought I saw one of the musicians from Penny Candy, and maybe Corelli, the new manager."

Sands's brows drew together, making him look grim. "I don't want you taking any more chances like this in the future. We don't know what delta slime we'll be digging into with Del's case yet. Understand me. You're not to run this kind of risk again." Sands's stern tone reminded her of her own father.

Recalling her own fright, she nodded. "I won't." She glanced at the dancers.

In the midst of a round-and-round, Corby miscalculated, swinging Dulcine a little too wide. The back of her oversized hoop skirt rocked up and caught on the tail of a green garland.

Instead of giving way, the garland didn't budge. Off balance, Dulcine stumbled, tried to catch herself, but down she went on her bottom. The garland released its hold. Her hoop skirt flew up in front, hiding the damsel's face but revealing lacy modern unmentionables.

The music cut off. The dance halted. Shocked gasps and laughter burst out. Meg pressed her hand over her own mouth, fighting the honest laughter but failing completely. The mirth burst from deep inside her, rocking her—jolting her—back to life. Her father's voice spoke in her memory, "I hear God in the laughter of children." Suddenly she felt the whisper of God inside her, felt the tug of life and happiness once again.

"*Oh! Oh!*" Dulcine's voice proclaimed her outrage.

Corby tried to help her up, and Belle rushed over too. Gabriel finally succeeded in lifting Dulcine to her feet.

The blonde's face, flushed hot-red, twisted in an ugly expression. "How dare you?" she shouted at Corby. "You clumsy oaf! Why didn't you watch what you were doing?"

Corby, glassy-eyed, tried to answer, but his mouth opened and closed wordlessly.

Belle stepped forward. "Dulcine, it was just an accident. I'm sure Corby's very sorry—"

Dulcine gave a fierce growl, silencing Belle. Reaching over, she snatched the pink satin cap off Belle's head.

A collective gasp went through the room like a switch thrown. All laughter died.

Meg thought, *Dulcine, you're a fool.*

Then Meg realized Belle looked different. "She's bobbed her hair!"

Sands grunted. "The fat's in the fire now."

CHAPTER 9

Teach us to number our days, that we may gain a heart of wisdom.
Psalm 90:12, NKJV

ARRIVING HOME IN SILENCE from Antoine's, Gabe, his parents, and his sister filed into Father's first-floor office. Orange-gold flames flickered on the hearth; a few low electric lights glowed against the dark wood and brown leather of the masculine sanctuary. Gabe knew why they had all assembled here. They wanted to close the door and open the unpleasantness over Belle's haircut. So still in costume—Gabe as an early nineteenth-century French gentleman, his mother as the medieval lady in lavender, and his sister as a pink powder puff—they found seats and faced Father, who had pushed his wheelchair behind his desk.

The thought flashed through Gabe's mind that they had arranged themselves as if the office were a courtroom. His mother took the place in the lone armchair to the right, as prosecutor, facing his father, who sat at the head of the court as the judge. Since Belle had settled down next to Gabe on the short sofa at the other side of the desk, she had evidently chosen him as her defense lawyer. If this had been a moment for humor, Gabe would have chuckled at the almost theatrical scene, complete with costume.

"Mother?" The judge prompted the prosecution.

"I am sick, physically ill over this." Tears seeped through mother's words. "How could you cut your hair, your beautiful raven tresses, without one word?"

Unable to forget the farce of Dulcine's "uncapping" of Belle, Gabe wondered if Belle felt ridiculous dressed as a powder puff for this confrontation.

Belle sat hunched, her pink-gloved arms crossed over her breast as though covering or protecting herself. "It's *my* hair," Belle grumbled.

"That attitude won't work here," Father replied. "This is a family. You are our daughter who is not yet an adult. Now I want you to explain to your mother why you cut your hair when you knew this would displease her."

Belle chewed her lower lip. She glanced at Gabe as though asking counsel if she should plead the Fifth Amendment.

Gabe shook his head.

Belle sighed deeply, "I went to try on my costume. My cap didn't fit over my long hair. It ruined the whole look of the costume! So I went across the street to Gray's Beauty Salon and had my hair cut and marcelled."

As a defense, it didn't have much to recommend it other than it proved lack of premeditation. Gabe grinned inwardly. He knew this matter was very serious to his mother, but he couldn't help feeling it was much ado about nothing. Delman, Meg's friend, faced murder. In the great scheme of things, the length of Belle's hair didn't amount to much.

"How could you do something like that without a word to me?" Mother sniffled. "A woman's hair is her glory—"

"I'm not bald, Mother." Belle folded her arms, tightening them around her silly shimmering pink costume.

Mother sniffed into her lavender handkerchief.

Gabe glanced at his father and found that he still looked unsatisfied.

"Belle," Father began, "I understand that you think differently than we do, but as a young woman, no longer a child, you must consider how your *every action* will affect others."

Belle hung her head.

Father's words unexpectedly stung Gabe's heart. For the first time, Gabe questioned his own actions in going to France and all the things he'd done there. He'd enlisted in the Army, in its Air Force, without a single thought for his parents. This realization rolled through him like a tank breaching a trench line.

"I'm sorry, Father, Mother," Belle said in a contrite voice.

Inside, Gabe echoed her, *I'm sorry.*

"Now, Belle, no more surprises. Promise us." Father stared at Belle.

"I promise."

Gabe couldn't make the same commitment. Right now, he hoped Marie would be on her way to New Orleans in a matter of weeks, at most a month. How, when, could he break this news to his parents?

Mother sighed. "Well, after all, it's only hair. It was just the shock."

"I think it was mean of Dulcine to embarrass me that way!" Belle grumbled. "She knew my hair had been cut because she was at Gray's Salon at the same time."

This piece of information didn't set well with Gabe. He'd thought Dulcine had pulled off Belle's cap in innocent retribution, but if she'd known . . .

Belle went on, "Corby just made a mistake, and she acted like he did it on purpose."

Mother frowned. "I'm afraid I must agree with you. But no doubt Dulcine is regretting it by now."

"I hope so." Belle grimaced. "I don't know how I can manage to be polite to her the next time I see her."

"You are a St. Clair woman." Mother stood and touched Belle's arm, drawing her up too. "St. Clair women have survived disease, wars, financial disaster. You will survive this."

Belle smiled grudgingly.

Father nodded in approval at his daughter. "Celestia, will you take Belle up with you? I'll come up in a few minutes."

Mother complied with Father's request, though as she left, she gave both Gabe and Father assessing looks.

Gabe wondered what the look meant.

Mother cast one last glance behind her, then left. Father turned his gaze to Gabe.

It penetrated Gabe like the rays of a hot summer sun. "What is it, sir?"

Father lifted his shoulder muscles, trying to loosen them. "What's bothering you, son?"

Gabe opened his mouth, but couldn't bring out any words. After three years of passivity, Father had moved forward again tonight, reclaiming his role as the head of the family. What did he want to discuss privately with Gabe? Had he read Gabe's mind, guessed his secret?

"You haven't been yourself since you got home. At first, I thought it would just take time for you to get over your experience in France. But lately you've been jumpy, inattentive. I say something and you don't hear me . . ."

Father's questions sank beneath Gabe's deceptively unruffled surface like a barbed hook, catching him by surprise. Gabe locked up inside.

"Son, I've heard you call out in your sleep."

Gabe swallowed, but his mouth was dry. He'd thought he'd done such a good job of hiding his ragged nerves and ghoulish memories.

Father's gentle voice continued, "I didn't see much action in the Spanish American War, but I did go. That's why I wouldn't let your mother say anything when you enlisted."

Gabe managed to nod. A buzzing sounded in his ears.

Father turned his chair to stare into the glowing embers on the hearth. "Your grandfather lost a leg at Chickamauga. Many men talked about serving in the War between the States, but my dad never said a word about his time of service. Then the day after I turned fourteen, he took me away on hunting trip. But

123

the real agenda of that day was to talk to me." Father now turned his attention on Gabe. "We sat, and he told me about the war. I'll never forget that day.

"It demolished my illusions about the glory of war. Maybe it was because my father had such integrity. I didn't doubt his story." Father gripped the armrests of his chair. "But it made it more difficult when it came time for me to leave for Cuba in '98. So . . ." Father looked Gabe directly in the eye. "I didn't tell you about your grandfather's and my war experiences. Should I have told you? Did I do wrong?"

As waves of unreality lapped over him, Gabe shook his head no.

Father propped his elbows on the arms of his chair, then his chin on his hands. "What is it, son?" Father's caring voice was low, barely a whisper.

Gabe couldn't find the words. His chest constricted. He couldn't take a deep breath. There was too much bottled up inside.

"I've read enough to know that this war, your war, differed greatly from any before. Tanks, trench warfare, bombing from the air, mustard gas . . . ." Father's voice faded. "Just remember. I'm always ready to listen."

"I know that."

The words scraped Gabe's throat.

Father closed his eyes. The ensuing silence, bit by bit, lost its intensity, and without any further words, Gabe found comfort in his father's understanding. Not everything had changed. His father, an honest man, still loved him. Maybe the God his father had taught him about would hear Gabe's prayers and bring Marie safe to this home. Soon he would muster the courage to tell his father.

Opening his eyes, Father broke the quiet. "You're upset with Belle and Miss Wagstaff's influence on her."

"I was."

"The world is changing. I think I saw it more clearly because of my accident. For nearly three years, I sat in this chair watching from the sidelines. I think the war, your war, changed everything."

Gabe nodded. "Everything changed." *Whether we wanted it to or not.*

"I want Belle to be ready to be a part of these new times. As her parent, I must not allow Belle to go out of my home lacking."

"And Meg Wagstaff is the woman of the future?"

"Yes, women may have the vote for this year's presidential election. I believe two-thirds of the states will ratify the Nineteenth Amendment. If I am correct, do you realize, in four years Belle will be old enough to vote in the next presidential election?"

"I hadn't thought of that." Gabe tried to imagine Belle walking into a voting booth. A different vision came instead. "I can see Meg Wagstaff voting." *Meg is equal to anything!*

A smile burst over his father's face. "Exactly. I want Belle to learn from her." Father grimaced suddenly.

Gabe wondered if this evening had brought on one of his father's headaches, which might put him in bed for a day or two. Gabe wished now he had given an honest answer to Meg's question, "What was her name?"

Father didn't mention any headache. He smiled at Gabe. "I've loved your mother since she was fourteen, but many times I have wished I could discuss my law cases and politics with her." Father sounded as if the final words he spoke pained him.

"Discuss politics with Mother?" This thought struck Gabe as revolutionary. "Do you think that will ever happen?"

Father shook his head. "She has always insisted she couldn't understand the law or politics." Father folded his hands and rotated his head again, stretching tight muscles. He sighed with audible weariness. "These social evenings take more out of me than a day in court. I'm tired, son."

Was father getting rundown with Delman's case and the demands of Belle's season? Maybe Belle going to fewer soirees had been for the best. "I'll get your man." Gabe rose, crossed the room, and squeezed his father's shoulder. He went into the hall-way and froze. A shock of electricity shot through him.

His mother stood just a few paces from the doorway. He didn't have to ask her if she'd overheard Father. Fresh tears sparkled in her eyelashes. Her hands covered her mouth.

He knew his father would be grieved to know his words had been overheard by his wife and had wounded her. Gabe tried to think of something soothing to say. Perhaps make light of it?   He parted his lips to speak.

She shook her head, then turned and slipped away, making no sound going back down the hall.

Gabe watched her retreat. Should he tell his father? Keep his peace?

"Is there anything wrong?" Father's voice came from behind Gabe.

Gabe couldn't tell the truth. His mother had signified that plainly. But he couldn't lie either. "Sorry. I'll get your man." *Mother, oh, mother.*

✹ ✹ ✹ ✹ ✹

Gabe allowed Meg's heavy, sweet fragrance to envelop him. Her French perfume made the gloomy parish jail less depressing.

"It's very kind of you to arrange this for me." Meg walked beside Gabe down the gray scuffed corridor to the cells.

"I knew you'd want to see your friend once he was moved out of the infirmary." His guilt over the attack on Del had prompted him. He couldn't get the sensation of her leaning close to him on the street in front of Alice's out of his mind. If he held Meg close, he wondered, *would her kisses . . .* He stopped this improper train of thought.

"What did the doctor say?"

"Delman will make a full recovery." *In time to hang.*

Meg glanced up at him as if she had heard Gabe's harsh thought. He recalled, as he had countless times over the past few days, her parting question to him after their supper the night of the Jupiter Ball—"What was her name?" How had she guessed about Lenore? No answer, no logical answer, was possible. He didn't believe in voodoo, so her needle-sharp insight must be because of their shared experience. *Who was Colin, and what happened to him?*

Gabe nodded at the grizzled jailer, who then, with a huge, old-fashioned key, unlocked the last door before the cells. The man's circle of keys clanked as the lock turned, a chilling noise.

Meg passed through ahead of Gabe. He recognized a tall burly man whom his father had often employed as a bodyguard sitting outside a cell. He murmured close to Meg's ear, "That must be Delman's guard."

As they walked down the cement floor toward the man, prisoners stood up in the cells and eyed them. A low wolf whistle came from a prisoner to Gabe's right. Gabe glared at the man.

Meg looked neither right nor left.

Gabe couldn't help but admire her aplomb. Not many women could look as cool, as composed, in this hellhole. He couldn't imagine Dulcine here under any circumstances. At this thought a smile twitched at the corner of his mouth. His father had been more than correct in his assessment of Meg Wagstaff.

Del's hired bodyguard stood up.

Gabe nodded to the man. "Miss Wagstaff, this is Mortimer Smith."

Meg startled Mortimer when she shook his hand. "Thank you for taking this job. I'm sure you're bored sitting here."

The ex-prizefighter grinned, showing two broken teeth. "Glad to have the work. Always like to work for Mr. Sands. He's a gent."

This pleased Gabe. His father's reputation had always been a shining example. If only he might not be a disappointment to his father. Rooney's recent behavior had caused Gabe, for the first time, to doubt his wisdom in taking a public position. He inwardly stifled this quandary. There had to be an explanation. "I'll leave now, but I'll be back in ten minutes to walk you out, Miss Wagstaff."

Meg nodded her assent. She would prefer to spend more than ten minutes with Del, but she realized St. Clair was doing her a favor by letting her visit Del in his cell. The man seemed almost human today. She wondered if he'd ever take her to Alice's again, and hoped that he would. This last thought unsettled her.

Mortimer motioned her to take his chair, then leaned back against the bars, staring at the other prisoners.

Gabe waved farewell and left.

His leaving chilled Meg. The oppressive atmosphere of the bleak, damp jail cells settled over her like a fetid miasma. Her spirits plummeted. She sat down sideways on the straight-back chair so she would be closer to Del as she faced him. Then stiffening her courage, she allowed herself to peer at him through the iron bars that separated them. "How are you?" The phrase sounded pathetic in her ears, and she longed to have something better to say.

His face looked drawn and ashen. He held himself stiffly. "I'm alive." Del's voice came out low. He cradled one of his arms in his lap.

"Is there anything you need or want?"

He stared at her, his expression stating clearly that she couldn't give him what he wanted—his freedom.

"How's Cecy? Has the baby come yet?" Del asked.

"I received a long letter yesterday from Father. Cecy is doing well, but still must stay in bed."

"You should be in San Francisco with them, not here with me."

She reached between the bars.

Del leaned away from her hand. "Don't touch me," he whispered.

"Can't keep your hands off him, can you?" One of the white prisoners taunted her with a vulgar name.

Del gripped an iron bar and scowled.

Meg turned to look at the man. Now she understood Del's warning. Her relationship to Del could only bring him abuse.

Mortimer straightened and glowered at the man.

Meg made herself focus on her reason for coming. She needed information about LaRae. She studied Del again.

Watching for his reaction, she whispered, "LaRae met me at the French Market."

Del's head jerked up. "Why did she do that?" He hissed. "Where did you run into her?"

Meg kept her voice so low only Del and perhaps Mortimer could hear her. "I went to Penny Candy."

"I'd like to shake you!" Though Del's face contorted with frustration, he responded in a whisper also. "Don't you ever go there again! Why did you go there in the first place?"

Meg understood Del's ire. When they were children, he'd always tried to protect her. Now was no different. She whispered, "I couldn't just sit here and let you wait for the noose. I will go wherever I need to and do whatever I need to get you out of this mess." Their conversation continued in heated whispers.

"Leave it to Mr. Sands."

"I went to Penny Candy *before* he took your case. Now shut up! And let me tell you what LaRae said. She wanted me to leave New Orleans. Why would she say that?"

"Because it's the truth."

"Is Corelli the man LaRae's afraid of?"

"Corelli. You met Corelli?" Del looked appalled.

"He introduced himself to me when I was at Penny Candy."

"Don't you ever go there again."

"You're repeating yourself," Meg snapped. "Who is Corelli? How did he get ownership of the nightclub after Mitch Kennedy was killed? Did Corelli kill—"

"Stop right there. Corelli is a snake, a poisonous snake. I told you to let Mr. Sands handle this."

Meg clamped her mouth shut and glared at Del. Why did men—even Del—have to be so stubborn? Father had never treated her like this, though at times she knew he'd had to fight himself not to. Should she ask Del about Pete Brown? She decided no. He'd just tell her to stay away from him. Why couldn't Del cooperate with her so she could help him? Wouldn't they *both* be better off out of New Orleans?

A thought occurred to her. "Is LaRae in danger?"

Del gave her a troubled look. "I hope not."

"Del, how close were you and LaRae?"

His mouth straightened into a line. "That's not for you to ask."

"I need to know. If she's dear to you, should I get her out of town? I could buy her a train ticket and send her to my father."

Frowning, Del looked uneasy. "She thinks she's in love with me. She's just a kid. I was letting her sing a song or two with us. She's got a decent voice. If she learned to sing with a band, she could get off the street."

That sounded like Meg's Del—always looking out for others. "Then should I send her to San Francisco?"

"You might put her in danger by trying to contact her."

A cold stone formed in the middle of Meg's stomach. "What if someone saw her talking to me?"

"That's unlikely."

Perhaps. Or had her bedeviled imagination just run away with her at the French Market? Had Corelli been there? Meg stared at Del. "If she's in danger, I think—"

"Did you tell Sands about LaRae?"

"Yes, privately."

"Ask him to handle it then." Del shifted his position where he sat on the end of the bed, and pain etched itself upon his face.

"Where can he get in touch with her?" Meg longed to ease Del's suffering, but she couldn't. Her oldest and dearest friend had been cast beyond her control. She couldn't even bring him a cup of water.

"I'll tell him myself. I don't want you getting in any deeper in this."

"Del, I'm not a girl just out of school. Why do you discount me?"

"I value you. Don't you see how dangerous this situation is?" His voice rose with his agitation.

"I'm not a fool." Meg fought tears. "This is life and death for you. Do you think this is the first time I've faced death?"

A strange expression passed over Del's face. He stared back at her, then bent his head. "Do you ever think of my grandmother?"

Meg nodded. Del didn't have to say the words. Meg knew he was remembering the day they lost her—Aunt Susan—the day they'd faced death together.

"Meg, do you ever pray anymore?"

The question startled her, but she had to admit the truth. "Yes." New Orleans had forced her to her knees. But her prayers had no power in them. She poured out her anguish and anger to God. Couldn't anything just go easy for a change? Hadn't she and Del suffered enough? *I can't lose Del, God. We've both lost too much.*

Del stared at the floor. "I have been praying. Sometimes I think I feel my grandmother's presence. I know she's offering prayers for me at the throne of God. I know God doesn't judge us here for what we do, but I think sometimes he tries to get our attention. Well, he's got mine now." His glance asked for her understanding.

She nodded, moved by his confiding in her.

"Would you find a church and ask them to pray for me?"

The question startled Meg. Del hadn't attended church since a few years before France. But once again she replied, "Yes."

CHAPTER 10

How long, O Lord? Will You forget me forever?
Psalm 13:1, NKJV

Gabe walked into the breakfast room, shadowy in the bleak morning light, and sat down beside his father. "What does the *Times Picayune* say today?"

"Parker is an angel of light in a world of darkness."

Breathing in the aroma of bacon and buttered toast, Gabe chuckled. "Really? I didn't think angels ran for governor in Louisiana, and that if they did, they would need votes."

"Thank heaven you're right."

Nodding his thanks to the butler, Gabe lifted his freshly poured cup of coffee.

"I'm concerned about New Orleans." Father folded the paper, but still held it with both hands.

Gabe looked to his father. The distracted expression he wore captured Gabe's attention. "Parker won't be better or worse than any other governor. Or do you know something I should know?"

Father shook his head. "Parker may shake things up for awhile, but the political machine will eat him up. The old Bourbons have run this state to suit themselves ever since Reconstruction ended. Parker won't change that." Father fell silent.

Gabe sipped his black coffee and waited. "What is it?"

"This Prohibition is coming in days."

"I know. We're invited to the Demon Rum Funeral."

Showing his distaste, Father made a face. "The *Picayune* barely mentions it. I can't believe that people really are convinced that humans will just give up spirits overnight. How can they? This Eighteenth Amendment should never have been passed. It will create a law enforcement nightmare. New Orleans is a world port. Liquor will be shipped in illegally—by the fleet. The city should be hiring new officers right and left."

Discouraged by his father's heated words, Gabe shook his head. "I don't see that happening, what with the post-war depression we're in. Nobody would dare raise taxes to hire more police, and that's what it would take."

Frowning, Father nodded and turned the page of his paper.

Gabe heard his father take in a sharp breath. "What is it?"

Father lowered the paper, his eyes pools of worry. "The body of an unidentified young black woman has been found in an alley in Faubourg Treme."

Gabe paused, his cup in midair. "That isn't the first time such a thing has happened in Storyville."

"She was shot in the back of the head and left behind Mitch Kennedy's Club, Penny Candy. It says here no one has come forward yet to identify the body."

Gabe's appetite dried up. He put his coffee cup down, fumbling it onto the saucer. "I don't like that."

"I don't either."

"It must be just an unfortunate coincidence."

"I don't believe in coincidences." Father tossed the paper onto the table. "Don't leave just yet. I need to call Miss Wagstaff." His father rolled away from the table.

"Why?" Gabe craned his neck to track Father on his way to the hall phone.

Father paused. "Because Miss Wagstaff must go see that body."

Gabe jumped out of his chair. "No! You can't mean to subject a young lady—"

Impaling Gabe with his gaze, Father pursed his mouth. "I wouldn't ask her unless it was absolutely necessary. And . . . don't you think she saw corpses in France?"

The gorge rose in Gabe's throat. He wanted to shout, *This couldn't have anything to do with Kennedy's death.* He'd questioned the officers who had arrested and questioned Del along with Rooney. There were eyewitnesses to the quarrel between Kennedy and Delman. The gun and money had been found in Delman's room. Delman had no alibi for the time of the murder. *It's an open-and-shut case.*

Without a backward glance, Father rolled out of the room, the one wheel beginning to squeak again as though mocking Gabe.

* * * * *

Almost two hours later, between Meg and Gabe, Father pushed his chair the few yards to the imposing brick building. The three of them had traveled here to the morgue—Gabe in his Franklin Touring Car, Meg and Sands in the family sedan. Though Gabe had his car's top up against the mist, it still penetrated his clothing. He hadn't wanted to bring his father out in this soupy weather. But father had insisted. Also, he'd insisted that Miss Wagstaff go along.

On arriving, they left the disapproving chauffeur by the cars. He didn't think gentlemen and ladies had any business identifying dead bodies who weren't members of the family. Gabe didn't blame him.

Inside the arched entrance of the hall, the three looked up the stairs. Gabe stooped and lifted his father into his arms. This act always disconcerted him. He never begrudged carrying his father, but he recalled too clearly his younger, robust father swinging Gabe, as a child, up into his arms. How strong and invincible his father had seemed then.

In her elegant black hat with a wisp of a veil over her eyes, Meg hoisted the wheelchair up step-by-step—bump after bump. "Did I ever tell you my stepmother is blind?"

"She is?" Father turned his head to glance at Meg.

"Yes, she took an awful fall and never recovered her sight."

"How long has she been your mother?" Father asked.

"Since 1906. I loved her the first time I saw her. She was so beautiful, so filled with life."

Gabe appreciated Meg speaking, distracting them all from the smell of formaldehyde. She was "whistling in the graveyard," and he admired her for it. "Is she still on bed rest?"

Meg looked surprised that he knew about this. "Yes, but she's doing fine. Father spends most of his days at the hospital with her."

Father spoke up, "He is a brave man having another child so late in life."

"He told me he's both overjoyed and terrified." With one last bump, Meg hoisted the chair to the last step, then onto the cement floor.

Gabe settled his father back into his chair. Under the glaring light, they fell silent. Gabe pushed his father to the door with a marbleized glass window. Gold leaf lettering read, Morgue. He twisted the cold brass doorknob.

The coroner, in a white lab coat, was writing at a cluttered rolltop desk. He glanced up over his gold wire-rimmed glasses, then rose. "Well, the two St. Clair men—the only honest lawyers in New Orleans."

"Kind words, Benjamin." Father shook hands with the white-haired man. "But an exaggeration."

Gabe observed Meg, hoping this ordeal wouldn't be too much for her. When they'd shared a meal at Alice's, she had seemed all skin and nerves.

"Not much of an exaggeration." The coroner eyed Meg. "Have you taken on a female partner, Sands?"

Father looked at Meg and smiled. "She hasn't graduated from law school yet."

Meg folded her arms in front of her. "I start this September at Stanford."

"Really?" Benjamin stepped to Meg and shook her hand. "I'm delighted to meet you, Miss."

Gabe sensed this banter was designed to delay or palliate the dreary circumstances. They'd come to view a body, a young woman's dead body. A tenseness grew in him, keying him up. He tried to shake it off. He failed.

Meg shook Benjamin's hands, wishing these pleasantries could be dispensed with. The bleak, unadorned room was making her heart skip in funny little jerks. *Please, Lord, don't let it be LaRae. Please!*

"Shall we get this over with then?" Sands asked.

"A policeman did finally find someone to identify this poor young woman, so if Miss Wagstaff would rather not . . ." The coroner stared down at Sands.

"I have to see for myself if it is who I think it is," Meg stated with a lift of her chin.

Sands nodded. "Have you examined her?"

"Yes." His heels tapping on the cement floor, the coroner led them over to a high metal table that had been covered with a dingy white sheet. "I was just writing up the report." Benjamin folded back the white sheet only far enough to expose the woman's head.

Hanging back with her head down, Meg battled her fear and stepped close to the table.

"Death was due to a gunshot to the back of her head at close range." The corner's voice droned on matter-of-factly.

Meg forced herself to look. *LaRae.* Dark, bloodless skin against white cloth. LaRae lay silent on the cold, metal table. A sinking feeling started at Meg's temples and lowered through her. Black spots wavered and danced before her eyes.

Gabe caught her.

Benjamin ran to his desk and hurried back with a vinaigrette. He pressed it into Gabe's hand, then he covered up the corpse with the white muslin again.

Gabe supported Meg's soft form with one hand and waved the pungent smelling salts under her nose.

She roused, moaned.

He handed the vinaigrette back to the coroner. "Meg, Meg."

She straightened up slowly.

But he held onto her.

She didn't push him away. The side of her slender body pressed against him, her perfume overriding the clinical odor and the last trace of the smelling salts.

"Miss Wagstaff, I take it you are able to identify this unfortunate young woman," Benjamin asked her.

"Her name is . . . was LaRae."

"Her surname?" Benjamin watched her.

She shook her head. "Del . . . Del . . ."

"Del would know?" Sands supplied, looking stern.

She nodded.

Gabe looked to his father. "Why?"

"My client, who is charged with Kennedy's murder, was close to the young woman." Sands returned Gabe's attention.

"Just because they knew each other," Gabe objected, "that doesn't mean the two deaths are related. It's just a coincidence."

"Not deaths—murders. I told you, Gabriel. I don't believe in coincidence."

Father looked up. "This development makes it necessary for me to consult with Del. I'll go over to see him now. If he and this young woman were more than mere acquaintances, I think it would be better if he heard the news from me."

The coroner nodded his assent. "Then I'm done for the day."

Father looked to Gabe. "Would you take Miss Wagstaff back to her hotel?"

Though Gabe nodded, he expected Meg to insist on going with his father. Instead, she remained leaning against him. Without his support, she would have fallen. A desire to protect Meg grew inside him.

Outside once more in the mist, Gabe sat in his car and watched his father being driven away, headed for the jail. Gabe's nerves spun like a propeller on takeoff. Seeing the sad earthly remains of LaRae had shaken him as well as Meg.

Beside him, Meg sat huddled next to the passenger door. Where had his sleek cat gone?

I can't leave her like this. She needs me.

Or did he need her too?

He started the engine and drove away. Instead of heading toward Meg's hotel, he found himself on the way to the Audubon Park. Turning off onto a campus street at St. Charles at Tulane University, he parked and watched young men in gray or drab green military trench coats crossing between red brick buildings on their way to and from classes.

Folding his arms, Gabe eased back and let the world go by. January had tested him. How much more could happen before Mardi Gras 1920? Minutes passed.

"Where are we?" Meg's voice broke in on his preoccupation.

Gabe sat up straighter and blinked. "Uptown. Tulane, my alma mater."

She stretched with distinct lethargy. "It's so awful."

He understood she spoke of the morgue, not the campus. "Yes."

"I saw her just days ago. So lovely."

Death had made a mockery of the young black woman's beauty. He knew he should comfort Meg, distract her. He couldn't. No sweet words could rub away what they'd seen today.

"How can someone want to be a coroner?" Meg's arms wrapped tighter around herself.

Was she chilled too? "Someone has to do it. I suppose doctors view it differently."

She nodded, her lips trembling. "I'm so afraid I caused her death."

He sent her a sharp glance. "Why do you think that?"

She rubbed her forehead. "I spoke to her . . . about Del. Maybe someone saw us together."

"That doesn't make sense. Why would that have caused her death?"

"I can't speak about this anymore. Not to you."

Gabe comprehended why. Meg believed someone other than her friend, Del, had killed Kennedy, and now she believed that same mysterious someone had killed Del's friend. Why? Gabe saw no connection between the two murders in Storyville. He didn't want to believe it was because LaRae had known dangerous secrets. Early violent death had always been one of the many hazards of a life of prostitution.

He wanted to discount Meg's reasoning. His mind insisted coincidence explained all. But his emotions matched Meg's. No doubt, seeing a corpse again had pinched a bruised nerve within him.

"Don't you have to be at your office or court?" She asked, sounding half asleep, so unlike the decisive Meg Wagstaff he'd come to know.

"It's Saturday."

Closing her eyes, she leaned back. "Saturday. My days have all lost their identity. I don't have a life here."

Again, he understood her cryptic explanation. But her sentence put into words what he had been feeling since he returned from France. *I don't have a life either.*

Gabe glanced ahead. "Do you want to go back to your hotel?"

"No."

That sounded more like the self-assured Meg he knew. "Want to take a drive with me?"

"Yes."

He gave a dry chuckle. "I do relish your pithy responses." He started the car and drove west. The reason he wanted to keep her with him still fluttered vague and uncertain in his consciousness. Somehow this woman had become key, but to what? "I'm taking you out to Spanish Fort."

"Spanish Fort?"

"An amusement park out on Bayou St. John."

"Oh, yes," she said satirically, "I'm in the mood for a Ferris wheel today."

"No, I'm taking you to Over the Rhine, a restaurant there." He looked sideways at her for her reaction.

She nodded, then bent her head as if too tired to hold it up.

He went on, "It will take us out of . . . away from—"

"From this place of death?"

He refused to respond. Death happened everywhere, not just in France.

Pushing away thoughts of Lenore in her lonely grave, he drove the length of Lowerline Street, then Earnhart to Carrollton, to New Basin Canal, to City Park Avenue, to Canal Boulevard, and finally to Adam Avenue near Bayou St. John. He read the street signs, one by one, focusing on the familiar, the mundane. Palm trees and live oaks with gray Spanish moss trailing from broad-reaching branches clustered around the amusement esplanade. He parked his car to the rear of the restaurant, a one-story building in the Louisiana style—many chimneys protruding from the roof and a low porch across the front of the white building.

At the entrance, Meg paused and looked toward the silent amusement park, desolate in the dismal drizzle. What was she thinking? And why did it have to be such a gloomy January?

Gabe gripped her arm more firmly and drew her onto the porch and through the door. Seated at a table for two beside a cozy fireplace, with heat radiating around their table, Gabe ordered coffee for him and tea for her. He waited for their drinks to come before he spoke to her again. He didn't know what he wanted to say to her yet, but her essence drew him like honey-bees to pollen—irresistible.

Meg sipped her tea and, finally, looked up into his face. "Thank you."

He nodded. Did he want to speak to her about Lenore? Marie? Words floated just beyond his reach. Instead of opening this painful topic, he reached for her. She let him fold his fingers around her black-kid-gloved hand. Touching her took the edge off his need. "You're cold."

"How is Belle?"

The question caught him off guard. "What do you mean?"

"Is your mother still angry over Belle's haircut?"

"She was that night."

"Though I came as Pandora, I didn't have anything to do with it. You know that, don't you?"

He said honestly, "I thought the whole fuss was ridiculous. Belle's bob is not world-shattering news."

She smiled at him.

This was the first true smile she had ever given him—not mocking, not teasing—a real smile showing her pleasure in him. The heat of it warmed him through his heart down to his toes. He yearned to draw her fingers to his lips.

"I felt bad for Dulcine," Meg said.

"Then why were you laughing?" Teasing, he squeezed her fingers.

"Who could help laughing at such a sight? Afterward, I sympathized with her. To be caught at such an occasion in so undignified a position would be humiliating."

"She should have laughed with everyone else." With his thumb, Gabe traced the mound beneath Meg's thumb.

"She may wish she had now, but I don't think Dulcine is accustomed to being laughed at." Meg slipped her fingers between his, weaving their two hands together.

This took his breath away. She craved his touch too.

The waiter came to take their orders. Still holding hands, Gabe ordered chicken and dumpling soup for both of them.

Meg sighed.

Gabe watched her relax. Her face lost its haunted expression. She leaned back in her chair, but she didn't release his hand.

"Do you know of a Negro church?"

Again, she startled him with a question. "A Negro church?"

"Yes, Del wanted me to find him a church and to ask for prayer."

With his fingertips, he traced her knuckles in circles, the kid leather soft as butter. "I believe the largest black church in New Orleans is the Mount Zion A.M.E. I believe that's where our servants worship." He studied her veiled face. He had no doubts that Meg would feel no awkwardness about contacting a black pastor. Meg Wagstaff was a unique woman, a slowly unraveling puzzle to him.

"Gabriel, do you believe in God? In prayer?"

Question after question. He wanted to respond archly, but the tenor of their conversation was decidedly serious, honest. "This must be your day for questions."

Lowering her chin, she gifted him with a genuine smile once more.

Her pleasure in being with him gave him new power, strength.

The waiter brought them generous bowls of rich creamy soup and a basket of warm hard-crusted rolls, white and pumpernickel. The waiter bowed and left.

"You seem to know all the best places to eat," she teased.

"I was hungry." More words, intimate ones, ribboned through his mind. But he needed to concentrate on his goal. The reason he'd wanted her with him stood up in his thoughts and wouldn't be denied. "That's my only explanation."

She nodded and drew her hand from his.

He felt the loss of her touch with a deep pang. But he couldn't put this into words. He watched her draw off her gloves, finger by finger. For the first time, he recognized how intimate this simple act could be.

To cover his uneasy awareness of her, he spooned up the first of the rich soup. Across the small table, his glances and hers spoke to one another. If he could only bring himself to begin, he knew she would understand about Lenore and tell him how to cope with Marie and his parents.

He looked across the table and asked, "Who was Colin?"

CHAPTER 11

The Lord is close to those whose hearts are breaking;
Psalm 34:18, TLB

Shocked, Meg searched Gabriel's intense gray eyes. "Why do you ask?"

"You said his name was Colin. Who was Colin?"

"I also asked *you* a question that evening. Do you remember it?" Meg fenced with him.

"You asked, 'What was her name?'"

"And?" Meg prompted. Was he really going to evade the opening she'd offered him?

"You won't tell me who Colin was then?"

Their white-aproned waiter paused at their table to ask if everything was satisfactory.

When they were alone again, she said in a cool voice, "Colin Deveril was a son of Viscount Lynton of Derbyshire."

Lenore Moreau was from Versailles near Paris. "Did he make promises to you he didn't keep?"

Her stomach tightening, Meg evinced no reaction to this impertinent question. She would have been justified in slapping his face. His question delved too deep. Her heart skipped a beat. Had Gabriel made promises he hadn't kept?

The words had come out sharper than he'd intended. What had this Colin been to Meg? Had he held her in his arms and kissed her? Of course, he had. Meg no longer possessed that giggling naïveté that still marked his sister. He didn't have to ask Meg if she had been in love before.

"Gabriel, I can talk to you about Colin, but not now. I've suffered too much strain today. The pain of Colin is too deep for casual conversation over lunch."

He nodded. His conscience nipped him. He'd been driven to push questions on her he had no right asking. He should have consulted her about Marie, how to handle . . . "I apologize. Eat. My mother says a light breeze could blow you away."

"For once, I agree with her." Meg swallowed some creamy soup. It warmed her as it went down. Aromas of chicken and beef wafted over her. She closed her eyes, savoring the chicken soup, with its celery and sprinkle of nutmeg. Maybe after she ate she would be able to think what to do next. How to help Del, how to judge what was evolving between her and Gabriel, Del's adversary.

Gazing into the blue-flamed fire, she swallowed mouthful after mouthful in the peaceful restaurant. Only a few other couples had driven out on this soggy Saturday. Meg watched a young couple, obviously in their Sunday clothes, sitting at a table behind Gabriel's left shoulder. Her heart ached for them—so young! Their hesitating movements and forced chatter broadcast their uncertainty about themselves and each other.

She'd been a better actress. Colin had thought her older and experienced in flirtation. Even now, the boldly handsome but secretive man across from her beckoned her without words. He wanted to know her secrets, but would he divulge his?

After a savory dessert, cinnamon bread pudding, Gabriel settled the bill. At the entryway, he helped her on with her black coat. She lingered with her back to him, reluctant to have him remove his strong hands from her shoulders. But she couldn't intimate that. Del stood between them. And Gabriel's secrets.

Outside in the sodden cold, she walked close beside him again. His height and breadth gave her a feeling of security. She knew it was only an illusion in this perilous city, but a welcome one.

He glanced down at her. "Are you still interested in buying your own vehicle?"

"What?"

He repeated the question.

She nodded. Why had he asked that today?

"Would you like to look at some now?"

She couldn't believe her ears. "Do you mean it?"

"Yes."

Smiling, she nodded. One more welcome delay; she wasn't going back to her lonely hotel room to await Sands's call—yet.

Soon they were driving back into town, the clouds to the west lifting. In the residential neighborhoods, Meg noticed the distinctive touches that made this French New Orleans. Peddlers walked the banquettes, hawking their wares. Chimney sweeps in their distinctive black frock coats and top hats paraded down the streets with their rope, bunches of palmettos, and broom straws over their shoulders, calling out "Ramonay! *Rrramonez la chimi-nee du haut en bas!*" Broom-makers carried Palmetto root poles and called out, "*Latanier!* Palmetto Root!" Washerwomen with bundles of clothing riding atop their heads waved at Meg as she rode by in the car. Meg waved back. "*Bon jour!*"

Gabriel pulled into a classy car dealership and parked. Inside the windowed showroom, Meg walked beside him down a line of three shiny black new automobiles.

"What can we do for you today, sir?" a well-dressed sales-man with his hair slicked back with Brilliantine asked Gabriel.

"Miss Wagstaff would like to buy a runabout for town use." Gabriel nodded to her.

"Well . . . well, how about that?" The salesman took a moment to digest this news. He firmed his square jaw, evidently ready to sell his first car to a lady. "How about a Cadillac? It's reliable and easy to drive in town."

"Could I see one please?" Meg asked. "I'd like to take it for a drive first."

This also seemed to throw the salesman off stride. "Of course," he recovered. "I have one ready. The gentleman will be accompanying you, won't he?"

Meg grinned. "Gabriel, do you trust me to drive you around the block?"

Gabriel grinned back at her. "That depends, Miss Meg. How long have you been driving?"

Meg recognized the subtle teasing in his tone. "My father began teaching me when I was fourteen, and I drove a YMCA truck all over France."

"Then I'll be happy to accompany you."

The salesman stared at them, aghast.

Meg bought the Cadillac.

Outside, the clammy weather had passed, leaving a sharp west wind in its wake. As she and Gabriel walked back to his car, she thought about all that had happened that day. Purchasing her first car had lifted her spirits, but she had to be practical. "I'll have to ask the hotel manager where I can park my new car."

"I've already considered that. I think you should hire a driver. Then he could park it near his residence and pick you up in the mornings."

"Driver? Why would I need a driver? I can drive myself." Was he showing his true old-fashioned colors again? What was in his mind?

"I don't doubt that." He smiled. "You drive excellently. But just think how hard it is to find a parking place in New Orleans. This city has old, narrow streets throughout much of it. You'd get to your destination, and then spend time looking and maybe not finding a parking place."

"I hadn't thought of that." She studied him, trying to judge his motives.

"A driver makes perfect sense," Gabe insisted.

"I will think about it." She still eyed him suspiciously.

He helped her into his car, then got in behind the wheel. "May I take you back to your hotel?"

Meg frowned and stared out her window. "I enjoyed lunch very much. I didn't thank you at the time—"

"Don't mention it."

She looked toward him. "I'm afraid I must ask you another favor."

"What?"

"You said your servants attended Mount Zion?" Meg felt her pulse speed up. LaRae's face in death was an image she wouldn't soon erase from her mind.

"Yes?"

"I'd like to talk to their pastor." She looked down at her black leather pumps. Had Del been in love with LaRae or only interested in helping the girl? He might not have wanted to tell her the truth.

"About Del?" Gabriel stopped to let an old carriage pass through an intersection first.

"Sort of. I'd also like him to help me contact LaRae's family." She stoked her resolve. "I'd like to offer to pay for her funeral."

"That isn't necessary." His eyes didn't stray toward her.

"Yes, it is." She folded her arms, lodging one hand inside each elbow.

Gabe recognized her tone, her most determined one. "If that's what you wish, I'll ask our butler to have his pastor contact you."

She heaved a deep sigh and smiled at him again.

He was glad he hadn't argued with her. He regretted having been on the receiving end of so few of Meg Wagstaff's smiles.

She'd also been easy to persuade into considering hiring a driver. He hoped she wouldn't discover the man's true purpose.

※ ※ ※ ※ ※

The evening of the Demon Rum Party had come. In her newest black evening gown, purchased at Maison Blanche— New Orleans' foremost department store—Meg dragged herself through the country club entrance. She was nearly two hours late, but she'd had a difficult time pulling herself together after LaRae's funeral that afternoon.

And to make her feel even worse, when she had asked for her key after the funeral, the hotel clerk had presented her with her first poison-pen note—anonymous, of course. The note had warned her about staying where she wasn't welcome and urged her to go home soon, very soon. Who'd sent it?

Now at the country club, the clink of ice cubes into glasses and the merry buzz of voices showed the party was well on its way. The ballroom was strung with black crepe paper streamers and red-gold silk draped along the walls and overhead like a canopy. Walking inside felt like stepping inside a blazing sunset with the cool, risky fingers of night just closing around her throat. The unusual decorations tightened Meg's already raw nerves. Had the party designers evoked images of hell on purpose? Just what had been planned for tonight's entertainment?

As she gave the hatcheck girl her wrap, she heard a voice from behind her.

"Miss Wagstaff."

Meg turned and smiled at Maisy, Belle's friend, wearing an ivory satin gown trimmed with exquisite lace. "Hello! You look lovely as usual."

"I just wish I could look as sophisticated as you do."

Meg smiled, her spirits lifting at seeing such youthful *joie de vivre*. Innocence still existed in the world. "I hear you have gone back to high school."

"Yes, and I can't wait to start Newcomb this fall! They have a notable pottery instructor, and I just know I'll make the most lovely things!"

Meg noticed Dulcine in a demure cornflower blue dress bearing down on them—no doubt intent on limiting Meg's influence on her dear, unsullied cousin. Miss Dulcine's oh-so-sweet-butter-wouldn't-melt-in-my-mouth mask was beginning to wear on Meg. Dulcine was one of those schemers who would never tell you honestly what they wanted or were feeling. Meg was starting to think Gabriel didn't deserve such a conniving woman as his wife.

"Miss Wagstaff," Dulcine greeted her with a prim smile. "Maisy, Jackson Gantry is looking for you. He wants a line on your dance card."

Maisy beamed and excused herself in a swish of satin and the tap of wooden heels.

"Very efficient," Meg commented. "I was just about to discuss Sigmund Freud and free love with Maisy."

"Who?"

"Sigmund Freud, a scientist interested in the mind. But I doubt you have heard of him."

"I don't always understand your droll sense of humor, Miss Wagstaff."

Dulcine's archness triggered Meg's frustration. It bubbled up and loosened her reckless tongue. "Call me Meg—please. After viewing your unmentionables, I don't think we need stand on ceremony."

Dulcine's eyes narrowed, but her evening-gala smile stayed tacked in place.

Meg started away, her silken gown rippling around her as she moved. A Frenchman had once advised her that in order to catch a man's eye, always to judge a dress in motion. Would Gabriel prefer chaste cornflower blue or sinuous black silk?

Dulcine followed along beside Meg.

Is there something you wanted to ask me?" Meg paused. LaRae's funeral had left Meg edgy, moody.

"No, I just wished to greet you." Dulcine's pretty eyes widened. "Oh, my mother is giving a tea party in two weeks. She wanted to know if you would still be in New Orleans. If you will be, she wants to send you an invitation."

"Well done." Meg gave Dulcine a measured look. "You veiled your curiosity about when I would leave town perfectly." The thought occurred to Meg that both the anonymous author of the poison pen-note and Dulcine wished Meg to leave New Orleans. Meg couldn't bring herself to credit Dulcine with the note. She couldn't have written it, could she? Taking a deep breath, Meg began walking again. "Thank your mother for thinking of me. I may still be in town, but I can't be certain. Everything depends on my friend's case—"

Dulcine pulled her face down into a moue, then shook her head. "I don't know if you realize . . ."

The insinuating tone Dulcine used made Meg halt. "What don't I realize, Dulcine?" Meg turned the full force of her attention on the blonde.

"Your involvement with that jazz musician, a Negro charged with murder, is affecting how people view the Fourchette and St. Clair families."

Meg's mouth dropped open. "You're making that up."

"I know what I'm talking about. This is New Orleans, not San Francisco."

Meg longed to wipe the sanctimonious, pseudosympathetic expression off Dulcine's face. "You know"—Meg leaned close to the blonde—"I was going to say 'Take him. I don't want him.' But this is too much. I *am* going to take him. You don't deserve Gabriel St. Clair."

Dulcine's pouty, pretty face turned fiery red.

Seeing red herself, Meg sauntered away, burning with unspoken insults.

Heedless, Belle rushed over. "Miss Wagstaff—"

Meg shook off her anger. Painting a smile on her face, she tucked an arm around Belle's slender waist. "I think it's time you called me Meg."

Her protégée blushed with pleasure. "Oh, thank you—"

"What do you looked so excited about?"

"I talked to Corby, and you won't believe it, but—"

The fanfare of a trumpet interrupted Belle.

Meg, along with everyone else in the ballroom, turned to view the entrance.

A young man entered, dressed all in black except for a crimson sash across his chest that read: Demon Rum.

Then Meg noticed it was Corby with an empty liquor bottle in his hand. Yesterday she had received a letter from her father. He too was deeply concerned about the effects of

Prohibition on crime. Being illegal wouldn't banish liquor, it would only raise the price! How could these people be blind to the fact that the devil was dancing with glee in Storyville already? "I don't like this," Meg whispered to herself. But beside her, Belle was lost in admiration.

Slipping away unnoticed, Meg wrestled with her turbulent feelings. LaRae's funeral this afternoon had left her shaken. And was Prohibition something to laugh about?

The band began to play "When the Saints Go Marchin' In." Corby swaggered around waving his bottle. Other young men dressed as policemen with nightsticks, bartenders, obvious drunks, and one man in an old-fashioned dress and bonnet with a hatchet impersonating Carrie Nation, pushed in behind him. All converged on Corby, either to protect or attack him. People laughed and shouted encouragement to the broad slapstick.

The scene from LaRae's funeral came back to Meg full force. After the funeral service, she had stepped out on the top step of Mount Zion Church. Gabriel had appeared at her side. Why had he come to LaRae's interment? Had he come as her friend, or as the parish attorney?

He had walked beside her the whole way to the peculiar above-ground cemetery. His presence had bolstered her poise, much shaken after LaRae's death. LaRae had left behind only a grandmother to mourn her. But many friends, obvious in their tawdry finery, women who also made their living in Storyville, had joined the procession.

She'd never seen a funeral procession like this one in New Orleans. As the cortege made its way to the cemetery, a band had played jazz, ragtime, and spirituals she had learned as a child.

"Miss Wagstaff."

Startled out of her reverie, she looked up into Gabriel's unwavering eyes. "I was just thinking of you," she murmured, unable to look away.

Gabe could tell from the haunted look in her eyes that she was recalling the funeral. His mood matched hers. After LaRae's funeral, he had found a telegram from Paul waiting for him at his office. "I don't think you or I are in the right mood tonight for this . . . party."

"It is dreadful." Meg pressed a hand to her forehead. "Doesn't anyone here understand that this is real life?"

Could he speak to her of Lenore and Marie tonight? The telegram sat in his pocket, a stick of dynamite to his life. "I don't think anyone here believes that there will really be no more liquor after tonight."

Squeals of laughter exploded behind them, pushing Meg to distance herself farther. "That's what I mean. Don't they realize that this means alcohol will . . . become more expensive, dangerous?"

Gabriel had gone to France looking for danger. He understood its lure for Corby and the other young men. "Let's go out onto the terrace. I think a breath of fresh air might help."

She let Gabriel ease her through the clusters of people who were laughing over Corby's antics. Outside, she stood beside Gabriel. "I shouldn't have come tonight, but I couldn't just sit at the hotel . . ." Besides, she had to talk to Sands here about what she'd been told at the funeral—and something she'd noticed.

"I'm glad you came." Knowing Meg would be here had made him join the festivities. If anyone in New Orleans could understand about Lenore and Marie, she could.

"I'm glad, so grateful, you came this afternoon to the funeral. Everything was so strange to me." Meg touched his sleeve.

"I know." He put a hand over hers, keeping her near.

"Why did you come to the funeral?"

To protect you. Her direct stare now made him want to loosen the tie around his throat. "I was curious to see who would show up for the funeral."

She frowned at him. The glow of electric light from the party illuminated his tense face. If what he said was true, she'd had the same curiosity. Pete Brown and Laverne Mason had come. LaVerne had watched her from afar with the same fascination one would concentrate on a cobra being piped from its basket by a charmer. Both men had steered clear of her until . . .

"I have someone in mind to take on the job of driver for you. Have you given my advice any thought?"

She stared at him. When she had come to New Orleans, her mission had been simple: she would get things cleared up and take Del home. How had matters gotten so complicated? She no longer felt equal to the task before her. "Yes."

"Yes, you want a driver?" he asked tartly. "Or yes, you thought about it?"

"Both." Was she doing more harm than good in New Orleans? Had she triggered someone to kill LaRae or was it just a coincidence?

"Good. I'll have him report to your hotel tomorrow morning. His name is Jack Bishop. I think you'll like him." In his mind, Gabe practiced an opening, *"Meg, I have a problem. I need some advice . . ."* Any way he introduced it, it made him sound like a shirker. *I didn't know! I wouldn't have left if I'd known!*

"Jack Bishop, okay." *Should I tell him what Laverne said?*

The vulgar uproar from within the ballroom spurred Meg, then Gabe, to turn back to look through the filmy curtains on the inside of the French doors. Meg watched the mock policemen struggling to push Demon Rum into a large coffin.

Overlaying this like a film negative, Meg saw again LaRae's coffin being slid headfirst into a stone mausoleum in the aboveground crypt. The mourners around her had sung, "Crossing over Jordan, what did I see, comin' for to carry me home? A band of angels comin' after me—coming for to carry me home. Swing low, sweet chariot. . . ." Closing her eyes, Meg had swayed to the spiritual, praying that LaRae was at peace, that a merciful God now cradled her within his arms. Then the mourners had sung, "On that great gettin' up mornin'—Allelu, Allelu."

A cheer rang out from inside the ballroom.

Meg's eyes flew open.

Demon Rum, Corby, had been shoved into the coffin. The policeman lowered the lid.

"No," Meg gasped. *I don't want anyone else to die.* "I'm so frightened."

"I know," Gabe whispered. Meg, so lovely in the moonlight, so vulnerable. *I must tell her, she'll help.* His impossible desire to hold Lenore gripped him.

He pulled Meg to him. Holding the back of her silken head in his hand, he bound her to him with an arm tight around her tiny waist. He kissed her as a man dying of thirst drinks water. He bruised her soft lips. Tears he hadn't shed for Lenore in France trickled down his cheeks.

She pressed closer to him.

His arms felt how frail, how delicate she was. This took the edge from his need. His hold on her gentled to a sheltering embrace.

"Gabriel?" A voice came from behind him, shocking him back to his present surroundings.

Meg looked up at him. With her gloved hands, she wiped away the evidence of his tears.

He let her go and turned to see his sister blushing in the doorway. "What is it, Belle?" His own voice sounded strange in his ears.

"Dulcine says Mother wants you."

She would, Meg said to herself.

Gabe excused himself and, without meeting his sister's eyes, went in through the French doors.

"I'm so sorry," Belle stuttered. "I would never have come out if I'd known Gabe was kissing you."

Meg walked past Belle. "He wasn't kissing *me.*"

CHAPTER 12

When Jesus saw him lying there, . . . He said to him,
"Do you want to be made well?"
John 5:6, NKJV

Ready to spit fire, Meg followed Gabe inside the ballroom but kept her distance as he spoke to his mother. When he reached his mother—surprise, surprise—Dulcine just happened to appear beside Gabe. The band struck up a lively two-step.

Did they deem her such a weak sister? She'd teach them to meddle. Meg strolled up boldly. "Gabriel, this is the dance I promised you."

Dulcine tried to hide her chagrin and failed.

Though looking a bit puzzled, Mrs. St. Clair smiled. "Of course, son, don't let me keep you from your dance."

As stiff as a tin man, Gabriel bowed to them and took Meg's hand in his. He led her to the fringe of the couples pairing up and beginning to dance.

In a businesslike tone, Meg demanded, "Don't I get a thank-you for getting you away from the persistent Dulcine?" With one hand on his shoulder and one in his other hand, she bounced in time to the sprightly rhythm.

He grimaced. "Didn't your stepmother teach you any society manners?"

"Yes, and in addition to learning which fork to use for which course, she taught me to be honest to others. It's time you were honest with me and with yourself."

"Who gave you the right to lecture me?"

"You did."

His neck turned beet red. "You mean when I kissed you on the terrace?"

"Did you kiss *me* on the terrace?" Meg raised one eyebrow.

"What do you mean? Of course I kissed you on the terrace. Who else?"

"You won't tell me her name."

He tightened his hold on her. "Don't pry."

"Don't lie."

He led her through a quick variation of steps. Did he mean to distract her? Did he still know her so little? One thing was sure: she wouldn't permit him to pry into her past while keeping his shrouded in secrecy.

They finished the dance in silence. At the end, he bowed to Meg. Smiling in spite of her true feelings, she nodded her thanks. She turned to find another handsome man waiting to ask her to dance. She accepted and stepped into his arms as the band started a fox-trot. She watched Dulcine take Meg's place in Gabriel's embrace, then Meg smiled up at her present partner. She didn't intend to let Gabriel play any more games with her. Something from France still bedeviled him. He would tell her what and soon. Then she shook her head. Why did she care about this stubborn man anyway?

✿ ✿ ✿ ✿ ✿

In the early morning hours, the Demon Rum Ball began to limp toward its end. Meg sat alone against the red-orange silk-covered wall and watched the last few dancers. Her earlier anger had slipped into the pervading ennui she'd felt since her first year in France. She told herself to ask to have a taxi called and go home, but that took too much energy. Besides, she hadn't talked privately with Sands yet. All evening, people had monopolized him, preventing Meg from stealing a moment alone with him. A swirl of white silk sat down beside her.

"Meg, may I have a word with you?" Belle said.

Meg glanced sideways at her young friend and nodded. Still, she hoped this would not be a heart-to-heart talk. She'd watched Gabe dance and laugh the evening away with young lady after young lady as if he hadn't a care in the world. He'd danced twice more with an exultant Dulcine. Now Meg burned for a heart-to-heart talk with Gabriel St. Clair. She had quite a bit to tell him about self-pity. But she shook off these stinging thoughts and gave her attention to his sister.

Belle blushed and wouldn't meet Meg's eyes. "Something wonderful happened to me tonight. Corby told me he thinks he's falling for me."

Meg didn't feel capable of dealing with this right now, but what choice did she have? "Oh?"

"We've known each other—forever. I've always liked him. And lately . . . he talks to me like no one else ever has—except you, of course."

Keeping an eye on Belle's parents, Meg needed to hurry this along if she were to have a word with Sands tonight. "What about you? Are you falling for him?"

"Yes! When we dance and he holds me in his arms, I feel lighter than a feather. I never knew love was so overpowering."

Was I ever this young? Unimpressed with these raptures, Meg tightened her hold on her patience. "Do you think your future lies with Corby?"

Belle fussed with the lace draped over her white silk skirt. "I don't know . . ."

Meg waited. Had Belle's burst of independence already failed with so little cause?

"I still want to go to Newcomb. I want to have a chance to be a nurse."

"I see. You aren't sure Corby will understand your ambitions." Meg crossed her legs and leaned back with a sigh.

"He's such a sheik; what if someone else decides to steal him away? What if he won't wait for me?" The words came out in a rush.

"Hadn't you considered how to handle this type of conflict when you decided to go against your mother's wishes and carve out a life of your own?" Meg couldn't conceal her exasperation.

"I should have. I see that now. You said that the kind of man *you* intended to marry wouldn't care if you had a law degree. How does a woman know if a man cares about such things?"

Meg stood up. Mrs. St. Clair had left her husband's side and was headed toward the hatcheck area. "There is only one way to find out, Belle. You must ask him."

Belle jumped up too. "What if Corby doesn't want to marry a woman with a career?"

Many answers popped into Meg's brain. She swiftly sorted and discarded them all; then she gazed at Belle's beautiful face. "You must find the answer to that yourself. I must speak to your father now, then go home." She smiled at Belle. "Being an adult means making difficult choices on your own. We all have to face these things."

I better take my own advice. Sands needs to know what I heard at LaRae's funeral. Leaving Belle by the love seat, Meg made her way to Sands.

He glanced up at her. "Miss Wagstaff—"

"I need to talk to you."

"Can it wait until morning, after breakfast?" Sands stifled a yawn.

"I don't think so. I'm worried." A shiver shook Meg.

"About Del?"

She nodded, then passed her hands over her face as though wiping away her cares.

"You've been pushing yourself too hard." Sands stared at her. "And you look more than worried."

Mrs. St. Clair came back with her dark sable evening wrap around her shoulders. "Oh! Miss Wagstaff, we were just leaving."

"Miss Wagstaff is coming home with us. I need to talk to her before bed—"

"Sands, it's so late. I don't want you to overdo—"

"Celestia, Miss Wagstaff will come home with us. I want a few moments alone with her in my office."

Mrs. St. Clair looked concerned, but said no more.

For the second time that night, Mrs. St. Clair surprised Meg. Why hadn't she objected to Meg coming home with them?

After thanking their host, the three of them started for the door. Soon Meg sat beside the chauffeur. "What about Belle?"

Mrs. St. Clair replied, "She didn't want to miss the last few dances. Gabriel offered to bring her home soon."

The granting of this concession surprised Meg. Perhaps Mrs. St. Clair was beginning to see her daughter as a young woman. The woman hadn't even frowned at Meg all night!

At the St. Clair home, Meg perched in the wingback dark leather chair in front of Sands's desk. One green-shaded desk lamp lit the room, casting deep shadows behind Sands and onto the bookcase crammed with leather-bound law books. "I'm sorry to have bothered you, but today has been dreadful."

"I take it that you are referring to the funeral?"

Meg nodded and let out a dejected sigh and lowered her chin. "I went to pay my respects and Del's, but I also wanted to see who else came to the funeral."

"I thought you would. Tell me, who—that you know— came to LaRae's funeral?"

"Two other musicians who played with Del—Pete Brown and LaVerne Mason."

"Did they speak to you?"

"Yes. Pete passed by me and said, 'This is all your fault.'"

Sands stared at her over his folded hands. "Go on."

"LaVerne told me, 'Leave town before you get us all killed.'"

"Interesting."

Meg's temper cracked wide open. "Interesting! How do you think I feel? LaRae's death is on my conscience!"

"Why? You didn't put a bullet in the back of her head. Did you think this was going to be a Sunday school picnic?"

This question shocked her. "I expected to get Del out of this and back home without more people dying."

"Then you were living in a fairy tale. Someone murdered Mitch Kennedy. Why? Someone killed LaRae. Why? I think the two reasons are separate, but the killer is the same, or connected to both. Murder begets murder."

Sands's harsh voice unnerved her again. But his words had already been proved true. "What should I do?"

"Keep your eyes and ears open. I don't want you going to Storyville by yourself again. If someone contacts you, I want you to come to me first—no matter what. I don't want you to take the risk of getting into cabs alone. I'm going to see about hiring a car and driver for you—"

Meg interrupted, "Gabriel . . . your son, helped me buy a Cadillac. I take possession tomorrow, and he has hired a driver for me."

Sands's eyebrows lifted. "He did? Who?"

"Jack Bishop. Have you heard of him?"

"Of course, I have. He's one of the men I hire as a bodyguard for my clients."

Meg recoiled as though she'd been slapped. "Bishop is?" Her voice shrilled in her ears. "Why do you need bodyguards for your clients?"

"Because I sometimes represent the unpopular or ones other people wish to silence."

"Like Del?" *Like me?* she echoed silently. She swallowed and found her mouth dry.

He nodded. "Someone once called me New Orleans's conscience. That, of course, was and is nonsense. But I'm not afraid of standing out in the crowd. I have gotten the feeling you aren't either."

Numbly, Meg nodded. "You think that I may be a target then?" She had rejected this idea before, but now she forced herself to believe it true.

"I think it is safer if we assume that."

Safer? She'd felt safer on the Western Front.

Mrs. St. Clair tapped on the door, then opened it. "Sands, it's really time you were resting. I'm sure Miss Wagstaff—"

"You're right, Celestia, but I think we should invite Miss Wagstaff to spend tonight in our guest room. I don't want her out in a car this late and alone."

Celestia nodded hesitantly. "Of course, she's most welcome. Sands, I will send your man in. Miss Wagstaff, if you will follow me, I will take you to a guest room."

The lady's easy agreement helped Meg accept. She wanted to refuse, but even staying here, where she didn't really feel that comfortable with her hostess, was less dismaying than riding through the deep night and returning to the lonely hotel. The thought that both Gabriel and his father believed she needed a bodyguard had sobered her, then alarmed her.

As Meg followed Mrs. St. Clair upstairs, she turned this fact over in her mind: even though Gabriel was the prosecution he had decided she needed a bodyguard. Did he know something that she didn't?

Outside, Gabe pulled to a halt in front of his parents' front door. He noted the light on in his father's office. Was Meg in there now? "Here you are, Sis. See you in the morning."

Belle pouted. "I'm not in the least tired. Why can you stay out after the ball, but I have to go to bed?"

"You know why. Good night, Belle." He reached across and pushed open her door.

"All right, I know when I'm licked." She got out and closed the door behind herself. "Don't do anything I wouldn't do!" she teased him.

"This younger generation," he answered in kind. He watched her go inside. Sliding the car into gear, he headed back for town. He had seen Meg leave the ball with his parents, so she should be safe for now. And in the morning, Jack Bishop would be on the job.

Tonight, Gabe wanted to have a look at Storyville for himself and do a little fishing. He'd recognized at least one unwelcome face at the funeral. Had the man merely been an acquaintance of the dead girl, or more? Gabe needed information. Besides, maybe some Basin Street jazz would settle his nerves.

He parked his car under a street lamp on Canal Street. From under his seat, he drew out a pistol, cool and heavy in his palm, and slipped it into his evening jacket pocket. Stepping out of his car, he set his shiny black top hat on his head at a jaunty angle. Unless someone recognized him as the parish attorney, he'd just be another *bon vivant* ending a Carnival evening with jazz—which just proved how deceiving appearances could be.

He had only walked a half block before he was approached by a young black woman wearing a very short purple dress.

"Want some comp'ny, gent?"

He wanted to say no, but experience had taught him that if he didn't have a woman on his arm, he would have to turn down many more such offers. "I'm in the mood for jazz. What about you?"

"It's your nickel," she replied.

He offered her his arm. She took it and they walked down the way to Rampart Street. Her cheap perfume hadn't lost any of its potency, even after 3:00 A.M. Gabe led her into one of the clubs and seated her gallantly at a table by the back wall. A six-piece jazz band played "Tiger Rag." Gabe ordered gin for two. "What's your name?"

"Philly." She downed her drink in one swallow.

Deciding to take a chance on finding what he really needed, Gabe pushed his glass toward her. "Philly, you look like a smart gal."

She looked at him a bit puzzled. "You need a smart gal?"

He nodded. "Less than a week and it's Prohibition. Who's going to have liquor? That's what I need to know."

"You and everybody else." She set her elbows on the table, which wobbled at her touch, and leaned forward.

"Mario Vincent?" Gabe named one of the notorious powers behind much of the crime in Storyville.

Philly eyed him nervously. "I don't know him."

Gabe leaned forward so he wouldn't be overheard. "Maybe you know someone who knows him."

"Maybe. How much you willin' to pay?" She sized him up with her eyes.

Gabe took a ten-dollar bill out of his pocket.

Philly reached for it.

Gabe held on to it. "I'll wait here. Come back with a man who knows Mario, and I'll give you the ten."

"What if he's busy?"

"Then you won't get this bill, a *lagniappe* for you."

Philly downed Gabe's second gin and left him.

Gabe settled his chair back against the wall and listened to "Canal Street Blues." He needed at least one new informant. The one he'd used till now had ceased to be informative. He wondered if someone else had begun paying the man better than Gabe could. Tonight, he might gain nothing new, or he might get lucky. He rested his hand on the gun in his pocket and remembered that Paul's telegram still remained there too. *I should have told Meg.*

❋ ❋ ❋ ❋ ❋

The next morning at nine, before anyone else had come down, Meg left the St. Clair home without breakfast. She couldn't face trying to make small talk. The St. Clair chauffeur drove her to her hotel. Surely she'd be safe in broad daylight. Jack Bishop, her bodyguard, would report later in the morning.

At the desk, Meg picked up her key and mail and walked upstairs in the quiet hotel to her room. Halfway up the steps to the second floor, she heard heartstopping shrieks coming from the top of the stairs. Her own heart racing, Meg hurried up the last few steps and found a black maid outside the door to Meg's room screaming, "*Gris-gris, gris-gris!*"

Doors on both sides of the hall were thrown open. People leaned out to see what was happening. Meg tried to calm the middle-aged black woman, but words didn't touch her panic.

The desk clerk rushed up behind Meg. "Stop this screaming at once, do you hear? Stop it or you'll lose your job!"

This broke the woman's hysteria. The screaming stopped, but she still sobbed and shook. Dramatically, she pointed her finger to the floor in front of the doorway to Meg's room. *"Gris-gris."*

On the floor, white salt had been spilled to make the sign of a cross. In the center of the cross sat a short white candle on a dish; the candle obviously had burned out hours before. At the end of each point of the cross lay a nickel.

A single glance at this hit Meg like a blast of cold wind. She shivered and took a step back. Elemental revulsion rocked her. She stooped to brush the offensive symbol away.

"Don't!" The clerk pulled her back.

"Voodoo!" The black maid shook her head. "Voodoo!"

CHAPTER 13

"These things I have spoken to you, that in Me you may have peace.
In the world you have tribulation, but take courage;
I have overcome the world."
John 16:33, NASB

STUNNED AND SICKENED, MEG repeated, "Voodoo? What are you talking about?"

"Black magic," the desk clerk replied. "Colored people down here believe in it."

Resenting his prejudice, Meg pulled herself from his tight grip. She noted that he—the white desk clerk—also didn't want her to disturb the *gris-gris.* So it wasn't just black people.

Last night she'd learned she needed a bodyguard in this city, and now someone wished to unleash the powers of darkness against her!

In a throbbing voice, the maid warned, "You cross *gris-gris,* anyone cross *gris-gris,* get bad luck, real bad luck."

Meg had never faced anything like this before. Flesh-and-blood peril already crowded her. Billows of anger and loathing threatened to sweep away her reason. Casting about in her memory for an adequate reply to this demented assault, she stared down at the salt cross and stubby white candle.

Leave it to evil to use religious symbols and pervert them. A quiet voice, her father's, began reciting the truths she'd been taught as a child: *Ye are the salt of the earth. If salt loses its saltiness, can it be made salty again? No, it is good for nothing but to be thrown out and trampled under foot. If any man loves me, he must take up his cross and follow me.* And a candle was an ancient symbol of prayer. A jolt of anger scorched through her. How dare someone corrupt that which drew one closer to the divine? She grappled with her outrage, trying to hit on a course of action. What would her father do in this situation?

The silence in the hallway became absolute. No one went back to their room. No one spoke. Everyone stared at Meg and the voodoo symbol.

Meg closed her eyes. *Father, what should I do?* She couldn't differentiate in her own heart—was she praying to God or appealing to her own father. In this moment, they'd become entwined in her heart. A battle raged around her. *Father, what should I do?* She could almost hear demons shrieking.

The answer came.

Meg opened her mouth and voiced the words that had come: "As the archangel Michael said to Satan: The Lord rebuke you!" Meg stooped and picked up the candle and dish and the four nickels. Then with one wave of her arm, she swept aside the salt, obliterating the sign of the cross. "Get thee hence, Satan!"

The black maid gasped and crossed herself.

The desk clerk cleared his throat.

Rising, Meg unlocked her door, stepped across the scattered salt, and entered her room. Then she turned and faced the horrified witnesses. "Greater is he who is in me than he who is in the world." She closed her door. The murmur of disturbed voices filtered in from the hallway.

The unreality of this wicked attack gripped her. She walked to her bed and sat down. She had heard of voodoo long ago from Fleur Bower but had never thought it would be something aimed at her. Meg knew that people paid a voodoo priestess for these powerful hexes against enemies. Someone in New Orleans hated her, really hated her.

Who had paid for and sent her the *gris-gris?*

A polite tapping on her door roused Meg from her thoughts. "Meg? This is Gabe. Will you come out?"

Meg still sat on the side of her bed trying to fit the latest development into the scheme of what had gone on before. Though tempted, she hadn't called her father. She needed to face this alone. Now she shook herself, rose, and opened the door. "Gabriel?"

As she looked up at him, a foolish desire to throw herself into his arms bolted through her. She took tight hold of herself. Gabriel's gaze traveled over her face, then searched her eyes. His obvious concern for her lifted her drooping spirits. Their acquaintance so fresh, so conflicted, had led somehow into a special intimacy. Gabriel was enemy, friend, and the man who last night had bruised her lips with a kiss.

Disquieted, she shifted her attention to a man standing behind Gabriel. A black man in his thirties, he stood a few inches shorter than the parish attorney but a few inches broader around his barrel chest. Though her throat tightened with foreboding, she asked, "Is this Mr. Bishop?"

Gabriel made the introductions.

Jack gave her a wide smile. "Please call me Jack, Miss Wagstaff."

"Very well, Jack." She struggled to keep her voice light, as though accustomed to needing protection. "I understand you're going to be my driver." She paused to give Gabriel a significant look. "And my bodyguard."

"So my father told you?" Gabriel didn't sound too disgruntled.

"Your father wanted to hire a car and a driver for me, so I told him you'd already taken care of that. He recognized Jack's name. Did you talk to your father this morning?" Meg turned a steady gaze to him.

"I missed him. I had to leave early. Though *you* left even earlier than I."

Jack let out a sudden wordless exclamation, then pointed down to the rug. "Is that salt?"

"Yes, someone had a *gris-gris* waiting for me when I came home this morning." Her pulse quickened, but Meg watched for Gabriel's reaction.

"That is bad," Jack pronounced.

Looking down at the white grainy remains, Gabriel nodded. "It's nasty, perverted."

"I'm gratified to hear that. Someone is taking pains to make me feel distinctly unwelcome," Meg pressed him.

Gabriel couldn't seem to stop glaring and frowning at the remains of the *gris-gris*. Finally, he shook his head. "I don't know what to say. I never expected anything like this."

So many things have happened here—a false arrest, a poison pen letter. What would you expect, Gabriel? A knife blade in my back like Del, or a bullet in the head like LaRae?

"Who got rid of the *gris-gris* for you?" Jack asked.

"I did." Meg answered the men's expressions of surprise with a steady focus.

Looking impressed, Jack studied her. "I hear from Mr. Gabriel that you got a lot of bad luck already, Miss."

Meg shrugged. "You might say that."

Gabriel cleared his throat. "I think you should call my father and tell him about this. He'll want to know right away."

And my own father, too, but she said only, "I should have thought of that." Meg passed a hand over her forehead, disturbing her bangs. "I was just so shocked. I couldn't think straight." She went to the phone at her bedside and asked the operator to dial the St. Clair home. The butler there informed her that Mr. Sands had been driven into town.

"Then Jack and I will take you over to pick up your Cadillac," Gabriel offered briskly.

She scanned his face. He wasn't as unruffled as he wanted to appear. His jaw had hardened and a vein along his neck bulged.

"Can you wait downstairs? I still need to shower and change." Motioning to herself, she continued in a humorous tone, "I don't usually pick up a car in evening dress. It's a touch pretentious, don't you think?"

She wouldn't give in to the flutter in her pulse. She'd faced an earthquake, then a war. Now New Orleans, even with its voodoo, wouldn't conquer Del or her. She wouldn't let it!

Jack grinned.

Gabriel shook his head, still looking tense and displeased with himself. "We'll wait downstairs."

"As you wish." Meg sauntered away from them.

Gabriel closed the door.

Within the hour, Meg joined Jack and Gabriel in front of the hotel. The dark St. Clair family sedan pulled up to the curb. Meg stepped over to speak to Sands, who had rolled down his window.

"I see Jack is already on the job." Sands waved at the black man.

Jack smiled and gave a slight bow.

"Sir," Gabriel cut in before Meg could speak, "Meg was greeted by a *gris-gris* this morning in front of her door here."

Sands grimaced. "Are you all right, my dear?"

"Certainly. *That* for black magic." Meg snapped her fingers to show her disdain. *Bravado, you mean, don't you, Meg?*

"What about evil?" Sands asked.

His question threw her off stride, but she recovered. "I was in France, remember?"

Sands nodded. "Meg, I've arranged for you to visit Del today." Sands motioned to Jack. "She has an appointment at 1:30 P.M. today at the jail. Stay with her at all times."

Meg—caught between two conflicting reactions, gratitude and fear—didn't speak. She wanted to see Del and reassure him, but she didn't want to have to talk about LaRae. She was glad to have Jack's protection, but his presence clarioned her inability to protect herself.

"Gabe, I'll take Jack and Meg to pick up her car. I know you have court today."

"Very well, Father." Gabriel took her hand.

Her skin tingled at his touch, disturbing her. *We have business to settle between us, Gabriel. I haven't forgotten last night.*

He said, "Jack will take excellent care of you."

Meg bit back barbed words, words railing against her need for a bodyguard. To her mind, this old city around her had become a dark cavern. To free Del, she had begun her journey down the cavern's broad path. But as she descended, the way had narrowed, darkened, and stretched deep into a murky abyss. The secret to regaining Del's freedom lay hidden deep in New Orleans' black heart.

This image chilled her.

"I'll leave you then," Gabriel said.

She reluctantly released his hand, wishing she could bind him to her. She couldn't. Sooner than she wished, they would sit on opposing sides in a courtroom. More to the point, she had no hold on Gabriel St. Clair. Though as she watched him stride away, the strand of emotion that connected her to him pulled taut and strained.

After trying to eat lunch and failing, Meg walked beside Jack down the corridor to the visiting room at the jail, their footsteps echoing in the heavy silence. She recalled traversing this same narrow, dingy hall the first time she came to visit Del at the jail only weeks ago. As she walked, images, sounds, voices from her time in New Orleans jostled one another in her mind: LaRae's lovely face in life, the gritty odor of the street in Storyville, the anisette tang of a Sazerac on her tongue, Del's swollen face in court, moonlight, and Gabriel's fierce kiss. Who was friend? Who was foe? At the end of all this, would she and Del crawl out of the pitiless New Orleans maze into the daylight—safe once again?

The police officer unlocked the door of the room. She stepped inside, followed by Jack and the officer. The large room, filled with the small scarred tables and straight chairs, today held only another officer and Del. Meg walked directly to him and sat down across from him. She folded her hands on top of the table to keep herself from reaching for Del's.

The officer standing behind him mumbled the instructions about her not touching the prisoner. Examining Del with her eyes, she nodded distractedly. Both officers stepped back, one behind Del and one behind her. With arms folded, Jack waited just inside the door.

"Meg, I want you to go home right now."

Del's onslaught didn't surprise her. "I won't leave you. Don't waste words."

"You're in danger."

"So are you. I know why you're frightened for me." She wanted to say, *It's because LaRae was killed.* But she couldn't bring herself to speak the dead girl's name.

Del, who understood her thoughts better than anyone else, guessed them now. "The same could happen to you."

His words intensified the dread she carried. Though she sat motionless and upright, inside she collapsed in a heap, moaning her regret. She pressed a hand to her trembling lips. "I'm afraid it's all my fault."

"Your fault! *I'm* the one who came to New Orleans. *I'm* the one who fought with Kennedy. *I'm* the one who made her a target—and you." The force he used on his words made him grimace. So thin and drawn, he fidgeted in his chair, still moving stiffly with pain.

She longed to comfort him, but what solace had she to give? Her own helplessness ground inside her, making her squirm in her seat. Whatever pernicious evil had sprung up in Storyville would continue until she or someone more powerful conquered it. Maybe only God wielded that kind of power. Would Del survive? Would she? Had they endured France for this?

Del stared down at the scarred tabletop. "I want you to leave New Orleans—"

"No. Your trial begins in days."

"Do you want me to have your death on my conscience too?" he growled.

"I have my own car and bodyguard now. I have my gun. I will not leave you."

"Why do you insist on endangering yourself?" Del folded his hands and pressed his fist to his mouth, masking how close he was to breaking down. She knew him too well to be fooled.

She lowered her voice, "We made a promise once. Do you remember?"

Lifting his chin slowly, Del stared into her eyes. "I release you from your promise."

Love for Del and faith in his love for her propelled her toward tears. Her voice came out gruff, "That's not possible. The promises we made that day were for life."

*　*　*　*　*

The first floor of Hotel Grunenwald had been reserved for the gala celebration of the election of the new governor, John M. Parker. Standing in the hotel's lobby, Meg let Jack take her wrap to the hat check area. She waited until he returned, then she, dressed in one of her raven black Parisienne designs topped with a lavish red fox collar, strolled into the packed room.

A band on the right of a stage blasted an ear-ringing arrangement of "Dixie." Red, white, and blue streamers looped overhead and crisscrossed between the chandeliers. A large royal blue banner reading *Victory* adorned most of one wall—all the standard trappings of American politics. This wasn't the first celebration of this kind she'd attended.

Standing amid laughter, boisterous shouting, and back-slapping, Meg didn't feel festive. Behind her, Jack took a place against one wall, his hands folded. His constant presence plucked her tense nerves.

All day Meg had looked over her shoulder, feeling hunted. Was it because Jack had always been with her? Or was it because she was indeed pursued? Someone had tried to kill Del. Someone had commissioned this morning's *gris-gris*. She had never experienced the sensation of being tracked down before.

On the Western Front, she had lived in danger from bombardment, pestilence, fear, and despair. But this present sense of pervading, active evil weighed her down, stretched her nerves, and heightened her qualms.

Underlying all this, her unfinished conversation with Gabriel St. Clair at the Demon Rum Party nipped at the edges of her mind and brought her here tonight. Though adversaries, the two of them had drawn closer and dearer. Gabriel still sought to convict her dearest friend, and she would give everything to preserve Del. But she also needed Gabriel to push away the emptiness that lingered in her after France, the vacuum that threatened to drain the life from her. With Gabriel, she could talk about what was central in her mind—and her heart.

What's more, he needed her. He denied it, but that didn't change his need. How these opposing truths could exert pressure on her simultaneously couldn't be sorted out now. Too much had occurred in too short a time. Who knew what might happen next?

Belle, in white wool, appeared in front of Meg. "I'm going to tell him tonight."

"What?" Meg couldn't take in what the girl meant.

Belle lifted one of Meg's hands in hers. "Oh! Your hands are so cold." As though to warm them, Belle took Meg's other hand in hers too. "I'm going to tell Corby tonight that I plan to have a career."

Meg squeezed Belle's soft hands, trying to make up for not speaking.

"I'm afraid. But I know I must tell him the truth."

Meg nodded. She didn't feel equal to handling anyone else's problems tonight. Her own loomed high enough.

The band halted midnote, then sped up the tempo to double-time. Everyone around Meg began applauding and whistling. Belle pulled away and left her. A cortege of well-dressed men pushed forward to the stage. The tumult reached a frenzy. Meg shoved against the crush of people and headed back toward Jack.

Jack had disappeared.

Where had he gone? Meg's heart pounded in her breast.

Agitated, she glanced one way, then another, pushing between people until she reached the wall where she had left him. From behind, a hand touched her shoulder.

Meg spun around. Jack. Her knees weakened with her relief. Against the noise, she shouted, "Why did you move? I thought you left me."

The noise of the crowd and the band deafened her. He motioned for her to follow him to the doorway. There he drew her away from the uproar.

"Sorry, Miss, but they don't want me inside the room. I have to watch from the doorway. I'm not the only bodyguard here tonight. Parker has a few on hand too. Except for the doors to the kitchen, this is the only entrance. I will stay and I'll be watchin'. Don't you worry."

Meg's stomach, contracted into a tight ball, eased. "Thank you, Jack." She turned and edged back into the crowded hoopla. Finally, broad gestures from men on the stage quieted the gathering. The winning candidate stepped to the front and began to address his supporters.

Meg paid little attention to the verbose new governor. She scanned the crowd for Gabriel. At last, she glimpsed him and began to slip her way through the crowd toward him. She saw that he was pressing his way through toward her also. This realization uncapped a delirious joy. *I shouldn't feel this way! I have no right.* Her chastising words couldn't staunch the bubbling flow of joy within. *Gabe, come to me, hold me.* She moved forward, her eyes tracking his erratic, but steady, progress toward her. Acquaintances interrupted him as he made his way to her. He nodded to them but kept his eyes on her. She imagined his excuses to them as he pulled away.

She longed to burrow herself deep inside his strong arms. She had wanted his embrace this morning at the hotel, but hadn't admitted this to herself until after he had gone.

Maybe he wouldn't put up a wall against her tonight. Somehow knowing he'd also suffered loss in the war gave her strength to face her own past.

Tonight, he would tell her what had happened to him, to his heart in France. Tonight, perhaps he would kiss *her* and not a memory. Just a yard from her, a man would not let Gabriel pull away. Instead, he tugged Gabriel back toward the stage.

Frustration shredding her, Meg balled her fists. *Gabe, no! Come here!* More applause, then the governor stepped from center stage. The band played again but more quietly, and people chattered to each other. The shouting and speeches had ended.

"Miss Wagstaff, I declare; I see you everywhere." Dulcine, in a light pink dress, didn't sound very happy about this either.

Then Meg realized the blonde had a new look. *Dulcine, you had your hair bobbed!* Meg played with the idea of mentioning this change, but rejected it. Dulcine had become a wild card in Meg's mind. With Dulcine's outrageous outburst at the Pandora's Ball, Meg was in no mood for a public display. Who knew what this blonde Southern belle was capable of?

And Meg dearly yearned to say what she really thought about this woman to her face. But she had to think of Fleur's family's reputation and Gabriel's. "Good evening, Dulcine."

"I saw Gabriel being drawn up to speak to Governor Parker."

Meg nodded.

"My own father and Governor Parker are second cousins."

"Your family must be very pleased tonight."

"Oh, yes, we're very proud. I'm sure you agree with me that Gabriel St. Clair might have a future in politics." Dulcine sent her a pointed look.

"I hadn't realized that he had political ambitions," Meg returned.

"I'm sure he must have since he has taken a public office instead of going into private practice."

Was Dulcine trying to tell her that Gabriel wanted to be a politician and that Dulcine's family could help him in this? "Why are you telling me this?"

"Just making conversation." Dulcine gave her an enigmatic smile and strolled away.

Bemused, Meg shook her head. Gabriel still stood talking to Parker. With a sigh, she wended her way to one of the tables around the fringe of the packed room and sat down. Before she could answer the waiter who came over to ask her if she wanted any food or drink, Mrs. St. Clair walked up.

"May I join you, Miss Wagstaff?"

Meg's heart sank. *I only want Gabriel.* "Certainly." In defeat, Meg ordered tea.

Mrs. St. Clair did likewise. "That's a very lovely dress."

The waiter walked away.

"Thank you." Meg didn't know how much forbearance she could muster tonight. The *gris-gris,* getting—or more to the point, needing—a bodyguard, helplessly witnessing Del's grief—how much more could she take?

Mrs. St. Clair worried her lower lip. "I hope you won't think me forward, but I would like to discuss my son with you."

Meg was dumbfounded. "Do you think you should?"

"Yes, I want you to understand why I have encouraged my son to take an interest in Dulcine."

From a cart, the waiter served their tea, then moved on.

"This is none of my business," Meg objected. "I can't understand why you wish to discuss something so personal with me, and here of all places."

"I overheard something a few days ago that has given me much food for thought." The woman pursed her lips. "I have not liked your modern ways, but I am trying to understand why you have had such a startling effect on my family."

"I wasn't aware that I have had any effect . . ." Meg stopped. Perhaps Mrs. St. Clair had a point. Meg hadn't intended to have any effect, but . . . She frowned.

"Miss Wagstaff, it is difficult for me to talk to you about personal matters. You may have harbored no distinct motive, but do not waste time trying to convince me that you haven't been the catalyst for the changes in my family over the last four weeks."

"I am sorry if you feel I have purposely tried to change your daughter's direction in life . . ." Meg halted, then conceded, "Very well. What do you want to tell me about Gabriel?"

"I've wanted Gabriel to marry Dulcine." The lady stirred her tea silently.

The image of Gabriel waltzing with Dulcine the night before stung once more. Meg flared, "All New Orleans knows that."

Mrs. St. Clair looked tempted to snap back, but she merely took a deep breath. "When Gabriel returned from the war, I could tell he'd suffered terribly there, not just from his wounds, but from some deep emotional . . . shock."

"Is that why you told him not to talk about the war?" Meg couldn't seem to stop herself from attacking this woman.

"I never said that." The woman looked honestly surprised. "What are you talking about?"

Meg smothered her irritation. She had been judgmental and evidently wrong too. "I'm sorry. Go on please."

"I don't think you understand how difficult it is to give comfort to an adult son. I couldn't pull him onto my lap and make everything all right! I had to respect his masculine pride, his independence—and still try to make him feel secure and loved. I thought if he would marry, a wife would be able to help him heal. She could . . . comfort him in a way I couldn't."

Meg hadn't been able to see past this woman's very obvious match-making ploys to the motivation behind them. Hearing her reveal these deep feelings made Meg uncomfortable. She had misjudged this mother in more than one way.

"Anyway, I knew Dulcine was interested in Gabriel even before the war. She had her first Carnival season in 1916; then we had two very dismal seasons while most of our young men trained or went overseas. You went to France, but Dulcine didn't have that option. If Dulcine doesn't marry in the next few years, she'll be considered a spinster. She doesn't have your ambition or scope. Her family and she both want her to make a good marriage. We lost so many young men from this city to the war. Gabriel showed a preference for her . . ." Mrs. St. Clair fell silent.

Meg sympathized, but Dulcine's fate wasn't in her hands or Mrs. St. Clair's. "I didn't come to New Orleans to fall in love and marry, Mrs. St. Clair."

"Love rarely comes when we plan for it."

These unexpected words kicked Meg in the stomach.

"Meg, I never thought to find love at a Y-canteen." Colin cradled her head in both his hands. *"Marry me."*

"I know that in my own life," Meg agreed in a whisper.

Mrs. St. Clair nodded, but looked unsatisfied.

"What do you want from me?"

"I don't want you to tempt Gabriel and destroy Dulcine's chances only to leave him—"

"Be at ease. Marrying Gabriel St. Clair isn't on my agenda on this trip to New Orleans." Meg rose and walked away. She couldn't take any more. *I just want to get out alive with Del.*

Gabriel met her. "Why were you talking with my mother?"

"She was just being polite." *And informative.* The woman's words made Meg uneasy about Gabriel, but being near him flooded her with a sense of waiting, wanting. His gaze on her brought an awareness of him, an aching to nestle close.

"I need to talk to you—alone." Gabe took her arm. He realized he'd wasted opportunity after opportunity to ask for her help, and now he was running out of time. *"Blast."*

She swung around to face the same way as he. "What?"

"My sister is bearing down on us." He cursed softly. "We're getting out of here. We have to talk!"

Meg began to object, but he tugged her along, hustling her toward the exit. From the corner of her eye, she glimpsed Dulcine looking daggers at her. "Gabriel, do you think—"

"Don't stop now. We're going."

His urgent tone sliced through her. "Where? What's happened?"

CHAPTER 14

The winter is over . . . the song of doves is heard.
Song of Songs 2:11, 12, TEV

OUTSIDE THE FORMIDABLE white-frame hotel, with the sounds of giddy laughter and the syncopated jazz band still around them, Meg pulled against Gabriel. The cool night air and her fear made gooseflesh zip up her arms, then the back of her neck. "Where are we going?"

Looking hunted, he paused and glanced around. "My father's office. We have to talk."

"What has happened?" her voice shrilled.

Without answering, he hustled her into his car.

From the passenger seat, Meg studied him, a sick feeling tightening her stomach. Of all the things that could go wrong, Del's danger loomed foremost. "Is it Del? Has he . . .?"

"Sorry." He gripped the steering wheel with both hands.

In spite of the pale light, she tried to study his profile for a clue.

"This has *nothing* to do with your friend! This is about . . .
this is about . . . I received a telegram today from France." He
shuddered once, then bent his head into his hand for a moment.

Paris? Whom had he left behind there? Moved by his agitated
tone, she touched his sleeve to comfort him, to urge him to trust
her.

He grappled with himself—obviously overwrought. His
words came out in a thick, edgy voice, "Her name was Lenore."

Meg sat very still. *He trusts me.* A wave of ice made her
shudder, then a burst of heat sizzled through her. His revelation
of Lenore's name plunged her back to the French Front—the
sound of machine guns spitting rounds of bullets, the whine of
airplane propellers, the sweet sickening smell of decaying flesh,
the ivory white of cold dead hands.

Her heart pounded her breastbone. Clenched in the wintry
fingers of loneliness and loss, she slid across the seat close against
him, seeking his strength and warmth. When he didn't object,
she lay her head on his shoulder.

"Stay close," he murmured roughly.

"I will."

Gabe leaned his cheek on the top of her smooth hair and
swung his car onto the street.

Meg's nearness made the miles shorter and easier to bear.
Gabe parked his car under the port cochere beside his parents'
home. The night breeze, though cool, held the hint of the
coming warmer weather. Would this winter end in joy of
homecoming or separation from those he loved most?

As he led Meg inside, it seemed natural for him to keep her
close to his side. His rioting pulse steadied. In the past few
weeks, he'd seen what this woman could stand up to. And she'd
served in France. If anyone could, she would counsel him—
understand and absolve.

With a curious eye, the butler received their wraps. Feeling
awkward in his own home, Gabriel nodded at him. "We need to
discuss something privately. We'll be in my father's office."

If the butler saw this as strange, he said nothing, save, "If
anyone should call?"

"Don't disturb us unless it's an emergency."

The butler bowed his head.

Taking Meg's slender arm, Gabe led her to the office. There, he switched on the green-shaded desk lamp. His father's office held the essence of Gabe's father—both a consolation and a prompting to proceed. Playing for time to frame words, he asked, "Shall I light a fire?"

"Please." As though at home, Meg curled up on the sofa.

Unable to hit on a graceful way of bringing up Marie, Gabriel knelt in front of the green-marble hearth and busied himself moving the wire screen away from the fireplace.

Meg asked, "How did you meet her?"

In the midst of arranging charcoal on the grate, he paused, still longing to conceal, to protect his past. "A surveillance flight over Argonne." His voice sounded wooden in his own ears. "I was hit, but still managed to land the plane in a field. I was banged up enough to put me in a hospital for more than two weeks. Lenore was a nurse there."

"With the Red Cross?"

He added a few more chunks of charcoal, then began building a tiny pyramid of sticks and wadded newspaper to ignite the charcoal. "No, she had completed only a year of nurse's training—before she had married."

"She was married?"

He heard her surprise. "A widow. Her husband, a doctor, had been killed in an accidental bombing of the hospital close to the front a couple of years before I married her." Each word he spoke registered like removing weights one by one off a merchants scale inside him. He breathed easier with each word—each one deducted.

"Lenore was your wife." Meg considered this. "What nationality was she?"

"French. Her home had been in Versailles." He struck a match and touched its flames to the paper.

"I visited there before I came home." Her calm acceptance refreshed him like waking from a deep dreamless sleep.

The fire lit, crinkling up the paper into orange flame and instant black ash that danced above the pyramid. With a scrape and a clink, he set the metal screen in place and turned. He rose, staring down at her. Her pale skin contrasted intensely against the black of her dress and her short brown hair. Her clear, luminous eyes looked like glistening pools in a moonlit, midnight garden.

She held out a hand to him, a sign of welcome.

Crossing to her, he received it as a boon, and keeping it, nestled down beside her.

"Tell me."

Her two words acted on him like drawing a cork from a bottle. Lifting her hand to his lips, he branded it with a kiss of appreciation. "I loved her; I still love her." He gazed into Meg's eyes, watching for her reaction.

She squeezed his hand. "I knew."

"Yes," he acknowledged. He recalled her question, *What was her name?* Words began to flow from him, "She was like you— not in appearance—but like you . . . strong . . . passionate . . . a woman who understood things without having to be told."

His words played in her aching heart, touching chords, evoking memories, linking him to her. Meg shifted her weight on the sofa, leaning into him. "It was the war. Such misery, naked inhuman suffering . . ." A remembered image—a field the day after battle, an upflung hand frozen in entreaty. She shut her eyes; the image remained. She had whispered, "Heaven, help him, help us all."

"Things I witnessed . . . I knew I would be expected to kill people. I thought I understood that. But knowing and doing are poles apart. Firing a machine gun at an enemy flyer—in the air." He pursed his lips. "We had to fly so close. I always tried to shoot the pilot, not the plane. A bullet in the gas tank turned a plane into a blazing coffin. The screams—I could hear them even over the engine noise—"

Hearing the anguish of his soul, Meg wrapped her arms tightly around him. *Comfort ye. Comfort ye my people.*

"I loved to fly, but I grew to hate it," his vehement voice shook. "The Germans, English, and French had parachutes—not the Americans. Our brass said if we had them, we would bail out too quickly and wreck too many planes," he railed at the injustice. "Easier to train more fliers than to build more planes!"

Tears oozing from her eyes, Meg pressed her face into the protecting harbor of the crook of his neck. "I know," she whispered.

"When I saw Lenore the first time, she took my breath away. I know that's a cliché, but it actually happened to me."

"What did she look like?" Meg tilted her head back to watch emotion play across his finely chiseled features.

"Tall, a Gallic brunette. Her beauty came more from who she was, what she did."

"How?" She wiped away one lone tear on his cheek, then drew off her sheer, black gloves.

He groped for words. "Undaunted . . . smiling . . . she knew my heart."

"I know." Bracing her hands on each side of his head, Meg bent his head forward and pressed her brow against his. "I felt the same with Colin. When we met, it was like we had known each other all our lives."

Words exploded from deep inside him, "We didn't have time to waste—"

"On getting acquainted," she finished for him. "We went from Hello to I-love-you in one evening."

"Facing death alters perspective, strips away—"

"Everything but the essential."

Her sweet musk perfume enveloped Gabe in heady fragrance. The white pillar of her neck arched within a fraction of his lips. Its creaminess tantalized him. Unable to resist, he pressed his lips to her soft skin.

His touch made her breath catch in her throat; she kissed the lobe of his ear.

The touch of her lips suspended his faculties—as though she had released him from the constraints of time and space. He felt himself drifting in the delicious sensation of Meg in his arms.

Then their intimacy charged his pulse, making it pound at his temples. Cradling her silken hair in both hands, he bestowed a kiss to each of her closed eyes, and with his lips, pushed back her bangs.

A red welt crossed her forehead—a shrapnel scar! His heart surged in his chest. "Meg, my poor sweet girl, *ma cher*—"

"No, don't." She put up a hand to prevent him from touching the wound.

Undeterred, he captured her hand and held it away from her head. Her resistance weakened, gave way. Along the angled red crease, one kiss, two, three kisses. Then he inclined his forehead to hers, warm skin against warm skin. "Colin died?"

Trembling, she rubbed her forehead against his. "Shot by a sniper two months before armistice." She swallowed tears. "Lenore?"

Wincing, he closed his eyes, not breaking their contact. He forced out the words, "The field hospital bombed . . . an accident." He folded her into his arms against the past and its agonies.

She whispered a sigh into his ear, then relaxed against him, trusting. The charcoal fire glowed on the hearth. His father's mantel clock ticked-ticked. Feeling the load he'd carried for so long lighten, he drew in a deep breath. "Thank you," he whispered. "I haven't had anyone to share this with."

Sighing, she pulled from his embrace, though staying curled beside him on the sofa; his sleek cat had returned.

With his index finger, Gabe traced the line of her cheekbone. Then, exhaling, he reclined against the soft leather back of the sofa and stretched his legs toward the fire, crossing his ankles. The relief of purging himself of all secrets had drained him, but Meg's nearness bolstered him. If he stretched out his arm along the back of the sofa, she would come closer. The clock continued to tick time away, then chimed the hour.

Meg looked to him. "Your parents will return home soon. I should go. Since you sent Jack home with my car, you need to drive me to my hotel."

Her words touched a nerve. He hadn't come to the main point yet. Gabriel sat up. "I need to ask you for advice . . . for your help. I don't know why I got sidetracked." He rubbed the back of his neck.

Meg knew why. Lenore had dominated Gabriel's heart and mind. When he finally decided to let go, a flood had gushed over them, washing him clean, even smoothing the jagged edges of her loss of Colin. What more did he have to reveal? She inhaled deeply. "I'll help. What do you need?"

Showing her his lingering hesitance, Gabriel stood and walked to the mantel. "Lenore had a little daughter, Marie— only three years old—from her first marriage. I adopted her."

The desire to weep squeezed Meg's breast. Another child in that war that had spawned so many tattered waifs. "Where is she?"

"I thought she was with Lenore during the bombardment!" he railed at himself. "Lenore's grandmother, her only blood relative, often brought the child to eat lunch with Lenore at the hospital."

She understood his sudden anger. Children shouldn't be in danger of bombs. She clung to the hope his words offered. "But Marie wasn't there?"

Gabe had been right to talk to Meg. The calm feeling brought by telling her about Lenore didn't falter or fade, even in the face of his outrage. "No. Lenore and the grandmother died. Marie's body wasn't found, but she was so small . . ."

Gabriel didn't have to explain. A German shell could obliterate a little girl. Meg folded her arms around herself. "Where is Marie now?"

"A neighbor, another old woman, had Marie in her care that day when the bombardment came. When this old woman died a few months later, Marie was sent to an orphanage. I would never have known she was still alive except that Lenore's first husband's brother, Paul, kept searching for Marie just in case a mistake had been made. He couldn't give up on the chance that his only brother's only child had been spared."

"Is Marie with him?"

"She was for a brief time. France is so depleted because of the war, so Paul is sending Marie to me. In fact, he telegraphed me that she is on her way to New Orleans with a nurse now."

Meg sat up straighter. "How soon will her boat arrive?"

"Three weeks."

"But your mother said nothing to me!" She stared at him, but he retreated from her.

"She doesn't know." His eyes wouldn't meet hers.

Meg gasped. "But why? Surely she'll be delighted to have Marie—"

"I never told my parents about my marriage to Lenore. We met so close to the end of the war. We married so quickly. I meant to tell them . . ." He stirred the fire with the poker.

"Why didn't you?"

Gabriel began pacing in front of the fireplace. "Can't you guess? Did you tell your parents about Colin?"

Caught off guard, she stared at him.

"Did you?" he demanded.

"No." Suddenly restless, she rose and walked over to stand by the desk. "I couldn't speak of it. The loss . . . cut too deep." Voicing each word stabbed her like a biting penance.

He nodded, resting a hand on the mantel. "How could we explain how it was in France?"

"And why?" she agreed, stepping nearer him. "They would only ask questions we wouldn't want to answer—"

"Like how could I know when I met her that Lenore was the only woman I'd ever want."

"Yes." Meg drew in a ragged breath, recalling her father's worried expression whenever he had looked at her. "But it makes it harder now . . . on everyone in your family."

"You're telling me?" he asked with a dry twist. "How do I tell them about Lenore when mother wants me to marry Dulcine?"

In her mind, Meg went over her recent conversation with Mrs. St. Clair. "Maybe telling them won't be quite as difficult as you expect." Then a thought startled Meg. She regarded Gabriel with a stern unwavering expression. "Do you plan to marry

Dulcine? What will she think about your having a child from a previous marriage—indeed, a child, not your own blood, one you adopted? Some people won't accept adopted children. Some never understood why my parents adopted my brother, Shad."

He stared at her, then down into the lambent flames. "I thought I could marry Dulcine, but no. Talking to her is like talking to a . . . moving picture."

Meg strode forward and took hold of his sleeve. "You shouldn't lead her on. She really thinks she has chance with you."

"I know." He grimaced. "You're right. Governor Parker asked to meet me tonight."

"I know. I saw."

"He told me his cousin—"

"Dulcine's father?" She took another step closer.

Gabriel nodded. "Dulcine's father thinks that I have a future in politics."

"Especially if you're married to Dulcine with her political connections?" Meg replayed in her mind Dulcine's cryptic sentences earlier at the gala. Is this what she'd been hinting at?

He shrugged dismissively. "Will you help me? How do I tell my parents, especially my mother, about Lenore and Marie?"

Her eyes widened. "You don't need me. You know how, and you can do this yourself."

"It's my mother. I'm not worried about my father—"

"Your mother might surprise you." Meg's opinion of Gabriel's mother had been shaken loose tonight. She gazed down at the sisal carpet on the floor. "Don't delay. You must give them time to adjust and prepare. Everything must be ready for your French daughter. Little Marie has lost so much. She must feel welcome right away. She'll sense it if she isn't."

He sucked in breath. "You're right. I think I panicked today when I got Paul's telegram. How will I manage to care for a daughter?"

"My advice is, don't delay. Your family will help you. Tell them tonight."

Gabe clasped her small hands in his. "How can I thank you? I knew you would understand . . ." Drawing up both her hands, he kissed the soft palm of each.

The world around the two of them receded, again, another notch. Now only her fragrance, her white skin, her frail elegant form filled his consciousness. He kissed the hands he held, then drew her nearer. She came without demur.

Once again, he folded her into his arms. Holding her so close somehow wrapped him in a warm coverlet of contentment. Though frail as a feather, Meg Wagstaff was a strong woman, admirable. For the first time in many months, he experienced peace, ease . . . desire.

His mouth became dry. *I want to kiss Meg—not out of need or affection, but passion.* This realization shocked him. *No, I can't desire her.* But his body rebelled against his mind. *Kiss her!*

"Meg," he murmured, then he was kissing her as though the dew from her lips would give him life and hope. He deepened his kiss; she responded in kind, whispering his name against his mouth, pressing closer to him.

"Gabe!" Belle's shocked voice shattered their privacy.

Meg stumbled backward and would have fallen if he hadn't kept his hold on her. Waves of shock vibrated through him.

"Oh, I'm so sorry! I saw the light when Corby brought me home. Then our man told me Meg was here talking with you . . ." Belle covered the lower half of her flushed face with her hands.

Sensitive to Gabriel's reactions, Meg took a deep breath. "It's all right, Belle." She tried to make her voice sound natural. "Corby brought you home? Did you have your talk with him?"

Belle came in, closing the door behind her. "Yes, we did. That's why I wanted to see you." She sent a worried glance toward her brother.

Gabriel frowned but said kindly, "You and Corby are becoming quite the thing, I see."

Gabriel's tone reassured her.

"Ye . . . s," Belle stuttered, then straightened up. "Corby is impressed that I'm going on to Newcomb in the fall," she announced with a defiant glance at her brother.

"I don't doubt it," her brother replied. "He seems to have good sense."

This comment opened Belle's eyes wide in surprise.

"Belle," Meg cut in, "where are your parents?"

"At the gala. But they said they'd be home soon." Belle blushed again. "Corby and I wanted a few moments alone, and father said he would be obliged if Corby would take me home for them."

"Gabriel." Meg touched his arm, reminding him of the urgency to speak about Marie. "I think you should take me home before they return."

He nodded. "Belle, would you tell our parents that I've taken Meg home and will be back very soon. I'd like them and you to wait up for me here in the office. I have something important to tell the family."

"Important? What?" Belle stared at them in obvious bafflement. When she received no reply, she agreed, "OK."

"Come, Meg, I might as well tell them tonight while I have the courage, but first I want to get you safely back to the hotel."

"Yes." Meg walked quickly toward the door. As she passed her, she patted Belle's arm.

Belle nodded and opened her mouth to speak.

Meg forestalled her with an upraised hand. "Gabriel will tell you everything tonight."

He whisked her outside into his car. She didn't speak, but watched the play of streetlamp light over his face as he drove her to the hotel.

She recalled the first day they had met. From that prickly moment of their first standoff over Del's case in his law office, who would have thought that she and Gabriel St. Clair had shared such similar experiences? She'd never anticipated his turning to her for advice and understanding, or what's more, her receiving back again the same from him.

Gabe parked across the street from her hotel. "Thank you . . . for everything tonight. I had no right to involve you in my affairs, but—"

She pressed her hand to his lips, stopping his words. "I was happy to listen." She lowered her eyes. "You helped me too. Now don't get out; just go home and tell your parents everything." Acting quickly, she got out of the car without his assistance, walked in front of it, and began to cross the dark street.

From behind Gabe's car, another car pulled away from the curb with a squeal of tires and curved around Gabe. One gun shot, then a volley of shots exploded the silence.

Meg screamed.

Gabe bellowed, "No!"

CHAPTER 15

A false witness will not go unpunished,
and he who speaks lies will not escape.
Proverbs 19:5, NASB

T HROWING OPEN HIS DOOR,
Gabe jumped out of his car.

The strange car—already past—roared away.

"Meg!" Gabe sprinted to her. "Meg!"

She lay face down on the street.

"Dear God . . . no." Kneeling, he lifted her limp shoulders to him.

She moaned.

"Were you hit?" He slid his panicky hand over her body, feeling for wet blood.

"No." She threw frantic arms around his neck and clung to him. "Hold me."

He crushed her to him—shock making him both fierce and weak. *I nearly lost her!*

People at the hotel threw wide their windows and called down questions. Men burst out of the door of the hotel and surrounded them, shouting questions, cursing, yelling: "Police, police!"

Gabe lifted Meg. Pushing through the crowd, he carried her into the hotel lobby. His heart hammering his ribs, he laid her on the first sofa. Sinking to the floor beside her, he knelt. The bright lighting of the lobby hurting his eyes, he swiftly examined her. But she'd come through near-murder with only scraped elbows and ripped black silk stockings.

Meg's large eyes looked wild. Her hands clutched his lapels. "After the first round, I hit the street."

With both his hands, he framed her face. Her head trembled within his grasp.

Though breathing fast, she returned his look steadily. "I'm fine."

He felt sick to his stomach. "Someone tried to kill you!" *And I was helpless!*

"I know." She bit her lower lip, pushing down a sob.

People flocked around them. Gabe urged Meg to remain reclining. He stood up. "Where's a phone?"

At the desk, he dialed police headquarters to summon Rooney. He then ordered the desk clerk, "When I'm done, call your manager."

"Yes, sir," the desk clerk replied, shaken.

Gabe couldn't avoid the implications of this foul act. He didn't want to connect this attempt on Meg's life with Del's case, but he knew Meg would. If he were in her position, he would too. But could it be a coincidence? These incidents did happen once in a great while. But why here? Why now—if this shooting weren't connected to Del's case? This wasn't Storyville or Basin Street at 2:00 A.M. The Hotel Monteleone's neighborhood had never suffered such an event before, at least not in Gabe's time. *No, this couldn't be a coincidence.* The intent to harm or frighten Meg had been unmistakable, monstrously clear. Rage at the injustice of threatening an innocent woman enflamed him. He wouldn't let anyone sweep this attack under a rug just because Meg was a Yankee who'd attached herself to an unpopular suspect.

Finally, Rooney arrived with another two police officers in tow. "What's all this?" he demanded.

When Gabe had called headquarters, he'd insisted to the night officer that Rooney must come himself to investigate this. Now, standing in front of Gabe, Rooney had the look of a man who'd scrambled out of bed—shirt untucked, uncombed hair, all topped with a belligerent expression.

"What did you get me out at this hour for?" Rooney barked.

"I wanted you here because this kind of shooting is something we don't want here in New Orleans." Gabe glowered at the man and raised his voice, "Or do you want our citizens to fear walking on a public street in danger of being shot down? This type of thing doesn't happen in New Orleans, especially this part of the city."

Holding tight to his temper, Gabe cast Rooney a sidelong glance, reminding him they had an audience. The elegant lobby was crowded with police as well as hotel guests in various stages of evening and night wear. Two reporters had appeared before Rooney's arrival and were interviewing anyone who would talk to them. They now approached Rooney.

Gabe knew the instant Rooney recognized the newsmen. The Irishman's face changed in a flash. "I'm glad you called me, Mr. St. Clair," he boomed in an official voice. "The safety of the citizens of New Orleans is the prime concern of the city police—"

"What about visitors," Meg interrupted him in an arch tone, "who have friends facing a charge of murder?" From her seat on the sofa, Meg gave Rooney a look of contempt.

Rooney's chin jutted out. He took a menacing step forward. "You! I might have known . . ."

With one heated glance, Gabe checked him. *Don't even think about it!*

The harassed desk clerk and the disheveled hotel manager approached. The manager towered over Rooney. "I insist more police be added to this neighborhood. My guests demand proper protection—"

Rooney waved his pudgy hand. "Don't give it another thought. I'll beef up the patrols in this area immediately. You must take into account that this young woman has unsavory connections and has frequented the seamier side of New Orleans—jazz clubs and—"

Meg piped up, "And I have a friend in jail who's been wrongfully charged with murder—"

"Don't bring that up now!" Rooney bellowed, forgetting the reporters who were scratching their pads frantically.

"And how do *you* know how I've spent my days and nights in New Orleans, Deputy Police Chief Rooney?" She pinned him with a suspicious stare. "I feted Governor Parker tonight. How would he view your classing *him* with the seamier side of the city?"

Gabe eyed Rooney himself. Had Meg been followed while in New Orleans? Things like that didn't occur in a free country, did they? But Rooney's own words convicted him. Meg had been under police surveillance. Why? And why hadn't Gabe been told of this? This was his case! But Gabe still rejected any direct link between the police and this assault. Did someone know she'd been at Gabe's home tonight? Why had someone parked in front of Hotel Monteleone waiting for her to return after the evening's festivities, waiting to shoot her? Or had the intent been to merely frighten her?

Rooney blustered a limp apology for his innuendo about her, then declared, "This isn't the time or place—"

Meg rose from the pale green sofa where she sat. "Why shouldn't I discuss Del's case now?"

"It's late. These people want to get back to their beds." Flustered, Rooney gestured vaguely.

None of the people he spoke of moved. Everyone stared at Rooney, including Gabe.

Rooney's neck turned red. "All right, you asked for it." He went on in an insinuating tone, "Maybe some of Mitch

Kennedy's friends are tryin' to tell you you're not wanted here. Maybe they don't like you payin' to defend a killer."

"Rooney," Gabe snapped, "you're out of line."

The hotel manager interrupted, "Have your officers finished this investigation here? This is a hotel where people come to rest. I can't have our guests kept up all night."

One of the older police officers who came earlier spoke up: "Mr. Rooney, sir, I've taken down statements from everyone who saw or heard anything."

Rooney glared at everyone. "Good. Make sure those reports are on my desk first thing in the mornin'." He looked up at the manager. "The increased police patrol will be out tomorrow night."

The manager nodded. The hotel guests moved away reluctantly, obviously afraid hostilities might break out again, and they didn't want to miss them. Gabe appreciated the pressure their presence had exerted on Rooney. But finally as the police left and the manager stepped over to speak to the Meg, they began to drift away. The reporters hung around the fringe, no doubt hoping to pick up an indiscreet word.

The lobby clock chimed three o'clock in the morning. Gabe watched the others leave. First, the shooting, then all the commotion afterward had keyed Gabe up, but now fatigue hit him. Shock doubled its punch. Drained, he swallowed a yawn.

With a concerned expression, Meg glanced at him. In a quiet voice, she said, "Gabriel, shouldn't you be getting home?"

He leaned forward so only she could hear his words. "Yes, but you're coming home with me."

Some deep emotion flashed across her face. How had this attack affected her? She needed him. He longed to hold her close again. But he couldn't. "It's all right—"

"I'm not leaving you here. That's final. Go up and pack an overnight bag." He wouldn't expose her to any further danger or terror.

"But—"

"Go." He turned her and nudged her toward the staircase. "I'll follow you."

With one last backward glance at him, she went to the steps. He walked beside her and saw her safely into her room, which he examined carefully—looking under the bed, behind the curtains, and in the bath. Leaving her alone even long enough to pack proved difficult. He stepped outside, then leaned against her door to wait. The memory of Meg in his arms made Gabe ache to hold her close again. But did he have a right to?

Who wants Meg dead? He walked to the bottom of the staircase, but remained vigilant—ready to leap to her aid at her slightest call. His mind replayed the sound of the bullets slamming and ricocheting off the street around Meg. *I nearly lost her. I just found her. Oh, Lenore, I can't feel this way.*

✳ ✳ ✳ ✳ ✳

"All rise," the bailiff's booming voice called Gabe back to the present time, to Simon LeGrand's white and oak courtroom for the first day of Del's trial, two days after the attempt on Meg's life. The judge sat down and began coughing into a large white handkerchief held in his clawlike hands.

Waiting, Gabe wondered where Meg was. He had slept most of yesterday morning away, then had come to court to select a jury along with his father. Afterward, he'd attended a meeting with the chief of police and visited the police station to get the facts about the attempted shooting of Meg the night before. The ensuing evening had been filled with an unavoidable political dinner that had stretched until the early morning hours.

The chief of police, who had also attended, had questioned him closely about the night before. For the first time, Gabe had suggested that the chief review Rooney's competence. Gabe had made the point that Rooney's behavior shouted bias and untrustworthiness. The chief had seemed impressed with Gabe's argument.

But in all those hours, he'd only seen Meg in passing in his home. His mother had welcomed Meg. He wondered at the change in his mother. She no longer pushed him toward Dulcine, and she didn't resent Meg. He hoped she'd been able to reassure Meg.

All this commotion had pushed his worry over Marie into the background. He still hadn't had time to sit down and discuss his daughter with his parents. His life was spinning out of his grasp like a coin flipped into the air. Was it heads or tails? Was Del guilty or innocent?

Judge LeGrand finished coughing and put away his white handkerchief. He stared down at Gabe. "Counselor, are you prepared to begin the prosecution of this case?"

"Yes, Your Honor." Worried, Gabe glanced over his shoulder. Meg and Jack still hadn't appeared in court. Why? Had something else happened? Maybe he should have added a second bodyguard. But he'd ordered Jack not to let her out of his sight except when she was in Gabe's own home. Even then, Jack was to remain on the premises until Gabe came home. Gabe would let no one hurt Meg. No one.

The judge barked, "Well, Gabriel, the court is waiting."

Gabe forced his mind to concentrate on the trial at hand. He owed the city of New Orleans an honest day's work. "Your Honor, the prosecution calls Patrick Rooney, the deputy chief of police, as its first witness."

Rooney, in a tight-fitting suit, swaggered to the witness stand, was sworn in, and sat down.

A wave of revulsion washed over Gabe. In a vague way, he'd never liked or trusted Rooney. Now, without question, he disliked him and distrusted him. Keeping his voice colorless, Gabe asked, "Mr. Rooney, would you please recount for the court your official activities early on the morning of January 2, 1920?"

"Me and two other officers were called to the scene of a murder around three o'clock. The body of Mitchell Kennedy had been found behind his Storyville club, named Penny Candy."

"How did Mr. Kennedy meet his death?" Gabe made himself follow the normal questioning procedure.

"He had been shot twice in the chest." Rooney shifted in his seat.

To Gabe's right, his father and Del sat stone quiet. What questions would his father ask of Rooney? Would he object to anything? Facing his father in court had an unexpected effect on Gabe. His father's gaze made him feel like a first-year law student. He cleared his throat. "What evidence did you find at the scene?"

"We questioned a couple of Kennedy's employees, and they told us—"

"Objection," Sands said. "Hearsay."

"Sustained." LeGrand stared at Gabe. "You know better than that."

Acknowledging the hit, Gabe felt his neck warm. "Mr. Rooney, did you find any other physical evidence at the scene?"

"Physical evidence?" Rooney looked surprised. "No. Just a dead body in an alley."

"What did you do next?" Gabe felt the judge's disapproving gaze burn into him.

Rooney grimaced at the judge. "Following a lead, we— Officers Bergman and Destry and me—obtained a search warrant and went to 83 Canal Street to a colored roomin' house there."

"Why did you go there?" Gabe proceeded as planned, but with a growing uneasiness.

"To question Delman DuBois, who'd worked for Kennedy."

"And what did you find there?"

"Delman—sound asleep. We found over two hundred dollars under his mattress—the amount of money subsequently reported stolen from Penny Candy's office—and a gun under his pillow." Rooney spoke as though he'd memorized his testimony.

Who coached you, Rooney? I didn't. Gabe grimaced.

For the gun and money, Gabe followed the appropriate procedure for identifying and admitting evidence in a trial. Then he continued, "What did you do next?"

"We arrested Delman for robbin' and murderin' his boss. I called it a neat arrest and a good night." Rooney grinned.

"This is no occasion for levity, Mr. Rooney." Judge LeGrand glared at the deputy.

"Sorry, Your Honor." Rooney looked unrepentant.

Judge LeGrand gave Gabe a contemplative look, as though he found him wanting too. "Is that all for this witness, Gabriel?"

The door at the back of the courtroom opened, the barest swish of the air around the door alerting Gabe. Distracted, he glanced over his shoulder and observed Meg and—his mother! She walked in beside Meg and sat down on the defendant's side of the courtroom. *What is my mother doing in a courtroom? Has the earth spun off its axis?* He'd been a little surprised at the warm way his mother had welcomed Meg into their home. But this?

Gabe tried to catch Meg's eye. She avoided his gaze.

"Gabriel, is that all the questions you have for this witness?" the judge asked in an aggrieved tone.

"Yes, Your Honor." Gabe sat down.

His father rolled around his table and approached the witness stand. "You found money and a gun in Mr. DuBois's room?"

"Yes," Rooney sneered.

"How do you know this gun belonged to my client?"

"What? It was in his room, under his pillow!" Rooney declared. "If it wasn't his gun, why'd he have it?"

"Did Mr. DuBois claim ownership?"

"No." Rooney gave a look of disgust.

"How did you connect the gun to this murder?" Sands asked.

"It's the right caliber," Rooney snapped. "And everybody knew this Negra had it in for—"

Father cut him off. "By that do you mean, it matched the bullets found in the deceased man's body?"

"Yeah." Rooney's eyes bulged.

Unperturbed, Sands rolled his chair over to the evidence table. "How about the money? Had there been any record of serial numbers kept by Mr. Kennedy by which we can connect this cash to him?"

"No, nightclub owners don't keep lists like bankers."

"So what you're really saying is this: Mr. Kennedy was shot two times with a gun of the same caliber as the gun found in Mr. DuBois's room?"

"Yeah," Rooney growled.

Sands nodded. "And that some money was missing from Mr. Kennedy's office and that you found some money in DuBois's room? That is your evidence?"

Rooney glared at Gabe's father. "It's enough! Down in Storyville some coloreds will knife you for two-bits—"

"Some maybe. But *not* Delman Caleb DuBois—a graduate of Howard University, the third such graduate in three generations in his family! A man who served his country bravely in France. Do you expect this jury to believe that Delman DuBois—who has enjoyed the patronage of the multi-millionaire family who raised him—would kill a man for a few hundred dollars? Why would my client—who has several thousand dollars of his own in a San Francisco bank account—commit murder . . . ?"

Gabe knew he should be objecting. Every word his father leveled at Rooney stung Gabe like a lash. But each word also slit the veil that had separated Gabe from the truth. *"There is none so blind as he who will not see."* He'd been blinded by prejudice. A black jazz musician in Storyville—that's how he'd seen Del. And only as that. He'd spent no time checking into the facts of the case, even when he knew the kind of man Rooney was. *God forgive me. Forgive me! What can I do now?*

Gabe's stomach soured. The evidence that had seemed so conclusive just weeks ago now sounded puny. Del didn't fit the crime he was charged with. Gabe should have known a woman like Meg wouldn't be the friend of a person capable of this type of crime. *Why couldn't I see it!*

Judge LeGrand stung Gabe a contemptuous glance.

Gabe couldn't disagree. His witness—this entire case—was worthy of contempt. Why had the chief of police chosen someone so biased, so inept, as Rooney for his deputy? And who had killed Mitch Kennedy?

✳ ✳ ✳ ✳ ✳

Dinner that evening at home was a giggling agony for Gabe. He longed to speak to Meg, but she remained aloof. Why? Maybe it was the company tonight. Belle had invited three friends—Nadine, Maisy, and Portia—over for dinner and an evening of . . . giggling.

After an embarrassing and essentially worthless day in court and a dinner in the company of four giddy debutantes, Gabe escaped with his parents into his father's snug office. Finally, he had a moment to tell his parents about Marie. His father sat behind his orderly desk, his mother on the chair, and Gabe on the sofa opposite.

Fleetingly, Gabe recalled the intoxicating sensation of holding Meg in his arms on that sofa two nights ago. He rubbed his forehead trying to erase that thought. The time had come for truth-telling—regardless the cost. Marie was counting on him, her "papa."

"What is it, Gabriel?" his mother asked.

Gabe looked at her. *How do I start? What do I say?*

"Does it have to do with Meg?" Sands asked.

Gabe glanced up in surprise. "No. We did discuss it though."

Sands pursued Gabe as if he sat in court, "Is it about Del's case?"

Gabe raked his hair with his fingers. "No, it's about France . . . about the war."

Both his parents gazed at him then. Their combined attention daunted Gabe, but he took a deep breath and began. "Things happened in the war that I never wrote you about or told you."

His father nodded. His mother sat like carved marble.

"Things I should have told you. I regret . . . keeping them from you."

"What things, son?" Sands folded his hands under his chin.

"I married a French woman." The sentence was so simple, yet it carried such impact. *I married for love, passion in the midst of carnage.*

His mother gasped.

"Where is she?" Father spoke as if Gabe had just said he'd invited a friend to dinner.

"We were only married a short time before she was killed in a bombardment near the end of the war." His heart twisted.

A gale of giggling filtering from another room made his grief more stark.

"Oh, Gabriel," Mother moaned. "Why didn't you tell us? I knew something horrible had wounded your heart."

He stared down at the sisal carpet. "We didn't know each other very long before we mar—"

"How did you meet?" Mother asked. "Who was she?"

"Her name was Lenore Moreau. She was a nurse at the hospital I was taken to when I was shot down." He reached into his pocket and pulled out his wallet.

"A nurse? You mean with the Red Cross?" Mother went on.

He drew out the one small photograph Lenore had given him. "No, Lenore was with the French hospital where her husband practiced medicine—"

"Her husband!" Mother blanched. "A divorcee?"

"No, a widow." Gabe gathered his courage and handed Mother the picture. "A widow with a small daughter."

Jazz music from the Victrola tinkled in the background. A girl's voice began singing along.

His mother stared at the photograph, then up at him. "The child; you didn't leave her in France, did you?"

Gabe gazed at his mother. Some of her questions he had expected. This one he hadn't. "I was told she was killed with her mother."

"But she wasn't," Father concluded.

"I received a telegram from Marie's uncle in Paris that he had continued to search for Lenore's daughter just in case she had escaped." Gabe turned his attention to Mother. "So many children just got lost or misplaced. Marie's body was never found—"

"So the uncle succeeded? He found her. Is that why you're telling us this? What does this all mean, son?" Father received the photograph from Mother and studied it.

Gabe lowered his eyes. The jazz song in the background stopped; then another melody began. "Marie never knew her father. He died before she was born, so I adopted her. Marie Lenore St. Clair is my legal daughter. Four days ago, Paul, her uncle, put Marie on a boat with a nurse. She's due here within three weeks."

"Three weeks!" Mother popped up from her seat. "How old is she?"

"She'll be four this year." He couldn't tell if his mother was happy or sad.

Mother beamed. "Oh, a child. My first grandchild!"

Gabe stared at Mother. "You're not upset?"

"I'm sad you didn't tell us about Lenore." Mother sat down beside him on the sofa and touched his arm tenderly. "Oh, Gabriel, I didn't know how to help you. I could see you were grieving, but I didn't know over what, over whom. . . . Dear, did you really think you couldn't tell us?"

Relief soared in Gabe. *Why didn't I trust them?* "I kept waiting for the right time. I couldn't seem to put the news of my marriage into a letter. Then Lenore died, and telling you seemed futile. You never met her. I thought it best to close the book and spare you my grief."

Both his parents gazed at him with sad faces. It cut him to his heart.

"But you didn't," Father spoke at last. "Both your mother and I sensed your sorrow and didn't know how to comfort you. Don't do this again. This is what your family is for. You are a grown man. You don't need us for everyday things, but for matters like this, you do."

Gabe nodded gravely. "It won't happen again."

Mother sprang up. "Oh, let's tell Belle. She'll be thrilled!"

The jazz song had ended, but no more giggling could be heard.

Gabe objected, "But she has friends over—"

"Excellent," his father observed. "That will save us deciding who to tell about Marie first. We'll let the grapevine take care of that task."

Gabe appreciated this grim humor, but he still hesitated. His father and mother led him down the hall toward the parlor where the four debs and Meg had been chatting.

Before his mother preceded them into the unusually quiet room, Nadine's hesitant voice stopped them, "But I don't understand, Miss Wagstaff. Why do you interest yourself so deeply with the son of a servant. I mean, we've all heard that the colored accused of murder was the grandson of your old nurse, but—"

"I'll try to explain. Ordinarily, I wouldn't because you may not understand even after I do, but in these circumstances, in light of what you've heard, I will try." Meg paused.

"Del and I were children when we moved to San Francisco. We'd only lived there a few months when the 1906 earthquake ripped our home in two. My father had had to go away that day, so I was home alone with only Del and his grandmother, Susan."

Meg's voice took on a distant quality, as though she were removed from them. "The quake hit at sunrise. Susan got us out of the house. I can remember an old woman across the street screeching and screeching. When the first shock ended, Susan put her hand over my mouth. I had been screaming, too, but didn't realize it.

"Susan started to take us to the Golden Gate Park, away from collapsing buildings. On the way, Susan had a heart attack. We didn't realize it at the time, but that's what it was. She died there on the curb. No one would stop to help us," Meg's voice faltered. "I don't know if it was because Susan was a Negro or if it was just a day of death and terror. No one acted normally."

Gabe watched Meg, his heart touched by her lost expression.

"Then an aftershock hit us. Del and I were thrown to the ground where we clung to each other. I thought we were going to die. I shouted, 'Stop! Stop!' When it finally did, we couldn't let go of each other. We made a promise to each other then. We promised to stick together. And we always have." She looked up then, and her voice hardened. "Now, is that a good enough explanation of why I will stick with Del no matter what? Do you choose to believe that nasty gossip, or me?"

"What gossip?" Mother demanded.

"Yes, what gossip?" Gabe echoed.

CHAPTER 16

*[Nothing] shall be able to separate us from the love of God,
which is in Christ Jesus our Lord.*
Romans 8:39

MEG CAST GABRIEL A WORRIED glance. "Just some rampant nonsense."

Raven-haired Nadine, who obviously had a taste for melodrama, said in a hushed but well-projected tone, "Someone started a rumor that Miss Wagstaff isn't a friend to Del, but his . . . his paramour." The girl blushed a fiery red.

"I pay no attention to rumors." Meg forced a relaxed smile. "My family has never lived just as everyone else, and this isn't the first time a rumor—"

Mrs. St. Clair spoke up, "Gossip is the hallmark of small minds. That's what my grandmother always said."

"But this could be—" Sands began.

Gabriel cut in, "When did you first hear this rumor?" He addressed Nadine as though she sat in the witness chair.

Nadine frowned in deep thought. "The first time I heard it was at the celebration for the new governor."

Meg watched the wheels turn in Gabriel's head. She had a suspicion of who had started this rumor, but it didn't really matter. She would be in New Orleans only as long as it took to get Del out of jail. Yet somehow this thought didn't relieve her as much as it had previously. She found herself studying Gabriel's stern profile. She shook herself mentally. "Don't let it worry you—"

"I won't!" Belle declared. "If anyone says it within my hearing, they'll get a piece of my mind!"

"That is very loyal of you," Sands said, "but remember Shakespeare: 'Methinks thou doest protest too much.'"

Even as his father spoke these words lightly, Gabe picked up the concern in his parent's eye.

"Exactly so," Mrs. St. Clair sniffed. "Treat it with sublime contempt."

Sands nodded. "Quite right, my dear."

Gabe ignored this pap, spoken no doubt for Belle's benefit. Who had spread such a misleading and malicious rumor? Even the hint of a liaison such as this could end in a lynching.

Meg read the ill-concealed worry in Gabriel's and his parents' expressions. She knew just what kind of reaction this rumor could bring. The KKK held sway in the South and was spreading north. Whoever had begun this rumor had done it to drive her from the state! But Del stood in the greatest peril. A black man accused of killing a white man stood almost no chance of acquittal. Finally admitting that cost her the tag ends of her peace. But this rumor multiplied into even greater danger to Del. If the jury heard of this and believed it, Del was a dead man. Suddenly in her memory, the sound of shots from two nights ago exploded. Shaken, she stood up.

Gabriel moved to her side.

Nadine glanced at the clock. "Oh, it's eight! Time for us to get on our costumes for the Momus Parade."

While the other three girls hurried out giggling, Belle hung back, looking at Meg doubtfully.

Meg forced another smile. "I'm looking forward to seeing your costumes."

"Yes, run along." Mrs. St. Clair smiled, though the strain she felt revealed itself in a tightness around the corners of her mouth.

Still shaken, Meg stood beside Gabriel.

With a backward glance, Belle paused at the door. "You'll still go with us to see us in the parade?"

Meg nodded.

"We wouldn't miss it," Gabe added.

Belle grinned, then hurried out with Mrs. St. Clair close at her heels.

Sands looked at them. "I'll be in my office. Gabe, are you sure you still want to escort the ladies? If you don't, I'm sure we could manage to get me through the crowd some way——"

"Leave it to me," Gabe insisted.

Sands nodded once, then left.

Gabe looked down at Meg. "Tomorrow is Mardi Gras. I'll have to take you to the French Quarter." Trying to speak normally, he said, "How are you? I was worried when you didn't come to court . . ." He stopped. He'd begun by making light conversation. Reminding her of Del's trial would only distress both of them.

"I wanted to be on time, but it took me so long to fall asleep after . . ." *After someone tried to shoot me,* she said silently. Meg braced herself. *I have a duty to myself and Del not to give in to fear.* "Your mother didn't want to disturb me. You and Sands were long gone before I woke."

"I was surprised that my mother accompanied you to court." Gabe couldn't have stopped these words even if he had tried. He was having trouble adjusting to the changes in his mother.

"She insisted. She said she'd not had time to attend court to see your father represent a client recently, and she wanted to see you also."

Meg's explanation sounded like pure fiction to Gabe, but he'd seen his mother in court with his own eyes—for the first time in her life. Had the night his mother overheard his father in the den motivated his mother to come to court, or was it out of concern for Meg? "Meg, I—"

Gabe's mother hurried in. "Gabriel, have you seen my sewing basket? Portia's side seam just gave way. It never fails!"

Meg helped his mother find it. Gabe waited until he and Meg were alone again.

Meg asked, "You told your parents tonight?"

He nodded, his eyes devouring her. She was always chic, always elegant, always in black. Now he understood. Meg was in mourning for Colin. But her black silk dress with its sleek lines—he couldn't look away.

"How did they take it?"

Belle's small Victrola upstairs began with a sudden burst of song, "I Wish I Could Shimmy Like My Sister Kate."

Gabe concentrated on Meg despite the loud music. "Mother is excited over Marie—her first grandchild!" He forced a wry grin. "I felt guilty for not telling them sooner. I thought I was saving them from my sorrow over losing Lenore, but they knew something had happened, and both were worried anyway."

Recalling her own father's drawn expression the morning she'd left San Francisco for New Orleans, Meg wrapped her arms around herself, wishing Gabe would draw nearer. *Father, why didn't I tell you about France?*

Gabe shoved his hands in his pockets. Again, he couldn't hold back words. "I don't feel like the same man who traveled home from France more than four months ago."

"I know. I lost Colin in September. I came home for Thanksgiving. I wanted to tell my parents—"

Gabe interrupted her, "But you didn't have the strength to explain what you'd seen, experienced—"

Meg faced him squarely. "I felt like I was drowning in sensations and images from the trenches—"

Pulling her closer, Gabe gripped her shoulders, affected again by her frailty. How could a slight woman pack such courage? The intensity of his emotions didn't fit the occasion or setting. But his feelings, now freed, wouldn't be denied. He looked into Meg's warm brown eyes. "I couldn't find my feet. I took the job as parish attorney to give me a life, a reason to get up in the morning and get dressed. I thought I could forget by keeping busy." His voice came out rough.

Meg pressed both her hands against his chest. How firm and strong he felt under her hands. "I was so frightened. I thought I'd never feel like myself again."

Am I falling in love with this woman? Is that why I can't hold back? Or is this just shared experience and sorrow? "I know. But I don't think we'll ever be exactly as we were."

"I wouldn't want to be. If I were, it would mean that Colin had no effect on me." *"This world is not my home, I'm just a-traveling through"*—the old spiritual sang in her mind.

Nadine, dressed in a bright green silk wrapper, dashed in. "I need my purse! Did you see it? It's black leather!"

Meg pulled away from Gabe.

To get rid of the girl, Gabe swiftly searched the parlor. "Here it is." He thrust it into Nadine's hands.

"Thanks!" Nadine vanished with a flash of bright green.

Gabe looked to Meg.

She lowered her eyes. "My poor father—he has me to worry about, my stepmother's difficult pregnancy, and Del being arrested . . ." Meg didn't raise her gaze. "Did it feel peculiar to face your father in court?"

Gabe wanted to shout, "I know Del isn't guilty! I've been a blind fool!" *But facing Rooney as a witness was impossible! The man disgraced himself and the New Orleans police. Thank God I'd mentioned Rooney's bias and incompetence to the chief of police!*

"This is an awful situation." Meg's voice came low and urgent.

Gabe took her gloveless hand in his. This contact alone moved him. In his pocket, he held information about the case . . . possibly helpful information. Should he give it to her? Would it help her? He kissed her hand and wished circumstances were different. They couldn't talk about what separated them, but Meg was so easy to open up to. The barriers between them had tumbled down two nights ago in his father's study. As he recalled the tender response of Meg's lips, he shuddered with awareness of her.

Meg spoke in a low, desperate tone, "What are we going to do? I can't discuss Del's case with you. But something dreadful is happening in this city."

The four girls clattered down the stairs and burst in on Meg and Gabe.

Meg pulled away from him again.

Gabe's frustration level spiked. *We need to be alone!* With extreme effort, he swallowed his anger.

The girls posed in the doorway. "How do we look?" they asked in a ragged chorus, then giggled at themselves.

Meg made herself smile, though the effort caused her physical pain. The muscles of her face and neck felt like taut steel cords.

Belle was dressed as the Statue of Liberty; the other three were a black cat, a veiled harem girl, and a Japanese Geisha with a powdered-white face.

Meg kept her smile in place. "What inventive costumes."

"Indeed," Gabe rallied.

"You girls, get your wraps now. The cars are in the port cochere," Mrs. St. Clair instructed from the hall.

The girls left in a flock, chattering and laughing.

Within minutes, they all were crowded into two cars. Mrs. St. Clair and three debutantes in the family sedan, and Belle in the backseat of the Franklin behind Meg and Gabe.

In the darkness, Gabe slid his hand over the front seat till he touched Meg's hand. He clasped it in his. The agony of their situation twisted his gut.

What am I going to do? Gabe asked himself. *I care about Meg. How can I prosecute her dearest friend with a flawed case?* What did a prosecutor do if he became convinced that the defendant was not guilty? It was the kind of question he usually would ask his father, but how could he? His father was the defense! What a coil!

The chauffeur drove behind Gabe to the corner of Canal and Rampart Streets near the edge of the Quarter. The debs flocked out of the family car and into the throng. Belle jumped out of Gabe's car and ran to catch up with her friends.

"The parade is gathering here," Gabe explained to Meg. She nodded.

Squeezing out of the sedan, his mother pushed her way back through the crowd to Gabe's window. She had to shout to be heard over the noise of the crowd. "A spot has been reserved for you on Felicity Street; you remember where?"

Gabe nodded.

His mother motioned broadly. "Our place in the pied-à-terre is on Rampart, right over there!"

"I remember," Gabe shouted back. "Meg and I will walk back and join you!"

His mother nodded and turned away to push her way to the nearby pied-à-terre.

Gabe threaded the Franklin through the packed streets and back to the Garden District. He found his spot at a friend's home and parked. He helped Meg out of the car. Only blocks separated them from the riotous celebration in the Quarter. But Felicity Street looked deserted. The night breeze rustled through the tall live oaks; the Spanish moss fluttered over their heads like tattered sleeves on an ancient shroud.

Meg looked up at Gabe, her eyes pleading for . . . what? What could he give her? The piece of paper in his pocket weighed him down. It might put her in danger's path again!

"I want you to hold me," she murmured into his ear.

Pulling her against him, he closed his arms around her. How he wished to protect her from the evils that nipped at her heels. With his forefinger, he tilted her quivering chin up. He paused to gaze into her tear-sprinkled eyes. He kissed her. Again, the pain of the past fell away in the joy of Meg's kiss, the coming together of their lips—thrilling, heart-stopping.

Meg swayed in his arms. Gabriel's kiss bound her in a sensation that momentarily shoved back the pain of losing Colin and the horror that she might lose Del. Then she recalled the evening and where they were. She pushed away from him. "We must go. Your mother will worry if we don't come soon."

Gabe allowed her to draw him along on the street cloaked in night's shawl. A half-moon shone above the city. The tap of their heels on the paved banquette gave sound to their hurried pace, a counterpoint to the cacophony of human laughter and jazz trumpets in the distance. Gabe wanted to pull Meg into his arms again and forget about the parade, his mother . . .

A flock of frightened sparrows swirled up suddenly from one of the oaks. Gabe tilted his head up to watch them land in another oak for the night. He wished he could settle his nerves as easily.

Soon Rampart Street was in sight. Gabe drew Meg closer to him. Sometimes young men tried to steal a lady from her companion. No one was stealing Meg from him tonight. They had too much left to discuss.

Finally, he led her past the doorman, who had opened the wrought-iron double gate and door for them, and into the apartment where they were expected. She walked up the curved staircase to the second floor.

"Gabriel!" At the top of the flight, Dulcine gazed down at them. "Gabriel's here!" she announced gaily.

She ignored Meg pointedly and reached for Gabe's hand as he topped the steps. "I've been waiting for you!"

Gabe evaded her hands as he bowed to her. "Good evening. Did my mother arrive safely?"

Dulcine looked disgruntled and cast a nasty glance at Meg. "Yes, she's on the balcony."

Gabe nodded his thanks. Taking Meg's arm, he led her through the happy revelers and out to the balcony. He greeted his mother, then drew Meg to the end of the balcony where they could be more private.

Meg leaned close to his ear again. "I think it's fairly obvious Dulcine isn't thrilled to see me. Go back inside. I'll just watch the festivities with your mother."

"Dulcine has no hold over me—"

A gin-flushed male voice bellowed from inside, "What? Did he bring that Yankee with him? Doesn't he know the truth about her yet?"

Gabe froze, anger flashing inside him like white-hot flame.

Meg gripped his arm. "Go sit beside your mother. I don't want a scene."

"I am my own man," he whispered back fiercely. "No one will tell me who I may or may not escort—"

His mother rose majestically from her nearby wicker chair and reentered the room. "Charles DuPuy, I heard what you said."

Meg gasped.

A hush fell over the festivities inside.

Mrs. St. Clair proceeded, "You are, what we called in my youth, foxed. Please take yourself away until you've recovered your proper sense." Then she returned and sat back down with every evidence of calm.

Gabe and Meg stared into each other's shocked eyes.

"Bravo, Mother," Gabe whispered beside Meg's ear.

"You should still go inside. Dulcine might . . ." Meg drew in a dismayed breath. She hadn't meant to reveal the name of the woman she suspected of starting the rumor Belle's friends had overheard. Images of the poison-pen letter and the *gris-gris* came to her, and she realized that deep down she'd suspected Dulcine of being behind those too. Could Dulcine be that senselessly cruel?

"Don't turn away. I suspect her myself. I have been to blame for encouraging her. Before you came, I was so broken up, I didn't know if my mother could be right and I should court Dulcine."

Meg tucked her chin low. "Perhaps it would be advisable for you not to make a clean break with her just yet."

"Why?"

"I believe—though I could be misjudging Dulcine—that if she thought we were romantically attached, she would spread more rumors—ones to your detriment too. Perhaps impugn your honor as Del's prosecutor."

Dulcine couldn't impugn my honor more than my own thoughts and actions! Gabe couldn't respond. What could he say to this?

Meg's every word rang true. How could his mother have wanted him to marry such a pedestrian and perhaps, spiteful woman?

The evening inched on forever. He and Meg bravely ignored the quizzical expressions of some and the cold stares of others. But after his mother's admonition, no one dared say or do anything slighting to Meg. He argued back and forth inside himself over whether or not to give Meg the piece of paper, the name he'd been given.

At last, he and Meg stood, alone, back home in front of his parents' fireplace.

"I should go up," Meg said with a weary sigh. She didn't move. "But there are things I want to say to you."

"Say them."

Meg drew in a ragged breath. "Maybe you don't see it because this is your home, your New Orleans, but I feel such a presence of evil. And it's not just because of Del being accused."

Gabe pulled her closer. "I feel it too. Or I did two nights ago when they shot at you. I couldn't talk to you about it then—it was too fresh."

Meg's voice went on, steady and calm, "I think if they had wanted me dead, I'd be lying in the morgue today. I was too easy a target, exposed on that empty lamp-lit street. Someone wants me to leave New Orleans and wants Del convicted."

Gabe wanted to shout, "You're right! But who?" He could say nothing. Frustration burned in his stomach.

Tears collected in her throat. "I feel like crying, and I don't know why." Giving way suddenly, Meg wrapped her arms around his back and buried her head within his suit coat. The stiffly-pressed cotton of his shirt felt smooth under her chin. She breathed in Gabriel's distinctive scent—shaving soap and bay rum aftershave, so reassuringly masculine.

Gabe kissed her hair.

Meg fingered one of the round buttons of his coat. "I don't want you to suffer because of my friendship."

He circled her tiny waist with his hands, drawing her against him. *Friendship? Meg, what I feel for you is much more than that. I want you. I need you. And if I let myself, I'll fall in love with you. But how do I reconcile our relationship with my conscience over Lenore, over Del's case?* "I think my only course is to resign from the parish staff of prosecutors."

"No, I'll just stay away from you!" She stepped back, out of his hold.

In spite of her reluctance, he took her shoulders in his hands and drew her closer again. "This won't be a sacrifice. I think I made a poor decision at the time. Now I would much prefer to enter into practice with my father. That wasn't a possibility before . . . before you came."

"No! I don't want you to resign."

"Why?"

She pulled from his grasp. "Don't you see? Resigning from the case could put you in danger."

"Danger?"

"Mitch Kennedy was killed—by whom and why? Del was stabbed by his cellmate, but why? LaRae was killed probably because she talked to me! Someone paid for the *gris-gris* to frighten me. Someone ordered that attempt on my life the other night—"

"I'm not frightened!" Gabe's hands balled into fists.

"Of course, you're not! You faced death in France! But what about your parents? You once warned me about kidnapping. Would your family be safe? What about Marie? She needs you. She needs to come to a calm home, a happy home, not one filled with mourning—"

"Stop!" He wrenched her to him. "I refuse to be frightened by evil! I won't tremble in my bed! I will do what is right! I will serve justice!"

She threw her arms around his neck and kissed him.

He reveled in the abandon of her kiss and swayed with her in his embrace. Her kiss shouted her trust in him, the possibility of a future. He deepened and prolonged the kiss. Passion eliminated the confusion of his mind, but it intensified the confusion of his emotions. *Lenore, Meg—you both tug at my heart!*

Finally, breathing hard, he drew back a fraction from her lips. "I will resign. We won't be afraid of the future. And I will give you and Father a chance to prove Del's innocence."

Meg stopped breathing. "What are you saying?"

His decision made at last, he pulled a slip of folded paper from his pocket. "This is the name and address of a man who may be able to give you information you need. I visited Storyville myself not long ago and decided to try to find a new informant. This man may be able to help you, or he might be worthless. I haven't spoken to him about Del's case, so I don't feel that it is dishonorable for me to give you his name. I pray he will help you."

She accepted the paper, gratitude swelling inside her. "Thank you. I want to ask you many questions, but I won't. You're not in a position to answer them, and I won't ask you to do anything against your conscience."

"I'm frightened for you. Be sure to go in daylight and take Jack with you." He cupped her now unwavering chin in his hands and gazed at her arresting face in the light from the house. How could he have thought her less than beautiful when first they met? He wouldn't let this woman go down into disaster or slip from his life. "Right now, I can't say all I'm feeling, but please know that you are dear to me."

❀ ❀ ❀ ❀ ❀

The next morning, parked at the curb on a misleadingly quiet daylight street in Storyville, Meg glanced at Jack beside her in the plush leather front seat of her Cadillac. "I'll be fine. I told you I got this man's name from a trustworthy source. You're armed. My derringer's in my purse. I've entrusted you with the cash, so he won't be able to get it unless he gives us some good information." In her mind, Meg pictured Gabriel's determined face in the light from his parents' fireplace.

"I don't like you hobnobbin' with lowlife people like the ones who live in this neighborhood," Jack grumbled. "Can't this wait? Court doesn't resume until tomorrow afternoon."

Dispensing with courtesy, Meg opened her own door and got out. The warm breeze spread a brackish odor from the nearby Mississippi River.

"Wait for me!" Looking affronted, Jack scrambled out and hurried to Meg's side. "We should have told Mr. Sands we were comin' here."

"I don't want to bother him unless we actually get lucky. The person who gave me Asa Dent's name wasn't sure this man would have anything worth paying for." Meg tugged her black velvet hat more firmly in place. When would Gabriel give his resignation in court? No doubt Del's case would be delayed again as another prosecutor took over. That would give her more time to scare up helpful information.

"Storyville is no place for a lady." Jack grimaced. "But I can see I'm not goin' to change your mind. Give me that address—please."

Meg chuckled. "Here it is. Don't get so upset. It's broad daylight and you're with me. What harm could befall me?" Gabriel had hired Jack to protect her. He'd taken her into his parents' home for her safety. He'd given her this lead. Had those actions been prompted by chivalry or love?

Jack grumbled wordlessly to himself, but studied the address and the doors along the seemingly deserted street where Penny Candy was. "Let's get this over with. Looks like he's across the street at the far end."

Jack led her to the corner. As they waited to cross, Meg recognized an open car as it turned farther down on the street and pulled into a parking place in the next block. Surprise zigzagged through her like an electrical charge. "Look there, Jack. That's Mr. Gabriel's Franklin, isn't it?"

Jack followed her gaze. "Yes." Then he whistled low.

"What is it?" Meg asked, staring as three men got out of the car along with Gabriel. The men, all in suits, gathered on the banquette beside the car and began talking.

"Mr. Gabriel keeps high company. That's the chief of police and the mayor with him."

"Really?" Meg's mouth formed a perfect O. "Why would he be with them here, and now—and who's the fourth man?"

Jack shook his head. "I don't have a clue why they'd be here. The fourth is probably a plainclothes cop. I think I saw him with Rooney. Here, let's cross now." He took her in hand and escorted her to the other side of the shabby street.

Meg hesitated, looking down the street. Penny Candy, Kennedy's Club, lay between Meg and Gabriel. *What had brought Gabriel to Storyville this morning and in such company?* Meg could think of no logical answer.

"Have you seen reason and changed your mind?" Jack asked in a hopeful tone.

"No, let's see if Mr. Dent is at home and awake." Meg started walking again. She felt as though she were being watched. She glanced around, but couldn't discern anyone interested in them—just a few drunks lying in doorways and closed cars driving through Storyville.

Jack followed her to the address where Meg tapped the peeling green front door. The landlady, an old black woman in a faded red housedress, greeted them warily and sent them upstairs to Dent's room. Meg sensed her suspicious black eyes following their every move.

The smell of stale smoke and coffee hung in the sour air. Being in such a rough boardinghouse made Meg uneasy, but she pushed her concerns to the back of her mind. She had to find more evidence to clear Del. Even after Rooney's biased testimony, Del's life still hung in the balance.

Jack knocked on Asa Dent's door hard enough to wake the dead.

A careless, tobacco-rough voice called out, "Don't break it down. The old girl will take it out of my hide. Who's there?"

"Jack Bishop."

"I don't know any Jack Bishop."

"Well, you might know my friends: George Washington, Abraham Lincoln, even Andrew Jackson—"

The door swung open. "You got some friends I like."

The landlady called up querulously, "Remember, rent's due today!"

"You'll get it, old lady!" Asa Dent, in wrinkled trousers and a stained T-shirt, looked to be in his thirties. "Come on in." Then he spotted Meg standing behind Jack, and his yellowed brown eyes widened.

Jack stepped aside and let Meg enter first. She glanced around. The sparsely furnished room was tidy but dusty. A cigarette burned in an ashtray by the still-rumpled bed.

"What brought you here?" Dent's eyes assessed them.

Pulling out his wallet, Jack slipped out a five-dollar bill. "We're looking for information."

"What kind?" Dent's gaze roved over them, puzzled.

Meg turned her eyes on him. "Anything to do with Mitch Kennedy or Corelli."

"Mitch is dead. Corelli's the new owner. That's all I know." He folded arms over his thin chest, putting up a barrier.

Meg couldn't have told anyone how she knew, but Dent was lying to her. Why would Gabriel send her to someone who wouldn't cooperate?

Dent looked nervous too. "Why you askin' me? I don't know nothin' about no whitey club owners. We got nothin' in common."

Jack took out another crisp five-dollar bill and added it to the first.

"Can't tell you what I don't know," Dent said sullenly.

Jack flashed a twenty-dollar bill.

Dent snorted and glanced away.

"Mr. Dent, we need information for my friend, Del DuBois. I was given your name as a possible source of information about what happened at Penny Candy just before Mitch Kennedy was murdered." A bad feeling lumped up inside her. Dent had knowledge, but he wasn't going to sell any to them.

"I told you. I don't know nothin'. I can't tell what I don't know." He turned and picked up his cigarette.

"That's true," Jack replied in a quiet tone. "But I hate to put these presidents back in my wallet."

Dent's yellow eyes turned greedy. He took a step closer. "Maybe you're interested in bettin'. I can line up some action for you, hot wagering. Better odds than the on-track bookies."

Jack shook his head and folded the bills back in his wallet. "Sorry, we can't do business."

"Maybe you know someone who could help us." Her hope shrinking fast, Meg grabbed at any chance that remained. "I'd pay you a finder's fee."

Dent shook his head. "No can do."

Jack took Meg's arm. "We'll be leaving you then. Sorry we wasted your valuable time." He led her out.

Dent clicked the door closed behind them and turned the lock.

Meg's tender optimism of this morning hit the floorboards. Her insides started folding up, shutting down.

Jack and Meg walked down the steps, bid the landlady farewell, and stepped out into the balmy day. Numbly, Meg paused and looked up the street again where Penny Candy lay between them and Gabriel's car. Another hope dashed. Why couldn't anything turn out right for a change?

"Miss?" Jack prompted.

"I want to walk around Penny Candy." The club drew Meg irresistibly. The answers to this riddle lay there, where all this had begun.

Jack heaved a big sigh in exasperation. "Why would you want to go where people have been killed, and what good will that do?"

"I just want to get a look at the alley behind it."

"Why?"

Meg couldn't give him a rational reason. LaRae had been killed in that alley. Meg should want to leave this sad, forlorn street. Instead, she started walking toward the club. Jack followed her, muttering to himself about women.

Meg had seen and smelled dirtier and narrower alleys in San Francisco's Chinatown, but she saw nothing here that sparked any inspiration about what to do about Del. Had Del been just a convenient party to pin a murder on? Or when he'd insisted on being paid, had he unknowingly stepped on someone's toes?

Back on the street again, Jack led her toward her Cadillac. Meg kept looking around. A black newsboy neared them, shouting, "Extry! Extry! Read all about it!"

"Jack, the answer lies here. If only I knew where to look, who to ask . . ."

"I don't think so."

But Meg paid no attention to Jack. The newsboy came abreast of them. "Deputy found dead in Storyville!" Across the way, Gabriel and his companions emerged from another doorway and vanished inside Penny Candy. Had Gabriel seen her?

"What's going on here?" Meg asked.

Jack shook his head. "I think we should be going."

"No." Meg stared across at the entrance to the club. Gabriel had told her that he intended to resign from the case, that he didn't have a future in public politics.

The tattered newsboy stopped in front of them. "Paper, lady? Paper, gent? Deputy found dead in Storyville." He waved the single sheet special of the *Times-Picayune* in front of her.

Absently, she took it and handed the boy a quarter. So why was Gabe here with the chief of police and mayor? Nothing added up. Why hadn't the informant had any information for her? Gabriel hadn't made any guarantees, but—

When Meg glanced at the headline, a name jumped out at her: Rooney. She cried out, "Jack, look here! That's why Gabriel's here!"

A soft curse.

Jack fell to the banquette in a heap.

Meg gasped. Searing pain. Her head! She was falling . . .

CHAPTER 17

Where can I go from Your Spirit? Or where can I flee from Your presence?
Psalm 139:7, NKJV

G ABE GLANCED AT HIS WRIST-
watch. Half past eleven. Mardi Gras festivities would soon fill the
nearby French Quarter.

"Mr. Gabriel!" a hoarse voice hailed Gabe.

Gabe looked up and down the street in front of the Penny
Candy. He, along with his three companions, had just come out
its door.

"Mr. Gabriel!" Jack Bishop waved to him and charged across
the street.

"Jack! Where's Meg?" Gabe froze, an awful premonition
shooting through him.

"They took her! Someone knocked me out and took her!"

"Who?" Gabe gripped the large man's shoulders. "When?"
His world began spinning out of control again.

"Here—on this street! The paperboy distracted me and
someone hit me from behind. I couldn't have been out long. I
can't believe they caught me nappin'!" Jack struck the air with

clenched fists. "How could I have been so stupid? I told her we shouldn't have come here!"

Gabe knew why Meg had come. By giving her Dent's name, he'd set her in danger's path. *I'm a fool! How could I have exposed her like that?*

"What has happened?" the chief of police demanded. "Who's disappeared?"

"Miss Meg Wagstaff." Gabe looked up and down the somnolent street, a ferocious anger igniting in his gut.

"You mean that young woman whose name has been linked to that black boy who's on trial?" the mayor asked.

"That rumor, sir"—Gabe spat out the words—"is scurrilous. Miss Wagstaff is paying for the . . . for Del DuBois's defense. His grandmother was her old nurse."

"I see." The mayor nodded, still eyeing him.

"I can't believe she's been kidnapped." The police chief glared at Jack with open hostility. "This must be a mistake."

"This is no mistake, sir," Jack spoke up. "I was knocked out from behind, and when I woke up, she was gone."

"What was she doin' down here?" the chief demanded. "Storyville is no place for a lady . . . *if* she is a lady."

Gabe held himself in check, but it cost him. "Miss Wagstaff is every inch a lady. This must be connected with Rooney's death."

"Is Rooney really dead?" Jack asked.

"Yes, that's why we're down here. I wanted to question Corelli about it."

"A wild-goose chase," the chief muttered.

"How is Rooney's death connected to Miss Wagstaff's disappearance?" the mayor asked.

"They must be connected," Gabe insisted, his stomach sinking steadily. "Why else would Rooney be found dead in Storyville and Miss Wagstaff kidnapped on the *same street* the next morning? Both of them are involved with Del's trial."

"Well, we can't argue with that," the mayor said.

The chief of police looked as though he'd like to, but he turned to the fourth man, who had remained silent. "O'Toole, you better call into the station and give them the particulars about this Yankee woman who's gone and gotten herself kidnapped."

Gabe bridled at the chief's negligent tone, fury over the man's lack of respect overriding his anxiety. He couldn't reveal his feelings for Meg, so he used the only tack he thought they'd understand. He declared in a heated voice, "Miss Wagstaff is a guest in my family's home. The St. Clair honor is at stake. I'm going to advertise a reward for her quick return—five thousand dollars."

O'Toole, the plainclothes police officer, gave him a startled look. "OK. I'll get right on it."

"Instead of calling, you may take the chief and Mayor Behrmann back to headquarters in my car. Just leave it in my assigned spot." Gabe handed the man his key. "I'll go with Jack in Meg's auto."

The police chief glared at him. "You should leave this investigation to the department, St. Clair."

Gabe fought the impulse to break the chief's jaw, but his voice came out stiffly polite, "I'm sorry, sir. The lady is a guest in my home. Southern chivalry demands that I do all I can to find her and bring her home safely."

This left the other three men nothing to say, which was exactly what Gabe had intended. He watched them retreat, then he turned to Jack. "Now, I want you to tell me exactly what happened—from the time you picked Meg up this morning until she was kidnapped."

Within minutes, Jack helped Gabe retrace Meg's movements, straight to the informant they'd come to question. Upstairs in Dent's boardinghouse, Gabe grabbed the front of Dent's shirt. "You'll tell me the truth; tell me what you know about the lady's disappearance or you will regret it."

"I told you I don't know nothin'. Getting' rough won't change that," Dent clutched Gabe's hands to keep his balance.

From where he stood by Dent's window overlooking the street, Jack cleared his throat. "Corelli just walked into Penny Candy."

"Don't leave your room. I may be back." Gabe released him. Dent stumbled backward.

Within minutes, Gabe stormed into the empty and hollow-feeling Penny Candy and confronted Corelli beside the bar. "All right. What do you know about the kidnapping of Miss Wagstaff?"

"I don't know what you're talkin' about. You called and told me to get here. I came over as soon as I was dressed." Corelli leaned against the bar smoking a cigarette.

"What do you know about Miss Wagstaff being kidnapped?"

"What?"

Gabe's right hand clenched into a fist at his side as he pictured himself smashing the man's smug face. "Don't play dumb. Everyone in New Orleans knows who Meg Wagstaff and Del DuBois are."

"So?" Corelli flicked the ash off his cigarette.

"I'm putting up a five-thousand-dollar reward for her safe return."

Corelli gave a low wolf whistle. "That's a lot of money. Sorry I can't help you."

Gabe would have paid five thousand dollars for a legal excuse to drag Corelli down to police headquarters. Controlling his temper, he slammed his fist onto the bar. He turned on his heel and marched out. Jack followed him.

Outside, Gabe looked up and down the afternoon street. Most of Storyville still slept. "Where do we go from here?"

"Well, I would go to Mr. Sands." Jack rocked back and forth on his heels.

Why didn't I think of that? Maybe Del or Meg had told him something that would give them a lead. "You're right." They got into Meg's car, and Gabe sped off with a squeal of tires.

※　※　※　※　※

Through the buzzing in her ears, Meg heard voices, men's voices, arguing. She tried to straighten up, but couldn't without making her head spin sickeningly. She gave up and let her head loll weakly forward.

She became aware that she was sitting on a chair, but she couldn't move. *I'm bound,* she suddenly realized. She tried to speak, but a cloth gag stopped her. These realizations nearly shocked her back into unconsciousness. But through the haze in her head, the voices intruded again.

"You're a fool!" An unseen man's sharp voice hurt her ears. "Did I tell you to kidnap anybody? Did I?"

"No, but—" a low voice that she thought she'd heard before tried to explain.

"But you took matters into your own hands!"

"She was nosing around the club. Then more showed up— the chief of police, the mayor—"

"So what?" the sharp voice demanded, sounding as though it came from below her feet.

"I saw her go to Dent's, then go behind the club. He may have told her something," the familiar voice tried to sound reasonable.

"What could he tell her? I've got Dent in my hip pocket. He don't tell nobody nothin' I don't want him to. You've made a mess of things. Rooney made a mess, and look what happened to him."

A silence. "You mean that was you—"

"Sure it was. Rooney messed this up from the beginnin'. But yesterday in court was the last straw—"

"You went to court?" the familiar voice asked.

"I got someone who did. Rooney picked the wrong fall guy. That jazz player is more than just a cheap Joe. He's got an education. He's got a family behind him worth millions. The guy who raised him runs a high-class magazine that blows the whistle on people who do things he don't like—one of those do-gooder muckrakers."

"Who knew?"

"*Rooney* should have known! He bungled this whole deal from the beginnin'. Now don't you bungle this." The sharp voice sounded stern. "Even if she is a Yankee, the death of a white woman—a lady—will cause big trouble. And her father's got enough money to make waves. I don't want to kill her unless I have to."

"Don't worry."

"I'm not worried. *You're* the one who should be worried. I want this taken care of today. One way or the other! Don't forget what happened to Rooney."

"Sure, boss . . ."

The voices faded from her hearing, and receding footsteps told Meg that they were leaving her. She opened her eyes and tried to focus on the room in which she was being held. One small window let in the only light from high above. She could see no door, but it might be behind her. How long had she been unconscious? Lifting her aching head made her feel woozy. She lowered it fraction by fraction.

Helpless, I'm helpless. What happened to Jack? Did they kill him too? Tears flowed down her cheeks. *What are they going to do with me? Kennedy, LaRae, Rooney have been murdered. Maybe Jack. Am I next?* "Helpless" echoed in her heart.

A vision from the past flashed in her mind—the earthquake! The porch on her first home in San Francisco tore away from the foundation and rushed after her as a child. Screaming filled her mind. She wanted to shout at God, "Stop! Stop letting things hurt Del, hurt me!" Her heart beat so fast it hurt. She cried out against the gag, "Oh, God, I'm so frightened. Who will defend Del if I'm killed?"

Her father's voice spoke in her mind, teaching her about God, the Father—*"Be still and know that I am God."*

Oh, Papa! I know what you taught me. Then she spoke to God himself, *I know you are God, but I am lost, alone, helpless. Where are you, God? I need you!*

What can separate us from the love of God? Can bombs, mustard gas, barbed wire?

Colin's face came before her eyes. Pain cut her in two. Her wrists and ankles pounded with sluggish blood. Only her bindings held her up. Her grief dragged at her like poisoned claws.

"Where could I go to escape from thee? If I went up to heaven, thou art there. If I go down into Sheol, thou art there."

Dear God, save Del. Save Gabe. Save me. Without you, we are lost!

❀ ❀ ❀ ❀ ❀

"Del?" Gabe stared in shock at his father, who sat behind the desk in his office at home. "I need to question Del to find Meg? What could he know about this? He's been in jail under a guard—"

"Yes, Del," Sands interrupted. "If you want the truth, son, you must go to him."

Gabe felt hot and cold. His fears for Meg's safety had shaken him to his core. He now knew the extent of his feelings for Meg. *I can't lose her. I can't face the future without her.* "You'll tell me nothing then?"

"I can't tell you what I don't know. I think Del knows more than he's told me." Father picked up the newspaper, folded it, then handed it to his son. "Take him this. I think the headline will loosen his tongue."

Gabe took the paper and walked out.

Belle, with Dulcine at her side, accosted him at the front door. "Gabe, I need to know if you will take me to the Rex Parade this evening—"

"Parade?" He stared at her.

"It's Mardi Gras today," Dulcine trilled. "Did you forget, Gabriel?"

Meg's kidnapping had driven everything else from his mind. "Meg has been kidnapped."

"What!" Belle exclaimed.

Dulcine looked startled.

"I'm on my way to try to get information from Del at the parish jail."

Belle clutched his sleeve. "Kidnapped? Why!"

"I don't know, but I'm going to find her."

"You must!" Belle pressed her temples as though her head ached.

"Isn't that a job for the police?" Dulcine asked in a brittle tone.

"No, Dulcine, it's my responsibility because I'm the one who put her in harm's way. Besides," he went on rashly, "I intend to ask Meg Wagstaff to be my wife."

Dulcine's face went white except for two spots of red, one flaming on each cheek.

"I'll be praying for her," Belle murmured.

Gabe touched his sister's shoulder, then left.

✹ ✹ ✹ ✹ ✹

Gabe faced Del alone in the jail infirmary. The wall clock read quarter past three—nearly four hours since Meg had been kidnapped. The clogged streets and a fruitless talk with the chief of police had gobbled up precious time. He'd had Del brought here so they couldn't be overheard. Del's guard and Jack stood watch outside the locked door.

"Why did you want to see me alone here?" Del stared at him suspiciously.

"Meg was kidnapped this morning."

Del reared up out of his seat. He cursed Gabe. "Mr. Sands said you hired a good bodyguard for her! What happened?"

"Jack Bishop is a good bodyguard, but they took him by surprise. You can't blame me more than I blame myself. I need you to tell me everything you know so I can find her."

"She might already be dead." Del clenched and unclenched his hands as if he fought the urge to throttle Gabe.

"I hope—I pray—not." Gabe pushed the paper into Del's hand. "My father told me to show you this. Read the headline."

Del took it reluctantly, but one glance at the headline caused shock to spread over his face. "Rooney's dead?"

Gabe nodded. "I saw Rooney's body at the morgue before breakfast."

Del slumped back into his chair.

Sitting down on a stool, Gabe bent over. Folding his hands together, he propped his elbows on his thighs. "Tell me anything you know that might help me to find her. Please."

Del glanced up. "Your father tells me that you and Meg are an item. Is that true?"

"I have fallen in love with her." Would Del be able to help?

Del looked at the paper again. "You say you love Meg. Rooney's dead. Why does that mean I can trust you?"

"Because my father sent me. Because Meg trusts me. Because only the truth can free you and save Meg. Tell me. Please." *Dear Lord, make him confide in me!*

"I don't like it. I don't know if I can trust you or not."

"I can only tell you that I love Meg, and I wouldn't do anything to hurt her—or you because of her."

Del stared hard at Gabe. "All right. I can talk now with Rooney gone. It took me a while to sort everything out, but . . ." Del paused, staring at the ceiling, then he looked down. He talked slowly, as though exhausted. "As I've figured it out, Rooney framed me. Late one night I saw him with Corelli and the man who wears a flashy diamond ring on his little finger. At the time, I didn't even know who the three of them were."

Del shrugged. "I didn't put it together until after my arrest when I found out who Rooney was. Then I asked other prisoners about the man with the ring. They told me his name is Mario Vincent."

Gabe tried to take in what he was hearing. *Kennedy, Rooney, Corelli, and Vincent?* "Vincent runs most of Storyville."

"That's what I've found out—*since* being jailed."

"When did you see them together?" The enormity of what Del was revealing shook Gabe.

"Two days before Mitch was killed, about an hour after closing, I think they thought everyone else in the club had gone home but Mitch. They didn't know I was in the back in what we called the dressing room. I heard raised voices—"

"They were arguing?"

Del nodded. "I didn't think anything about that. I came out, ready to leave. I just nodded at them and left. They were talking to Mitch. The thing is, I don't think I would ever have put it all together if they'd just let me go north."

"They needed someone to charge with Mitch's murder." Gabe burned with the injustice of Rooney's treachery. He'd betrayed the public trust. For how long? *Dear God.* Corruption this close to the chief of police!

Del nodded. "Yeah, you're right."

"Do you know why Mitch was murdered?" Gabe looked into Del's eyes.

"I pieced that together too. I think someone is trying to challenge Vincent for control of the new gin trade."

Gabe repeated, "New gin trade?"

"There will be more dirty money than ever selling illegal liquor. Storyville will be a boom town with cash rolling through it. What I've heard in jail is that someone from New York City wants in. Mitch must have decided to back Vincent's competition. I think they were trying to convince him not to when I saw the four of them together. Evidently Mitch went with the competition. That must be why he was killed—a warning to the other club owners—to remember who they paid protection to and why."

"I've been afraid of what Prohibition might bring." *God, how can something meant to do good, do so much harm?*

Del's jaw hardened. "Well, whatever you have imagined, the reality will be worse. Big money draws tough predators. It will be a bloody fight for control of the smuggled liquor trade."

"It has already fostered three murders and a kidnapping." Gabe stood up, suddenly restless. *Meg, where are you? How will I find you? You're swimming in the midst of gators!*

"You've got to find Meg. She is one in a million!" Del stood up, kicking his chair back. "You realize they killed LaRae just for talking to Meg. Probably a warning to me and Meg."

Dear Lord, help me find her alive! But Gabe asked, "Did you tell my father about Rooney and his criminal connections?"

"*No.*" Del looked at Gabe as if he were insane. "Why would I sentence someone else to death? *I didn't tell anyone.* What I knew got me arrested for murder. Why would I endanger anyone else?"

Gabe faced Del squarely. "My carelessness in regard to your case makes me as culpable as Rooney. I want you to know that I intend to resign my position as parish attorney. If I had taken the time to do any investigation of you, I would have known that that evidence had been planted on you."

"You thought I was *just another colored jazz player* in Storyville," Del said bitterly. "But I was as foolish as you. I thought I could come back to the States and bury myself in my music—and forget the Klan and Jim Crow. In the war, the French army welcomed us with open arms—after Pershing handed us over to them. He wouldn't let his precious white divisions reinforce the French and English troops, but he was glad to get rid of us.

"I don't know what I was thinking! I was a fool to come home to face the same old bigotry. France was the first place I've ever lived where I wasn't judged by my color. That made coming back ten times worse. Meg told me I should have stayed in France. She was right."

Gabe could say nothing. Hearing Del's bitterness for the first time, Gabe felt ashamed of standing by while black soldiers received such treatment. *I saw it happen myself. The Black Swallow, the black American who'd flown for the French air force before the U.S. had entered the war, wouldn't switch to the American air force—they would have taken his wings!*

But Gabe could right no wrongs now except to free Del and find Meg. *The mystery is solved, but that doesn't help Meg.* Both their lives were at stake now. Gabe shoved his hands into his pockets. "Who do you think kidnapped Meg?"

"Corelli. He may have panicked. Or Vincent himself. I don't see that anyone else has a motive, do you?"

"No, but I've missed so much of what is going on around me that I don't trust myself. Now, how do I go after them?" Gabe slammed his fists onto a nearby cot. "I have no evidence against either of them. Even if I bring them in for questioning, that won't protect Meg! I could have them here in front of me and someone could . . ." He broke off, unable to say "kill Meg." "What are we to do? Every minute lessens her chances."

"Well," Del let out a deep breath, "my grandmother always said there'd come a day when I would be pushed beyond what human flesh could bear. I know what she meant now. We're there. We can do nothing in our own strength."

"What did your grandmother tell you to do then?" Gabe ground the words out in a voice that didn't even sound like his own.

"You either give up and go down in defeat or . . ."

"Or?"

"Or you hand everything over to God and take whatever he decides."

"That doesn't sound . . . hopeful." Gabe stared into Del's eyes and saw his own fear and despair reflected there.

"We can always trust God—even in the face of death."

Del's last words froze Gabe's insides. *I can't face losing her, God. Please send her back to me. I need her.*

"Are you ready to accept God's will?" Del stood up.

"Are you?" Gabe countered.

"I already have. I've been powerless since Rooney framed me six weeks ago. I'm still powerless now, even though Rooney's dead."

Gabe stared at Del.

Del stared back.

Gabe rubbed his forehead. "I have no choice."

Del lowered his head, then raised his hands. "Oh, Lord, you know our sister, Meg. You have tried her like gold and found her pure and faithful. She's in your hands, Lord. Bring her safe through this testing. Bring her back to us. Please, Lord, please."

Gabe stared at the floor, pressing his fingers to his eyes, forcing back tears. His insides still felt tied in knots. "I know you have the power, Lord." He prayed silently, *I've buried my head in the sand too long, Lord. Please help me find Meg, or let someone else find her before it's too late.*

✻ ✻ ✻ ✻ ✻

In his office on the second floor of the courthouse, Gabe looked out his window at the waning light of day. He'd come here to think. Jack had gone to tell Sands everything. When he returned, the two of them would venture out again through the swarming holiday streets. Even from the distance the festivities and excitement of Mardi Gras could be seen and felt. Gabe heard strains of raucous jazz and glimpsed a flash, a sparkle, here and there of the revelry. Mardi Gras: New Orleans' highlight!

Fear and regret gnawed at him. Every minute Meg's danger increased. Hope ebbed inside him. *Meg, Meg, where are you? God, protect her. Help me find her. Only you know where she is and how dear she is to me.*

✺ ✺ ✺ ✺ ✺

Staring up toward the dimming light of day, Meg ached within her tight bonds. The blood in her wrists and ankles throbbed from the pressure of the ropes. The sensation of pins and needles prickled in her hands and feet. From outside came loud jazz, laughter, and shouting. Mardi Gras. New Orleans was celebrating while she waited alone to see if she would live or die. *Oh, God, help me. I don't want to die—not when I've just found hope again. I have done all that I can do to help Del, to help myself. I have tried to take care of Del and to shoulder my grief over the war and Colin without you, but I can't.*

You did not forsake me in the quake or in France. When you promised never to leave me or forsake me, I was foolish to turn away. Do not forsake me now. Only you can help me now. "Trust in the Lord . . . and lean not on your own understanding"—Father taught me that years ago. Why did it take a war, a death, a murder charge, and a kidnapping to make me really know it? "Seek ye the Lord while he may be found." "I do trust you, Lord. Am I too late?" She hung her head limply and sobbed.

✺ ✺ ✺ ✺ ✺

Gabe paced his office. Night had closed around him. The shouts and laughter of Mardi Gras reached him through closed windows. Jack sat slumped in a chair, his head down in defeat. He and Jack had searched for Meg for hours—by car and then on foot. But Mardi Gras had clogged the streets and banquettes of the French Quarter and Storyville.

The police search for Meg—desultory at best—had given way to crowd control. When Gabe and Jack had returned to Penny Candy, they'd found Corelli gone and had received evasive answers to their questions: "Come back tomorrow after Mardi Gras. We're too busy trying to keep up with business." Mardi Gras had become Gabe's adversary—and in the end, it had won!

Someone banged on the outer door of Gabe's office. Gabe's secretary had left hours before. Startled and wary, Gabe went to answer it. He opened it.

Dent faced him. "Still offerin' five grand for information about the Yankee woman?"

Gabe's heart jerked and began pounding. He hauled the man inside by the lapels of his coat. "Do you know where she is?"

"Sure do." Dent smirked. "What about the reward?"

"Tell me where she is, and if I find her there alive, you'll have your money."

*　*　*　*　*

Because of the holiday, it took Gabe four excruciating hours to get a search warrant. It was nearly eleven at night when Jack Bishop, O'Toole, Asa Dent, and one uniformed policeman accompanied Gabe. They pushed their way on foot through the Mardi Gras revelers jamming the French Quarter. Dent had fingered Corelli as the kidnapper and had given Gabe an address of a house on Royal Street.

The Rex Parade was in full swing, snaking its way through the Quarter. All around them people in shimmering and outrageous costumes and masks greeted one another and danced to the music that filled the air. Prohibition had been forgotten for the day. People openly shared bottles of liquor and toasted Mardi Gras!

Because of the din, Gabe pointed to the number that matched the one on the search warrant. The uniformed policeman pounded on the door. When no answer came, he tried it, found it locked, and kicked it in. Gabe rushed in first, with his gun at the ready. The house had a musty, closed-up odor and no electricity. Fireworks burst over Royal Street and lit their way as Gabe led the search through the first floor. No one. Gabe felt his stomach twisting in agony. Had Dent brought them on a wild-goose chase?

"I hope you didn't bring us here for nothing, Dent," Gabe growled. "You'll be sor—"

"She's here; just go on." Dent pointed to the next flight of stairs.

Gabe nodded and started up. Second floor. No one. Gabe turned to Dent, ready to rip his heart out.

Another rapid explosion of fireworks lit the sky. Jack pointed upward. Though the din from outside was muted, he still had to raise his voice, "An attic?"

Gabe caught a flickering glimpse of the outline of a hatch. Before Gabe could act, Jack dragged a chair underneath it and pulled at the handle, drawing the hatch downward. Gabe grabbed a ladder that had been left propped against the wall. Jack stepped aside, and Gabe placed it in the hatchway and climbed up the ladder into the attic.

He nearly collapsed with relief. In the dim light, he saw Meg on a chair. But she showed no signs of life. Was she alive? Pulling himself up, he rushed to her side. He tenderly lifted her head in his hands.

Meg's eyes flew open. She tried to shout, "Gabe! Gabe!" but the gag prevented her.

He kissed her hair. Then with his pocketknife he stripped away her bonds. Lifting her, he clasped her close to him— shaking with relief. "I thought I'd be too late! You're alive! Thank God!"

Trembling, Meg clung to him, gulping air. "I never thought . . . I'd see you . . . again! I love . . . you!"

His kiss cut off her labored words. His kiss deepened as though the world were to end in seconds. She swayed within his embrace. "Meg, I thought I might never get the chance to tell you I love you! I need to get you out of here. You need food and water. Don't worry, dearest. As God is my witness, I'll never let you down again."

"I can't . . . stand."

Sweeping her into his arms, he carried her to the hatch and lowered her to Jack's waiting arms, then scrambled down the ladder after her. "O'Toole, I think you should stay here and secure the crime scene. We might get some evidence to convict Corelli—"

"It was Corelli," Meg croaked with her dry throat. "I overheard him speaking . . . with a man."

"Dent here gave us a tip on Corelli. This house belongs to him too. But why did he have you kidnapped?"

"He panicked . . . saw us around . . . Penny Candy." Meg leaned against him, her limbs like soft butter.

"We can take care of him later." With Meg in his arms, he hustled to the stairs. As Gabe descended the narrow curved staircase, the noise of the celebration bombarded him. At the front door, Jack pushed and kicked aside the debris left from the splintered door. Gabe stepped out onto the street with Meg.

She screamed, "He's got a gun!"

Gabe dove for the cold pavement, taking Meg down with him, his body covering hers. Gunshots roared above them. Screams, shrieks, bellows exploded.

Dent fell, lifeless, on the banquette beside them.

❈ ❈ ❈ ❈ ❈

Two days after Mardi Gras, Gabe sat behind the prosecutor's table in Judge LeGrand's austere courtroom. "All rise," the bailiff's voice boomed in the full-to-bursting room.

Gabe rose.

Judge LeGrand entered and seated himself with a flourish. He steepled his hands and gazed at the array of eyes before him. He gaveled the court into session and everyone sat. "You newspaper men, no picture-taking. None!" He turned to the prosecutor. "Gabriel, are you prepared to resume the prosecution of Delman DuBois?"

"Your Honor, the parish withdraws all charges against Mr. DuBois."

LeGrand stared at Gabriel. "Does this mean that the state now considers Delman innocent of all charges brought against him in the murder of Mitchell Kennedy?"

"Yes, sir, that is true." Gabriel couldn't help grinning.

The judge turned his stringent attention to Delman. "Delman DuBois, please rise."

Del rose.

"'Since all charges have now been dropped in the death of Mitchell Kennedy by the parish of Orleans in the state of Louisiana, Delman DuBois, you are free to go."

Del nodded gravely. "Thank you, Your Honor."

Judge LeGrand hit the gavel, then departed. As soon as the door closed behind him, the courtroom erupted into exclamations and excitement.

Meg flung herself in Gabe's arms. He caught her and hugged her close. "It's all over, dearest."

Del stepped close and pumped Gabe's hand. "Thank you. I know you're the one who managed this. I never expected to be cleared like this—even after all that's happened."

Gabe shook Del's hand. "The chief of police and Mayor Behrmann decided proceeding with such a flawed case would only bring disgrace on the city. After Rooney's murder and Corelli's disappearance, the chief decided a new investigation should be started. You wouldn't have killed Mitch for the reasons Rooney had concocted. The whole case had become too suspect, too flawed, too dangerous in light of public opinion."

"Do you think Corelli was killed too?" Del asked.

"We'll never know, but we haven't found a body."

Meg broke in, "I think Corelli fled out of fear of Vincent. And I think Vincent gave Dent my location and ordered Dent killed to make certain no one would be left to testify to anything." She shivered, thinking about the ruthless men. "It's just fortunate that I didn't see anyone when I was kidnapped. My ignorance saved me."

Del squeezed Meg's shoulder. "You never gave up on me, Meg."

She turned to him. "Our promise stands."

Del blinked away tears. "I'm going back to France."

Meg frowned. "Go to San Francisco first. Little Leland William was born last night. I received the telegram first thing this morning. My parents want you to come home before you do anything else."

"All right. When are you leaving?"

"I'm staying for another month or so."

Gabe smiled. "She has an engagement ring to pick out."

Nodding, she looked up at Gabe. "And I have a little girl to welcome."

Epilogue

Therefore the LORD will wait, that He may be gracious to you.
Isaiah 30:18, NKJV

Three weeks later
March 3, 1920

IN THE WARM SPRING SUNSHINE,
Meg and Gabe stood in the midst of his family—not just his
parents and Belle with Corby at her side—but a crowd of aunts,
uncles, and cousins, all in their Sunday best, overflowed the
dock. The regal-looking ocean liner surged up the slip toward its
berth in New Orleans harbor. The sight of it caused a buzz of
questions and comments around Meg:

"That's it!"

"Oh, I hope the little thing hasn't been seasick. I remember
when I . . ."

"The poor little thing lost her mother at such a young
age . . ."

"It's God's will. If Gabriel hadn't married her mother . . ."

Meg tried not to listen. She closed her eyes and took a deep, calming breath. She already loved little Marie, but the poor child would be scared to death by all these people!

Gabe's lips tickled her ear. "I still don't know why the whole clan, in fact both sides of the family, had to come. Marie is a shy little girl."

Looking up at him from under the brim of her jaunty new blue hat, Meg grinned and touched his arm. "We'll just keep her with us, your parents, and Belle. When she arrives, you must pick her up and not let go of her. That should reassure her."

He nodded, but concern for his adopted daughter tightened the lines around his mouth.

Sounding a blast of its deep horn, the ship, with the help of surrounding tugboats, slid up beside the pier. Still holding her hat in place, Meg tilted her head back to look up. Automatically she waved in greeting. Many hands on board waved back. The ship was secured. Customs and immigration officials gathered below the ramp. Slowly a trickle of people coming down from the ship began to pass through customs and immigration.

More than an hour later, a woman wearing a nurse's white uniform and cap holding a small child by the hand stepped off the ramp.

"Marie!" Gabriel shouted and ran forward. He scooped the little girl with brown curls into his arms.

The rest of the family surged forward, but halted as an immigration official stepped up to Gabriel. The two men spoke. Shifting Marie to one arm, Gabriel pulled out her adoption papers and his discharge from the army. After perusing these, the man nodded and shook his hand.

Gabriel carried his daughter back to the family. They all fell silent. "Everyone! This is my daughter, Marie Lenore St. Clair!"

The family around Meg applauded and called out, "*Bon jour,* Marie!"

The little girl hid her head in Gabriel's neck. This made everyone laugh.

Meg stepped forward. "Marie? I have a baby for Marie." She held out a brand-new porcelain-headed doll she and Gabriel had picked out together.

The nurse translated what Meg had said.

Marie nodded shyly and opened her arms for the doll. "*Merci,* madam."

The family cooed over and celebrated the child's two words. By this time, Meg began to think that the worst thing that might happen to little Marie would be that the family would love her to death.

Gabriel's mother, the recent founder and president of New Orleans' first Ladies Political Discussion Society, came forward in a chic new purple dress and hat. "Nurse, please tell her that I am her grandmother."

This was translated to Marie. The little girl studied her new grandmother, then reached out for her.

Mrs. St. Clair burst into tears as she hugged the little girl to her breast. "Oh, my sweet, sweet little baby girl. We are going to love you so much."

"Papa!" Marie looked around for Gabriel. "Papa!"

He caught up with her and patted her back. "Don't worry. Papa won't leave you."

Everyone blinked back tears. Meg felt like chuckling out loud. After all that had happened, all the danger and all the deaths and disaster, God had brought them safely through as he had before.

Gabriel took Meg's arm. "Everyone, let's head home for the party."

The relatives shouted in agreement and surged away from the water's edge.

In the Franklin, Meg sat beside Gabriel with Marie in her lap. He drove them toward home.

Meg thought her heart would burst with happiness.

"I'm still sorry you couldn't go home to San Francisco right away," Gabriel apologized again as he tickled Marie under her chin.

"My parents understand, and Cecy is fine. My new brother is healthy, and Del is with them and is recovering from his ordeal here. Right now, making Marie feel secure is our most important task. When she's settled in, I may go home for a week or two. Or my parents will come for a visit when they can."

"When does our wedding come in that plan?" Gabe quizzed.

"As soon as Marie knows me and can enjoy the wedding." She chucked Marie's chin, making the little girl giggle.

"What about the honeymoon?" He grinned at her.

"You're very naughty," Meg replied in a prim tone, "but if you marry me, I'll consider a honeymoon."

"How very kind of you."

"Don't mention it." Meg fluffed Marie's soft brown curls.

"And you're still going to law school?" Gabe glanced at her sternly.

"Yes, but not this fall. I think a husband and babies will come before a law career in my life's agenda. I have plenty of time—"

"All right, but remember, part of our marriage bargain is that you will practice law with me and father."

She chuckled. "Don't worry! I won't forget!" Her heart sang a joyous, but wordless, tune. "I didn't know I would ever be this happy again."

"Neither did I. Probably neither did Marie."

Hearing her name, the little girl said, "Papa. *Je taime,* Papa!"

"*Je taime,* Marie," Gabe replied. He traced Marie's cheek, then Meg's. "I need to fatten you two up." Joy swelled inside him. *Thank you, Lord. I probably don't deserve this happy ending, but*

I thank you for it. Help me be the father and husband you want me to be.

Meg caught his hand and kissed its palm. With a heart over-flowing with joy, she began to sing, "Blessed Assurance, Jesus is mine! . . . all is at rest, I in my Savior am happy and blest; This is my story, . . ."

Gabe joined her in singing the chorus.

Little Marie clapped her hands and clambered to her knees to kiss Meg.

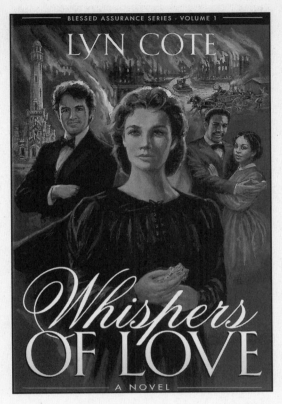

WHISPERS OF LOVE
ISBN#0-8054-1967-5
$12.99

A Civil War widow, Jessie Wagstaff, raises her son alone in Chicago until a mysterious stranger enters her life. He seems like the answer to a prayer, but is he? Jessie will find the answer amid the flames and ashes of the Great Chicago Fire, 1871.

Blessed Assurance Series – Three stories of love and struggle. The world pits itself against them with fire, earthquake and injustice. But God's love is sufficient in life, death and love.

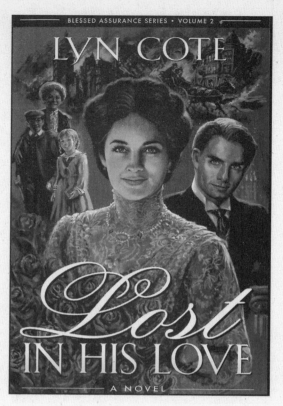

LOST IN HIS LOVE
ISBN#0-8054-1968-3
$12.99

Jessie's son, Linc Wagstaff, leaves Chicago after the death of his wife.
God has a mission for him in faraway San Francisco. A beautiful heiress
holds the key which can open the doors to his goal. Will she succumb
to God's call? Will Linc find his heart can love again? The Great San
Francisco Quake of 1906 will shatter barriers and open eyes.

Blessed Assurance Series – Three stories of love and struggle.
The world pits itself against them with fire, earthquake and injustice.
But God's love is sufficient in life, death and love.